TAKING THEIR
POLITICAL PLACE

Recent Titles in
Contributions to the Study of Mass Media and Communications

Advertising, Alcohol Consumption, and Abuse: A Worldwide Survey
Joseph C. Fisher

Beyond Agendas: New Directions in Communication Research
Philip Gaunt, editor

The Press and Politics in Israel: *The Jerusalem Post* from 1932 to the Present
Erwin Frenkel

The Disabled, the Media, and the Information Age
Jack A. Nelson, editor

Censorship of Expression in the 1980s: A Statistical Survey
John B. Harer and Steven R. Harris

The U.S. Media and the Middle East: Image and Perception
Yahya R. Kamalipour

Advertising, Alcohol Consumption, and Mortality: An Empirical Investigation
Joseph C. Fisher and Peter A. Cook

The Press in Times of Crisis
Lloyd E. Chiasson, Jr.

Native Americans in the News: Images of Indians in the Twentieth Century Press
Mary Ann Weston

Rights vs. Responsibilities: The Supreme Court and the Media
Elizabeth Blanks Hindman

The Press on Trial: Crimes and Trials as Media Events
Lloyd Chiasson, Jr., editor

Personalities and Products: A Historical Perspective on Advertising in America
Edd Applegate

TAKING THEIR POLITICAL PLACE

Journalists and the Making of An Occupation

PATRICIA L. DOOLEY

Contributions to the Study of Mass Media and Communications,
Number 52

GREENWOOD PRESS
Westport, Connecticut • London

Library of Congress Cataloging-in-Publication Data

Dooley, Patricia L.
  Taking their political place : journalists and the making of an
occupation / Patricia L. Dooley.
      p.   cm.—(Contributions to the study of mass media and
communications, ISSN 0732–4456 ; no. 52)
  Includes bibliographical references and index.
  ISBN 0–313–30062–3 (alk. paper)
  1. Journalism—United States—History.   2. Journalism—United
States—Political aspects.   I. Title.   II. Series.
PN4871.D66   1997
071'.3'09—dc21   97–16713

British Library Cataloguing in Publication Data is available.

Library of Congress Catalog Card Number: 97–16713
ISBN: 0–313–30062–3
ISSN: 0732–4456

First published in 1997

Greenwood Press, 88 Post Road West, Westport, CT 06881
An imprint of Greenwood Publishing Group, Inc.

Printed in the United States of America

The paper used in this book complies with the
Permanent Paper Standard issued by the National
Information Standards Organization (Z39.48–1984).

10 9 8 7 6 5 4 3 2 1

For Jon and Sarah.

Contents

Illustrations   ix

Acknowledgments   xi

1. Journalism as an Occupation in American History   1

2. Journalistic Work as Occupation in Eighteenth-Century America   45

3. Discursive Construction of Journalists as Political Communicators
   in Nineteenth-Century Newspaper Prospectuses   71

4. Discursive Construction of Journalists as Political Communicators
   in Nineteenth-Century Libel Courtrooms   93

5. Discursive Construction of Journalistic Occupational Roles
   During the Era of Good Feelings   109

6. Conclusion and Implications of Historical Study of the
   Journalistic Occupational Group   125

Appendix: Newspaper Prospectuses   139

Bibliography   145

Index   163

Illustrations

FIGURE

1.1 The Historical Sociological Development of
     Journalistic Work as Occupation   10

TABLES

3.1 Claims to a Political Journalistic Role by Authors of
     Newspaper Prospectuses   76

3.2 Claims to Provision of Journalistic Work Products in
     Prospectuses   78

3.3 Journalists as Political Protectors and Educators   78

3.4 Political Positions of Prospectus Authors vis-à-vis
     Journalistic Independence   82

3.5 Claims to Political Journalistic Standards in Nineteenth-
     Century Prospectuses   85

4.1 Statements About Journalists' Occupational Duties
     in Libel Trials   97

4.2 Political Affiliations of Libel Plaintiffs and Defendants   103

Acknowledgments

Since this book was developed and written over a number of years, the people to whom I am grateful are numerous and their contributions are much greater than can be reflected in the pages and ideas of a single book. To all of those at the University of Minnesota who have taught and believed in me, I owe a debt of thanks. I am especially grateful to Professor Hazel Dicken-Garcia, who served as my adviser throughout graduate school and who has continued since I graduated to help me in so many ways. She has read and commented on numerous drafts, and has always been more than willing to discuss relevant issues with me. She has helped, inspired, prodded, and encouraged me, and I will always be grateful to her.

Other colleagues and friends at the University of Minnesota's School of Journalism and Mass Communication who have given me much important advice, encouragement, and support are Professors Nancy Roberts, Philip Tichenor, and Roy Carter. In addition, as a teacher and mentor at the University's Silha Center for the Study of Journalism and Ethics, Professor Donald Gillmor, was so helpful. At the university's Department of History, Professor Paul L. Murphy worked with me both as a teacher and reader of my work, and I am thankful for his help and inspiration. Because he inspired me to pursue studies that probe the sociological history of journalism as a powerful occupation, thanks are owed to Professor Larry Griffin, a former teacher at Minnesota's sociology department. And Department of Sociology faculty member, Professor Barbara Laslett, has also served as an important and insightful reader of the original manuscript.

In addition, I owe thanks to the University of Minnesota's School of Journalism and Mass Communication for supporting me in my doctoral program, not only with generous financial support in the form of stipends and fellowships, but with faculty who inspired and prodded me to follow their marvelous examples; the many dedicated staff at countless libraries and archives who have provided me with the wealth of rich historical materials used in this project; and my colleagues and friends at the University of Maine, who have seen this study transformed from a dissertation to a book and have supported me with their advice and friendship.

Other friends in Minnesota, Maine, and others parts of the country who have not only supported me, but given me invaluable feedback on the project include: Susan Buzzell, who generously read and commented on the final drafts of this book; my colleague at the University of Maine, Paul Grosswiler, who encouraged me to keep working on the manuscript and who joined me in publishing an essay that takes the approach presented here in a new direction; and my friends in the field of rhetoric who offered me new ways of looking at my research, including Professor E. Anne Laffoon, University of Colorado, Boulder; Professor Raymie McKerrow, University of Ohio; Professor Karen Whedbee, University of Maine, Orono.

My deepest gratitude goes to Jon and Sarah; without the seemingly endless loving support they have given me, I could not have begun, let alone finished, this project.

Finally, I am thankful to Jeanne and Lee for all their interest and words of support; I only wish Lee were here to see this finished.

Journalism as an Occupation in American History

If asked today to answer the question "Who is responsible for the provision of political news?" most Americans would have no trouble thinking of an answer. "Journalists" would be our most frequent response, despite our knowledge that politicians, political handlers, and a host of others also disseminate political information. Americans, however, have not always turned to journalists for political news, nor was it preordained that they eventually would. Indeed, questions about whether journalists, rather than politicians or other political communicators, should serve as the nation's primary providers of political news probably would not have occurred to early nineteenth-century American citizens. For during this earlier era, the work of newspaper journalists was intertwined with the work of politicians. In effect, many of the country's newspapers were largely political organs, funded and used by politicians for political reasons, and the livelihood of journalists during this period often depended on the fortunes of the political factions or parties they were tied to. Virtually from the nation's beginning, journalists and politicians were tightly associated, with the former being so integrated with the political system as to be all but indistinguishable from the latter.[1]

Thus, not only journalists, but politicians, were involved in newspaper journalistic work from the time a multi-party system began to develop in America late in the eighteenth century, since newspapers would take an important place among the various communication vehicles adopted by politicians, vehicles that included a number of communication forms such as speeches and pamphlets.[2] But a century later, the occupational situation of journalists had changed, along with the character of the group's membership and the contents of the newspapers they published. Not only did a journalistic group with more clearly defined boundaries begin to form, but its societal roles were transformed, a process that afforded its members more occupational authority. Although journalists were often still involved with politics and politicians in both their work and personal lives, the nature of the relationship had changed, for journalists had wrested from politicians the role of providing political content in newspapers.[3]

While journalists are today just one of a number of sources of political communication in America, their perceived influence in shaping the nation's political agendas has led to many concerns.[4] Indeed, since the nation was formed, there have been critics of the press's performance in the political arena. But today's journalists are increasingly subjected to questioning that goes far beyond mere debates about whether political news is comprehensive and fair. Critiques that question the legitimacy of journalism as an institution are not uncommon today, and calls are being issued for the by-passing or replacement of journalists in the political communication process, journalistic predicaments exacerbated by the emergence of new electronic media.[5]

Whether one hopes to preserve or destroy journalists' legitimacy as America's primary providers of political news and analysis or to simply study the more general histories of journalism, mass media, or politics, it is important to understand the process by which journalists acquired jurisdiction over the tasks involved in the dissemination of such forms of political communication. To gain insight into this process, scholars should ask questions about how, when, and through whose agency it became commonplace for Americans to differentiate between the political communication work tasks of journalists and politicians. In other words, what was the process that led Americans to turn to journalists rather than politicians or other political communicators for political news?

This book studies this historical sociological transformation of journalistic work. Starting with theory from the field of sociology on occupations and professions that has been tailored to emphasize the role of communication, the model articulated here situates the emerging journalistic group within a broader political environment. Journalists are defined as those who enter newspaper work from the ranks of the broader printing and publishing establishment. Politicians are defined as party members or leaders, elected or appointed government officials, who entered newspaper journalistic work from outside the field of printing and publishing. Although the careers and activities of selected journalists are described and discussed, this book's emphasis is on the boundaries and legitimacy of the journalistic group on the broadest macrostructural level rather than on individuals.

Society's vital interest in journalists as political communicators has prompted scholars to explore the close proximity of press and politics from the nineteenth century and to ponder how this relationship changed over time, and this work depends heavily on their rich contributions. Relatively few historians, however, have examined the history of this relationship as one that existed within an occupational structure. Furthermore, most studies on the history of journalism as work, occupation, and profession have characterized the work products and organizational structures of journalism as indicators of occupational and professional development, rather than considering them as part of the process whereby the group, its boundaries, and its legitimacy have been constructed. Finally, few historians of the journalistic occupational group have considered the role of journalists' discursive strategies as part of the history of the formation of journalistic work boundaries and legitimacy. Such strategies, also referred to at times in this book as occupational communication and journalistic discourse, have played at least as important a role in the construction of the occupation as have the work products and organizational forms that emerged during the eighteenth and nineteenth centuries. Embodied within such printed and oral forms of communication as newspaper prospectuses, autobiographies, libel courtroom testimony and speeches, occupational communication has assumed an important role in the history of journalism as work, occupation, and profession.

In its simplest terms, all work, including that in journalism, consists of sets of tasks performed by workers in particular environments under specific conditions. But the more complex concept of work inevitably brings up questions of occupations and professions, social organizations, the public, and myriad events and developments in broader social and cultural environments. While histories of work often start with identification and description of work tasks and those who accomplish them, they must also study the complex processes that precipitate the emergence and development of occupational groups.

Occupations, defined here as the social and cultural organization of work and workers, do not reflect or implement fixed or natural differences between work roles. Rather, occupation is cultural knowledge and social organization that define differences between work groups, and such knowledge is volatile. Occupations coalesce through complex processes that vary across time, cultures, and social and demographic groups.[6] While work tasks acquire occupational dimensions from isolated events or more general developments in the broader environments they are embedded within, occupational knowledge or meaning is also constructed through the agency of workers themselves, including discursive strategies. At times, such meaning is constructed oppositionally in that the cultural meanings of occupations come out of processes that involve group conflict between different but related groups over questions of who ought to have authority over work tasks. Often debated in public media, these work-related disputes can lead to creation and reconstruction of occupational boundaries that differentiate various groups of workers. At other times, such work-related disputes are less public, occurring in less visible legal and workplace domains.

If applied to the field of journalism, these definitions raise myriad questions, including the following: When did American journalistic work begin to emerge occupationally; that is, when did a group whose work regularly included provision of certain categories of political communication begin to be connected to journalistic work tasks? What conditions have led to the legitimization of the journalistic group and its politically-related work? What discursive or other strategies have journalists engaged in that might have led to construction of self-serving definitions of political communication-related work? How might such rhetoric have impacted the group's legitimacy as providers of political news? What events or developments outside the boundaries of journalism might have affected its occupational boundaries in relation to political communication work? In short, has there been a process whereby the journalistic occupational group has been constructed over time as Americans' regular provider of political news and editorial opinion that may be instructive in the present?

An exploration of the approaches of sociologists on the development of professions reveals a rich mine of perspectives that can be plumbed by historians interested in answering questions such as these concerning the history of journalism as an occupation. But despite the important role sociologists' models on professional development have played in this study, it must be stressed that the purpose here is not to explore whether journalists are professionals or nonprofessionals. This debate has for too long overshadowed study of journalistic work. The perspective here is that journalistic work is professional because of its abstract nature, but also because of the journalistic group's discursive linking of such work to its members. To be considered professional, journalists, like all occupational groups seeking higher legitimacy, have engaged in discursive strategies that under certain circumstances and in various time periods have afforded them certain measures of authority. Finally, any measure of success journalists have enjoyed in their pursuit of professional power has been vulnerable to erosion from the effects of unexpected events in the broader systems within which the group resides, and the efforts of other groups who have sought to encroach on their work territory.

SOCIOLOGICAL THEORY ON WORK, OCCUPATIONS, AND PROFESSIONS

While generally agreeing that the professions make up a special category of occupations, sociologists have differed on the attributes that make them special, as well as why and how groups achieve such designation.[7] Until the late 1960s and early 1970s, scholarly attention to occupations and professions was largely focused on identifying "traits," such as development of codes of ethics, that supposedly differentiated professionals from nonprofessionals.[8]

But out of the political and cultural turmoil of the late 1960s and 1970s a more dynamic model began to emerge and gain prominence in sociology. An important precursor to these newer approaches was Everett C. Hughes, one of the leaders of the "Chicago School," who, during the 1950s, revised his thinking on professional groups. Such redirection foreshadowed the later ferment that reshaped basic questions in studies of professional and occupational groups. In reflecting on his career in a 1958 book, *Men and Their Work,* Hughes revealed how his thinking about occupations changed over the years: "In my own studies I passed from the false question, 'Is this occupation a profession?' to a more fundamental one, 'What are the circumstances in which people in an occupation attempt to turn it into a profession, and themselves into professional people?'"[9]

Hughes sought to understand how members of occupations, in their day-to-day activities, negotiate and maintain their special positions. For him, the key characteristics of the professional phenomenon could be identified from the observation of occupational groups at work. Such thinking reflected a changing sociological environment and signaled the new directions occupational sociologists would pursue.

Despite Hughes's influence, his approach to studying professions did not begin to filter into the explanatory models of sociologists until a decade after *Men and Their Work* was published. During the late 1960s and the 1970s, a new cadre of scholars began to search for different paradigms and explanations in studying professions.[10] The labels they used to describe the work of their predecessors offer clues to the newer direction: Such adjectives as "time bound," "culture bound," "inaccurate," "antitheoretical," "simplistic," "ahistorical," "unexplicit," and "unsystematic," suggest their impatience with previous inquiry about professionalization.[11]

One of the most important recommendations of the more recent occupational sociologists was the call for historical analysis of occupational and professional groups. Julius A. Roth, for example, described history as the "best antidote for the attribute rut."[12] He continued:

If we can see in some detail how present-day professions developed, we would be less inclined to conjure up a vision of a list of characteristics toward which certain lines of work are moving and see it rather as a long-term process of negotiation. Sociologists in the occupational area have so far made little use of historical analysis. We will have to draw on writings from other disciplines to develop a historical perspective.

Roth's comment symbolizes an old marriage between history and sociology that has been reconsummated in the last two decades. But while sociology has always been to some degree a historically grounded and oriented enterprise, until recently sociologists who strongly emphasized history were not considered a part of the mainstream.[13]

Historical sociologists differ in their explanations of when, why, and how occupational groups emerge and coalesce. For example, one argument asserts that occupational groups emerge primarily in response to broader environmental movements, events, structural changes, or processes. Among this group is Hughes, who posits that occupational groups are precipitated by technological development, social movements, and new social institutions.[14]

A second explanation is that groups form and are strengthened due to the efforts of the groups themselves. Among the strategies groups use to establish themselves are social actions, including the formation of occupational associations, the issuance of occupational-related communication, and group negotiation of a system of interdependencies with other groups. Boundary formation and maintenance are important, claim these sociologists, since the various forms that boundaries take help delineate and empower the group's members as they seek occupational power. [15]

Certain categories of work become known as professional work, and differing explanations of this process reflect a second important difference between the approaches of the old and new schools of occupational sociologists. A group of recent sociologists see professional development largely as a matter of group struggle and control — rather than the mere accumulation of traits — and use what can be called a power model. Trait theories, they argue, suggest too many categories of traits. In a review of trait theory literature, Geoffrey Millerson, for example, identified twenty-three elements included in various definitions of profession.[16]

One of the earliest proponents of a power model, Terence J. Johnson, contends that, rather than serving the "disembodied social needs" of consumers, aspiring professionals attempt to impose their own definitions of human needs fulfillment on groups of "atomized consumers."[17] Emphasizing that sociologists' preoccupation with professional traits diverts their attention from more important questions, he stresses occupational power as the important factor in evaluating the professional status of occupational groups.[18]

Julius A. Roth also finds serious deficiencies in the work of trait theorists.[19] He criticizes their focus on identifying supposedly unique characteristics of professional groups, maintaining they ignore more important questions. Claiming the older scholarship was antitheoretical and avoided the social problems inherent in the professional ideology, Roth faults his predecessors for being "apologists for the professionalism ideology, justifying the professionals' control over their work situation."[20]

Sociologist Andrew Abbott has also critiqued trait theorists' approaches, arguing that a primary difference between occupations and professions lies in the nature of their work rather than their abilities to accumulate traits. Two categories of work, he claims, coexist in occupational structures: technical and abstract. Often referred to as crafts, technical work includes purely physical or rote tasks that do not require the acquisition and/or control of abstract knowledge. Professional work, on the other hand, depends on the acquisition and manipulation of abstract knowledge. Here, practical skill grows out of an abstract system of knowledge, and control of the occupation lies in mastery of the abstractions that generate the practical techniques. Professional work, according to Abbott, functions to solve "human problems amenable to expert service . . . problems for individuals, like sickness and salvation."[21] As such, some human problems, such as illness, are in expert hands throughout much of the world, while others vary in definitions and treatments from country to country. For example, the human problem of discovering the meaning of life is secularized in some countries but is in the domain of organized religions in others. Professional work jurisdictions emerge when groups amass enough power to garner some level of control of both the abstract knowledge and the skills needed to do the work. Jurisdictions form the ties that bind occupational groups to work tasks.[22]

Depending on their theoretical orientations, scholars whose models stress groups' accumulation of power have adopted different approaches in studies of professionals. Magali Sarfatti Larson, for example, who adopts a critical Marxist approach, defines professional power as the ability of certain occupational groups to create markets for services and accumulate monopolies over the dispensing of such services.[23] Of central importance is a group's ability to meet the needs of various groups as it sells its services.

The possession of skills, usually based on specialized knowledge, according to a number of occupational sociologists, is also an important aspect of the power model. Through the adoption of various strategies, occupational groups attempt to win, enlarge, and capture the largest markets possible for their skills and services. Knowledge and special skills thus become important commodities. Such ideas conform to those advanced by Max Weber, who viewed skills as modern forms of property.[24] John B. Cullen, for example, in such a Weberian vein, has related professional development to the abilities of certain groups to accumulate and manipulate scientific and technological knowledge.[25]

Another group of scholars has stressed various professionalizing groups' abilities to form and maintain occupational boundaries, which are social or cultural divisions that help signify a group's work, societal roles, and legitimacy. Although generally intangible, boundaries are at times clarified and anchored by social structural mechanisms such as occupational associations and laws.[26] Learning how occupations come to have boundaries requires studying how the group and its work have been constructed or legitimized within complex and broader social and cultural environments.

This process of establishing and maintaining boundaries is one that is central to an occupational group's amassing of societal legitimacy. To establish and maintain occupational boundaries, groups must define, claim, and seek to control certain work tasks; they must devise strategies to ward off the members of other occupations seeking to encroach on their work terrain; they must control the process of admitting new workers to the occupational fold; and they must strive to become solely responsible for penalizing those who violate the group's standards. In addition, occupational groups seeking to establish and maintain boundaries must create markets for their particular skills and/or products.

Thus, it is assumed that such boundary-building activity is part of a foundation from which an occupational group may ultimately be legitimized as one whose work is considered indispensable. To form and maintain boundaries, aspiring professionals must adopt various strategies, including the dissemination of professionalizing rhetoric in a variety of forms and venues, and become involved in social actions designed to influence public opinion and legislatures.

If successful in forming and defending the boundaries through such communication strategies, the groups' members are able to do the following: define its members' work tasks, as well as the normative values that guide the work of the group; control the admittance of newcomers to the group; retain the power to punish occupational members who do not meet the group's standards; design and oversee the process of educating those who seek entry into the group; accumulate and control the raw materials and other resources, that is, capital, labor supplies, equipment, technology, and information, required to produce the work product or service; prevent competing occupational groups from encroaching on the group's work territory; resist the efforts of economic, societal, govermental, or political institutions whose representatives seek to control the occupation's members; and, finally, supervise the occupation's licensing process, if one is required by state or federal authorities.[27]

The more control the members of an occupational group have over these processes and resources, the more occupational power they amass. To survive, groups must be able to adapt to the changing demands and conditions of the social system in which they reside, including economic, political and social forces outside their control, and this generally involves further dissemination of occupational rhetoric in public media or legal and workplace spheres.[28]

These various processes and actions do not occur separately in steplike succession. Instead, they occur in conjunction with each other, the occupational group's ultimate goal being control of all the necessary facets of work required for autonomy. In such an analysis, certain organizational forms and group rhetoric play dynamic roles rather than being merely static dimensions of the professionalization process. Freidson, Larson, and Abbott, for example, assert that professionalizing occupational groups attempt to use their claims to cognitive and normative superiority in certain areas in a process that involves both struggle and persuasion. In this process, groups negotiate the boundaries of a task area in the social division of labor and attempt to establish control over it. Persuasive rhetoric is directed outside the group to relevant elites, the public, and political and governmental authorities, among other audiences.[29]

SCHOLARSHIP ON JOURNALISTIC WORK, OCCUPATIONS, AND PROFESSIONS

This plethora of promising sociological perspectives on occupation and profession has had little impact on American scholarship in journalism and mass communication. Mirroring earlier sociological trends and approaches of the authors of American journalism textbooks, most writing on the journalistic occupation portrays it as a progressively developing entity striving for professional status through gradual acquisition of the accoutrements of professionalism such as codes of ethics and university training.

Some mass communication scholars have discussed the question "Is Journalism a Profession?" rhetorically, such as Penn Kimball in his well-known essay "Journalism: Art, Craft or Profession?"[30] Another common thread in writing on the journalistic group comes out of reaction to the intense public criticism of professions during the 1970s, urging journalists to strive for greater professionalism.[31] Finally, a few scholars explain journalistic professionalism in terms of the group's ability to acquire legitimacy, while yet another group studies the professional orientations of media workers.[32]

Of the myriad studies of the conduct of journalists and of issues of importance to the journalistic occupational group, relatively few have examined occupational change apart from specific journalistic industries, organizations, and practitioners. Scholars studying patterns of occupational change in journalism generally have used microstructural, rather than macrostructural, approaches, studying single well-known institutions and journalists, rather than groups of journalistic institutions, journalists, or other larger social structures such as occupational groups. In addition, scholars have frequently studied occupational history in narrowly constructed time periods, rather than longitudinally, over longer time periods. And studies of the journalistic occupational group and its development tend to focus on the group's relatively recent history, particularly in the twentieth century, rather than its earlier development.[33]

More recently, a number of promising studies have examined the historical sociology of journalistic work, arguing that most journalism history fails to recognize and study the rank and file in the history of the journalistic industry. While these studies contribute a great deal to the literature, they do not always examine the fundamental processes that would lead to the construction and reconstruction of journalistic work and the journalistic occupation over long periods of time.[34]

A MODEL FOR STUDYING THE HISTORY OF JOURNALISM AS WORK, OCCUPATION, AND PROFESSION

Derived from the work of sociologists previously discussed, the model explicated here will help fill a gap in the literature on the history of journalism, a gap that scholars have called attention to for more than a decade.[35] Represented in Figure 1.1,[36] this model is primarily concerned with the history of the general newspaper journalistic occupational group, that group whose members over time acquired legitimacy as providers of political news and editorial opinion writing. It could also be adapted to study other areas of journalistic work, such as broadcast news or photojournalism.

This model is predicated on the idea that the construction of the journalistic occupational group and its work is a cyclical and interdynamic process, rather than a linear and progressive one. Discursive strategies of emerging groups, and conflict between competing work groups for control of work tasks, are crucial components of this process, which can lead to definition, or construction, of occupational boundaries (i.e., public definitions of the tasks, roles, and legitimacy of particular work groups). Within histories of construction of occupational boundaries, four interrelated elements are of central importance:

Figure 1.1
The Historical Sociological Development of Journalistic Work as Occupation

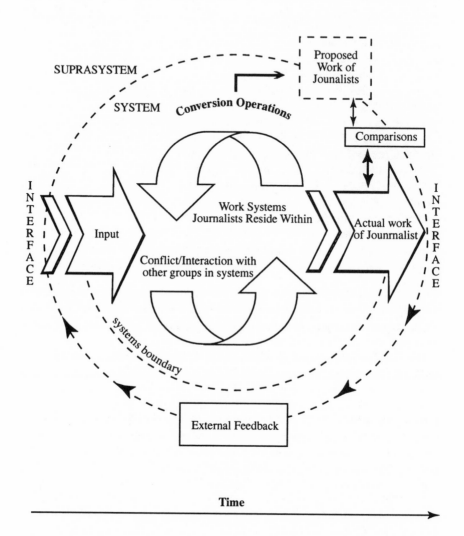

1. The fundamental work tasks and cultural and social aspects of journalistic work and those of adjacent occupational groups in professional work systems (work systems are constellations of related tasks and the various occupational groups that emerge to do them).
2. Changes within the broader technological, cultural, social, economic, and political, environments that journalists reside within.
3. The cultural and social values and norms of journalists' clients, such as the public, advertisers, or other patrons.
4. The occupational communication or other strategies of members of the journalistic occupational group who engage in competitive jurisdictional contests over work with related groups within broader work systems.

Study of development of the journalistic occupational group ought to begin by describing journalistic work and the historical conditions under which it emerged and coalesced into a set of collective tasks with particular cultural definitions and social organizational dimensions. Journalistic work is defined simply as any tasks or activities involved in the gathering, preparation, and dissemination of news, while definitions of the journalistic occupation embody concepts of the socially organized world of journalism and cultural knowledge of definitions of journalists as workers with particular societal occupational roles and authority. Neither journalistic work tasks nor the occupational and professional forms such tasks have taken have ever been fixed by their natures or in history. Rather, journalistic work and occupations are cultural and social constructions that are subject to redefinition and reconstruction that can come about through complex processes involving agency of journalists, the public, and events outside their control.

The work of occupational groups such as journalists can be considered professional if the work involved fulfills basic human needs that cannot be met without expert assistance; if the work tasks involved in such expert service require collection and manipulation of abstract, rather than technical, knowledge; and, finally, if the work group achieves some measure of jurisdiction over these work tasks.[37] To gain additional insight into how or when journalism became occupation or profession involves further description and analysis of the tasks and cultural and social aspects of journalistic work.

CULTURAL ASPECTS OF JOURNALISTIC WORK

Journalistic Work as Fulfillment of Human Need

Professionals are experts who serve humanity by fulfilling human needs that can only be met through the manipulation of abstract knowledge. Using this definition, one may say that the tasks involved in journalistic work are professional to the extent that they surpass nonjournalists' abilities to acquire and disseminate news, i.e., fresh or current information about the world outside their immediate environments.[38] Like other groups who during the nineteenth century sought professional status, journalistic work tasks were delineated and promoted in such a way that they would serve a particular human need.

Some human needs are innate, such as the need for food, while others are at least in part related to social and cultural conditions. Some of one's thirst for news may be intrinsic to human nature, but historically, people's news requirements were also likely affected by changes or events in economic, political, cultural, and social institutions.[39] Transformations that could have affected Americans' news needs over the eighteenth and nineteenth centuries include the shift from English colony to independent nation and a democratic representative form of government, from traditional to modern society, and from geographically disparate local rural communities to a largely urban society. In the eighteenth century, people received much of their knowledge of the community informally through friends, family, and neighbors. By the end of the nineteenth century, Americans could not depend alone on these sources to meet their news and information needs. The solving of this need for knowledge of a more complex and interconnected world would in time become considered by many to be the responsibility of journalists.[40]

For any given time period, then, one may study occupational forms designed to fulfill human needs. For example, in response to the American Revolution, the community's providers of newspapers, to fulfill a need created by political events, provided more politically volatile materials than they or their predecessors had, and newspaper work thereafter was altered as a result. Over the nineteenth and twentieth centuries, journalists responded to needs created by a continually evolving political, commercial, and economic environment by providing diverse narrative and visual forms of news and entertainment content.[41]

Throughout their history, journalists have communicated with the public about the work they perform and have created various organizational forms and practices that reinforce the idea that they ought to be the sole providers of the various categories of news and information that they claim people need.[42]

Abstract and Technical Dimensions of Journalistic Work Tasks

Professional work is distinguishable from other work in that its tasks depend on the manipulation of abstract knowledge. Many tasks in journalistic work meet this definition of professional work because workers must acquire and manipulate abstract ideas and concepts to gather, prepare, and dispense news and editorial content. Nonprofessional work, on the other hand, is accomplished through physical processes or techniques that do not depend on such abstract knowledge.[43]

The abstract and technical requirements of journalistic work have varied according to time periods and news medium size. Early journalism encompassed both. Those who produced early newspapers, for example, were often responsible for the actual printing, but early journalists also often completed tasks that depended on abstract knowledge. Maine newspaper editor Joseph Griffin described this in his book on the history of Maine's press:

The printer, combining intellectual with mechanical employment, — *composing* typographically, and at the same time, mentally, — elaborating or criticising the written ideas of others in the copy before him, — often putting his own thoughts, without copy, directly into form, — must have a dull, heedless head if he does not gain the tact of a ready and good writer.[44]

But as newspapers changed and circulations grew across the nineteenth century, the abstract and technical work tasks were often separated so that eventually, most tasks of a technical nature were largely delegated to nonjournalistic printers.[45]

In professional work systems, work is largely tied to systems of abstract knowledge gathered and manipulated by workers so that people's needs for certain expert services are met. Several examples of professional work systems are those related to political communication, medicine, law, and information. Work systems, which can include both professional and nonprofessional work tasks, are broadly defined as occupational structures that include certain elements that together engender work products. Such elements include the following: occupational groups (journalists and politicians, for example) and their work tasks (writing news articles and editorials) and products (the actual news articles), societal institutions and agencies (the newspaper industry, political parties, and government), and other societal groups (citizens or patrons). Whether an occupational group attains jurisdiction lies partly in the power and prestige of the abstract knowledge its workers use. Such knowledge legitimizes professional work by clarifying its foundations and tying it to major cultural values. For example, the medical profession is legitimated in part by its development of medical science and technology; law has legal theory; the military has military science; and politicians have political science and philosophy. Such abstract systems of knowledge are usually developed over long periods of time. [46]

Since journalism involves gathering and disseminating information about the world, it differs from such professions in that it has always depended heavily on the knowledge systems developed by others. The medical profession, for example, which from its early history developed its own abstract knowledge systems, has in part based its quest for legitimacy on its body of medical science. But journalism has no comparable body of knowledge from which to draw in its practice. Because a comparable body of knowledge has not been developed for journalism, the journalistic occupational group has based its quest for legitimacy on its handling of abstract knowledge from others.[47]

Dependence on abstract knowledge systems originating largely outside journalism has made the group's work especially vulnerable to both attacks from encroachers and to major shifts in institutions outside journalism's boundaries. For example, because journalists have been so dependent on political sources for knowledge about politics, they have been especially vulnerable to politicians and governmental officials who refuse to provide information. Additionally, journalists and their work are particularly sensitive to major shifts in political and governmental systems, such as the development of new party systems, political revolutions, or changes in the ways government officials manage information and communication.[48]

Subjectivity of Journalistic Work

In addition to the abstract and technical dimensions of work, it can also be analyzed according to its levels of subjectivity. Occupations such as theology and politics, for example, are highly subjective in that the tasks required to accomplish such work depend largely on abstract mental activity. The engineering and computer programming occupations, however, while still requiring intellectual work, are more closely tied to technological developments than theology and politics. The subjective or objective nature of work is important because subjective work is highly vulnerable to jurisdictional attacks from competing groups whose members would like to gain control of another groups' work tasks.

Certain journalistic work tasks, including those reporting, writing, and editing, are more subjective than journalistic tasks like printing and news dissemination, which are more closely tied to technologies. Because of their highly subjective nature, journalistic tasks such as newswriting and editing, have been particularly prone to jurisdictional attacks by competing groups whose members seek to invade journalists' work terrain or establish control over journalistic workers. [49]

Cultural Stages of Journalistic Work

Professional work can be conceptualized as consisting of three culturally defined overlapping stages: the diagnosis, inference, and treatment of human needs amenable only to expert service. Diagnosis is that part of professional work where workers take information into their knowledge systems. Treatment, which comes at the concluding stages of professional work, brings the information gathered in the diagnostic process back out from the work system in some form to solve the basic human problem addressed by the professional. Inference, a purely professional act that occurs somewhere between diagnosis and treatment, "takes the information of diagnosis and indicates a range of treatments with their predicted outcomes."[50] Occupational groups, including journalists, create links between their group and these cultural aspects of work; that link is jurisdiction, and it is constructed principally through a complex process involving occupational communication and other factors.

The "diagnostic" aspect of the process of journalistic work involves taking information into the knowledge system, or reporting. Journalistic work has always involved gathering observations and information from the broader environment. For example, today journalists observe, and otherwise gather information and knowledge about, politics and politicians. This "diagnostic" process puts journalists in close contact with those politicians and governmental officials who possess political knowledge and other occupational groups, including politicians and public relations experts, whose work also involves communication of political information.

Newspaper journalists' work has met the criterion of this diagnostic stage differently depending on such factors as the period under study, type of newspaper (whether daily, weekly, special, or general-focus), or stated editorial policy (whether it includes coverage of foreign affairs, national affairs, or primarily local affairs, for example). The earliest journalists, although not thought of as information gatherers because they rarely ventured outside their newspaper offices, nevertheless observed the world and collected information. Routinely exchanging newspapers with their peers, they were able to obtain a regular supply of items that they evaluated for possible reprinting. Additionally, early journalists depended on correspondents who provided essays or reports. Politicians often served as correspondents, writing letters or essays that reported on legislative sessions, meetings, and events. In addition, world travelers served as correspondents, as well as anyone else who had witnessed a significant event or attended important meetings.[51]

Over time, as newspapers and the news industry evolved, the diagnosis stage in journalism also changed from a largely passive, to a more proactive, one. In the nineteenth century, journalists would become more active as observers and news gatherers. This was part of the development of the journalistic role of the reporter, a role that began developing early in the nineteenth century, especially in America's urban areas, but would not become widely practiced until later in the century.[52]

Journalists, however, even today depend on other suppliers of information and impressions of the world. It is common today, for example, for a newspaper's reporting and editorial work to depend on a system of sources or to be supplemented by cooperative news agencies and related industries. Thus, services such as the Associated Press and New York Times News Service have come to play important roles in the diagnostic process in journalism.

The inference stage in journalistic work involves the evaluation of the knowledge gleaned in the information gathering stage and consideration and determination of which of a range of possible treatments will best remedy various groups' news needs.[53] This might involve using the knowledge in a news story, feature, editorial, or some other treatment. The inference stage constitutes a purely professional act, since it does not typically involve the public or others, except in the sense that the worker keeps the public's needs uppermost in mind throughout the process.

There is rarely a clear separation between the diagnostic and inferences stages of journalistic work. Often, those involved in gathering information make judgments as they do their work. The diagnostic process involves continuous evaluation in terms of what will be the most effective proportion of news and editorial content based on what might be conflicting needs of the public and publisher.

The final stage in the process of journalistic work is the treatment stage, where whatever treatment has been decided on in the inference stage is applied. Examples of treatments include news stories, editorials, or some other form of journalistic content, which are designed to fulfill the public's need for news and other forms of related communication. This process solves the human needs of the public and patrons, advertisers, and politicians for example, that journalists are required to cater to. Journalists, through their collection and manipulation of various categories of abstract information, create many forms of news and other content to fulfill these needs.[54]

The forms of journalistic treatments vary depending on the time period and the category of newspaper (daily, weekly, country, or urban). For example, during the American Revolution, newspaper proprietors published more letters and essays than did their late-nineteenth-century counterparts. During 1775, such content comprised more than 20 percent of a typical newspaper, whereas local news comprised only 7.95 percent.[55] But by the end of the nineteenth century, journalists considered local news stories to be a more appropriate treatment for the information needs of the public.[56]

The narrative styles in journalistic treatments have varied as well.[57] For example, early news items often resembled essays. Not until the Civil War did the modern form of the news story, embodying the inverted pyramid form's introductory statement, or lead, that summarizes important news elements including what happened, to whom, where, when, and why, begin to appear.[58]

SOCIAL STRUCTURAL ASPECTS OF JOURNALISTIC WORK

Jurisdiction (that is, links to work) consists of more than cultural aspects and tasks, since it also includes social structural elements, including systems for training and remunerating workers, emergence of legal protections for workers, and certain nonlegal entitlements, such as the right to define the group and its work; public financial support; unconstrained employment; and control of recruitment, schools, ethics codes, and associations.[59]

Rather than being viewed only as indicators that an occupational group has coalesced and might be developing as a profession, such social structures are better viewed as tools that serve occupational groups as they seek jurisdiction over certain categories of work. In the very least, the existence of such social structures indicate that work groups are socially organized and culturally defined. But additionally, members of emerging groups are free to incorporate mention of such attributes in the various public communications they engage in that contribute to public definitions of their work and roles.

Development of social structures that would serve to contribute to the process whereby journalism began to acquire occupational definition began early in the eighteenth century. Sets of tasks and systems for remuneration and training of journalists began to evolve, and late in the century, a printers' guild was established. In addition, another major social structural supporter of journalism dating from the eighteenth century is the First Amendment to the U. S. Constitution.[60]

Journalists developed normative values and organizational structural forms that underpinned their claims to being trustworthy and respectable. They formed occupational associations, the first of which was a national association formed in the 1860s, and it was followed by myriad state, local, and special purpose journalistic associations, such as those specially designed for certain categories of journalists. These issued statements that reflected the normative values of journalism and helped in the training of journalists. Later, in the nineteenth century, colleges and universities began also to develop curricula for journalists.[61] Through these education functions, occupational associations and college training programs served as mechanisms of group social control, and by their very existence, they reinforced the legitimacy of the journalistic occupational group and its various specialties.

Among other social structural mechanisms, the U. S. Supreme Court, in the twentieth century, began to apply the First Amendment to state and local cases. Other social structural mechanisms were continued, such as occupational associations and education programs, and some were created, such as news councils.[62]

While identifying examples of journalistic work in history is not difficult, understanding when and how early journalistic tasks and other social structural elements coalesced into occupations is more difficult, since these processes occurred centuries ago over long periods of time. Examples of some of the earliest journalistic workers, for example, may have included the creators of Roman news sheets in the first century, as well as later authors and distributors of news ballads.[63] To determine when journalistic work tasks began to assume occupational dimensions requires exploring: when various journalistic tasks were carried out by individuals on a somewhat regular basis for monetary remuneration; when individuals accomplishing such tasks began to be assigned a general responsibility and social status in relation to the work; when journalistic workers began to formulate methods for training recruits, or otherwise passing on knowledge related to the accomplishment of journalistic work; and, finally, when journalistic workers with greatly disparate demographic backgrounds (such as education, social class, ethnicity), began to exhibit similar occupational practices, values, and standards despite these differences.[64] Studying historical evidence, such as journalists' business and personal records, autobiographies, and newspaper prospectuses, will aid in discerning when journalistic workers began to coalesce into an occupation.

Journalistic Work Tasks

Out of these three broad cultural aspects of journalistic work evolved tasks that together would come to comprise the process of journalistic work.[65] News gathering, for example, became an important task in the diagnostic stage, whereas editing became part of the inference and treatment stages. In part, the more specific tasks delineated here, and the particular workers responsible for them, have varied according to the journalistic medium and the stage of journalistic development. Eighteenth- and early nineteenth-century journalistic tasks were completed largely by printers, whereas such tasks were increasingly differentiated during the nineteenth century. Such work came to be completed by different categories of workers rather than being bundled together and completed by the printers only.[66] However, today there are still journalistic enterprises small enough that tasks are bundled as they were in early newspaper history.

Publishing. Publishers are involved in establishing and at times supervising the overall editorial direction of the newspaper. Some publishers do not get involved in the day-to-day supervision of the staff, while others do. In early newspaper journalism, the publisher often completed all the other tasks defined in this section; however, over the nineteenth century, the publisher role was gradually differentiated from the other tasks. By late in this period, those filling such a position often performed only broad management responsibilities.[67]

Printing. Newspaper printers complete the technical and practical tasks necessary to physically operate printing machinery and produce the newspapers. Printers were among the first journalists, since they often completed all the tasks necessary to issue newspapers and other journalistic forms. According to nineteenth-century journalist Thurlow Weed, for example, the typical printer of the late eighteenth and early nineteenth centuries was "seldom satisfied until he had demonstrated his ability to compose articles, editorials, or advertising matter directly into type, without relying on written copy."[68] But, as the nineteenth century progressed, newspaper printing became a full-time technical task delegated to nonjournalists.[69]

Observation and Information Gathering. Journalistic work has always required observation and information gathering, even before reporting was to develop in the nineteenth century as a particular job category in journalism.[70] The reporters' special task is to gather information and/or serve as observers of the world in a proactive process. They are at times paid employees of the newspaper publisher and are often supervised by editors, while at other times they work on a freelance basis. In addition to their roles as newsgatherers and observers, reporters usually are also responsible for writing the news stories based on their research.

Unpaid correspondents historically have also served as reporters in the sense that they have provided to particular newspapers their observations and experiences as travelers or witnesses at important political and governmental events or meetings. While correspondents such as these were common on early papers, and were often highly valued in the newsgathering process, they are rarer today. Early newspaper correspondents were educated, literate individuals whose stations in life took them to distant, even exotic, places.[71]

Writing. Writing is integral to journalistic work, since all forms of journalism begin from written news accounts or other narrative forms like editorials. Nonjournalists did much of the earliest newspaper writing; that is, the writers were not regular workers in the printing offices that produced the earliest newspapers. Such individuals were especially equipped through education and/or career to serve as writers. As such, they fashioned their experiences and knowledge into essays and letters, much of which became the most essential components of early newspapers.[72]

Some of these individuals wrote under assumed names. One well-known example is John Dickinson, a late eighteenth-century Whig philosopher.[73] Although not a publisher or printer, his writing for newspapers certainly is an example of early journalistic work. (Technically, he was not a journalist in that he was not a paid newspaper staff member such as was the printer and editor, so far as is known.) Today, essays written by community members still appear on some newspapers' editorial pages, but they are always printed at the discretion of the editorial staff.

Editing. The editor's work consists of decision-making tasks, in conjunction with publishers and patrons, about the editorial direction of the newspaper. Such tasks include decisions about how and where news should be gathered, journalistic reports to be created, copy editing of materials to be published, creation and/or selection of headlines, or other important news elements. The editorial role emerged in its most basic form in conjunction with the earliest forms of newspapers. At first it was subsumed within other tasks completed by the earliest journalists-printers.[74]

Distribution/Dissemination. The work task of distribution, or dissemination, involves the printing and distribution of newspapers to the public. Largely technical in nature in modern newspaper work, distribution has rarely been considered part of the work of the journalist. However, in early journalism history, journalists were often responsible for delivering newspapers when an apprentice or other assistant was not available to do so. As the newspaper industry grew across the nineteenth century, this task was increasingly handled by nonjournalists, although even today, in some circumstances, these tasks are still performed by journalists.[75]

In sum, studying the emergence and development of the American journalistic occupational group and its work requires considering the conditions under which these fundamental journalistic work tasks have been transformed into an occupation and then further developed into various occupational specialties. Among specialties today are foreign correspondence, editorial writing, copy editing, cartooning, illustrating, photojournalism, documentary film or television journalism producing, sports journalism, and wire service and press association work.

IMPACT OF BROADER ENVIRONMENTS ON
JOURNALISTIC WORK

Journalistic work tasks have coalesced into occupations in part due to broad environmental movements, events, or structural changes such as technological, economic, and political development, social and cultural shifts, and movements and new social institutions.[76] Sociologists and historians claim that development within many occupations has been fueled by what has been called the "Great Transformation," a process in America over the nineteenth century that included industrialization, urbanization, and a fundamental shift from an economic system based on patronage to one dominated by capitalistic markets.[77]

The timing of this transformation varied from country to country, and other important industrial, technological, scientific, political, and social revolutions were a part of the same process. Such associated revolutions brought advances in knowledge in science and other disciplines; improvements in literacy rates; a revolution in religious thinking that precipitated other social movements, which were in turn fueled by political and economic phenomenon; new technologies that precipitated new work tasks and, ultimately, new products and services; and bureaucratization of institutions, including development of modern political systems based on popular rather than elite patronage. With these changes also came increases in populations and immigration.[78]

Looking at journalistic work long before it was established in America by the colonists, a particularly important technological development in its history has been the printing press. The oldest surviving regularly published newspapers were published in Germany in 1609. But the workers who issued these were only one category of early journalistic workers, since their medium was only one among several media that developed as a result of the printing press innovation. Printed books, pamphlets, and other media that at times disseminated journalistic content, for example, proliferated after Johann Gutenberg's invention began to spread throughout Europe and England in the late fifteenth and early sixteenth centuries.[79]

After the establishment of printing presses in the American colonies and the emergence of newspapers and other news products, other important events and developments would also come to have profound effects on its history. For example, the American Revolution played a particularly important role in the history of the American journalistic occupational group. However, such events alone rarely explain occupational development, especially when work groups have already emerged and acquired jurisdiction over certain work tasks. Development instead results through a complex process involving events or other changes that originate outside the group along with a group's discursive or other strategies in relation to work.

AGENCY AND COMPETITION IN WORK SYSTEMS

In addition to technological, social, and other broad environmental structures, emerging occupational groups also coalesce in response to the efforts of their own members. Among strategies they use to establish themselves within their communities are forms of occupational communication, formation of occupational associations, and negotiations of systems of interdependencies with other groups. These activities constitute boundary formation and maintenance, which are important, according to sociologists, since social boundaries delineate and empower the group's members as they seek occupational power.[80] The journalistic occupational group, like other developing groups, formed strategies that would spur the formation of occupational boundaries. One example of such was their issuance of newspaper prospectuses, a practice that ultimately constructed the meaning of the group and its work and helped give it social and cultural legitimacy.

Thus, over and above the basic nature of journalistic work and emergence of various social structural elements, a determining factor in the occupational development of the journalistic group has been its members' efforts to acquire jurisdiction over such work. Part of this struggle for power has involved efforts to amass market power through the development of products that attract patrons and advertisers. A second integral part of the process has involved attempts to form and maintain occupational boundaries, defined as social or cultural divisions that help define an occupational group's work, societal roles, and legitimacy. Boundaries are often lacking in tangibility; however, they can be clarified by such things as occupational associations and various laws or other legal mechanisms that serve as anchors. Boundary establishment and maintenance is a process that some occupational sociologists claim is central to a group's amassing of societal legitimacy.[81] Exploring such a process in the history of the journalistic occupation requires studying journalists' efforts to define and control their work tasks, overcome competition from neighboring occupational groups, and amass the raw materials and other resources needed to overcome other groups' efforts to control them and their work.

For example, one essential question becomes this: How did journalists obtain unrestricted access to the materials and technologies required to do their work? In the newspaper business, the needed raw materials include paper and other printing supplies and various technologies such as printing equipment, type, cameras, and the many other mechanical and computerized devices that have come to play important roles in the production of journalistic products.

Other less tangible resources essential to maintaining occupational power include enough labor and capital to carry on the business of printing, or producing, or other media output, and all the categories of information used to present news stories. Such factors raise questions about the ability of the members of the journalistic group to attract potential workers and to obtain funding from political patronage, government contracts, advertisers, or any others. How journalists acquire and maintain access to the important information they need to produce news stories or other newspaper content is also of importance. To succeed in these ventures, journalists seek to interact with, and manipulate to their advantage, various groups, such as readers or other clients; various political and legal bodies, including legislatures, courts, and local law enforcement authorities; "owners" of the desired raw materials and resources; and, finally, competing neighboring occupational groups.

Journalistic work, along with those who accomplish it, coexists with adjacent related tasks and professionals within broader professional work systems. Examples of work systems that journalism has been part of include the one studied here, the political communication professional work system, which includes politicians, journalists, and governmental communicators, among others, and a more general information work system, where journalists coexist with librarians and accountants.[82]

Development within professional work systems occur when groups accumulate greater measures of jurisdiction over work tasks that are professional in nature, meaning such work involves the collection and manipulation of abstract knowledge.[83] The history of the journalistic group and its work has in large part been determined by their interrelationships with other occupational groups who also reside within the same broader professional work systems. Examples of important occupational groups in the history of journalists include politicians and public relations practitioners. Like journalists, the essence of these groups' work is communication to various publics. Explaining the history of the journalistic occupational group requires studying it within these broader professional work systems.

The central phenomena of the work of newspaper journalists have been the links, collectively called jurisdiction, they have established between themselves and their work tasks. To understand the development of the journalistic occupation, one must study how journalists have sought to establish such links, including their issuance of jurisdictional claims in the public, legal, and workplace spheres.[84]

Any authority or legitimacy acquired by the journalistic group should be considered volatile by its members, since work systems are affected by changes or other developments that can upset their equilibrium. Also, challenges come from other groups who seek to wrest control of work from them, such as politicians and public relations experts. While journalistic work has always included some form of gathering, preparation, and presentation of information, the actual steps in such processes have changed in part as a result of the various settlements of such disputes.

The development of the journalistic occupational group has involved a series of jurisdictional contests, which generally consist of three interlinked stages: (1) the creation of a jurisdictional vacancy, (2) a jurisdictional struggle between journalists and a related group within a broader work system over the control of such vacant work, and (3) a new jurisdictional settlement. Crucial questions concern how such contests were precipitated, fought, and settled. Each of these three stages is defined and discussed here.

Journalistic occupational development occurs in cycles, which start with work vacancies that essentially are openings in work jurisdictions. Journalistic work task vacancies are created through three processes: technological innovations; changes in institutions or structures external to the journalistic occupation; and efforts of the members of the journalistic group who for some reason leave a particular jurisdiction, or open a new one.[85]

Early nineteenth-century technological events that precipitated development in newspaper journalism included various improvements in the printing press. For example, certain technological advances speeded up the printing process, making it possible to serve larger groups of readers. This, in turn, eventually was one of the factors that helped precipitate jurisdictional vacancies in journalistic reporting. In the 1830s and later, for example, the owners of the largely urban penny presses increasingly hired crime and police reporters to serve on their staffs.[86]

A second example of a technological innovation that ultimately led to changes in journalistic work was the camera. The camera and methods for reproducing photographs in newspapers led to the emergence and development of a new category of journalistic work — photojournalism.[87]

Innovations or other changes in newspaper journalistic work have also been closely tied to conditions in the social, cultural, technological, political, and economic environments. New technologies, for example, when coupled with such developments as urbanization, improved literacy rates, and other complex social, political and economic shifts, can lead to new forms of journalism and reconstructions of old ones. Advocacy journalism, emphasizing social issues, was a new form of journalism that emerged from a combination of social, cultural, and technological changes.[88] The abolitionist movement, for example, coupled with improvements in printing beginning in the 1820s, created a new category of work within journalism — abolitionist journalism.

The simple completion of journalistic tasks does not necessarily mean that journalists hold jurisdiction over such work. Jurisdiction has to be won, and this involves struggles with other groups for control of work.[89] After a vacancy occurs for whatever reason, jurisdictional contests, which eventually result in some category of jurisdictional settlements, develop between journalists and other groups with an interest in controlling the vacated work. For example, journalists have likely engaged in jurisdictional contests with politicians and government officials, public relations workers, and other occupational groups that may have been interested in controlling journalistic work in one way or another.

Jurisdictional contests have generally been over control of some cultural aspect or task within journalistic work. For example, newspaper journalists struggled with politicians over control of publishing and editing tasks during the nineteenth century. Politicians, especially early in the century, served as publishers and editors or provided funds for the operation of newspapers, making it dfficult for nonpolitician journalists who worked on such papers to exert authority over journalistic work and form an authoritative occupational group. The jurisdictional struggle between journalists and politicians thus involved journalists' efforts to gain control of the gathering, production, and dissemination of political content in newspapers and to become widely known as the legitimate providers of such. Nineteenth-century courtrooms became common forums for these disputes, since they were an arena where politicians often challenged not just the legal, but occupational, authority of newspaper journalists in their courtroom testimony.

Not all occupational groups acquire full jurisdiction over work. In the case of journalism, five categories of jurisdictional settlements between journalists and other occupational and professional groups are possible: (1) subordination of one of the two groups to the other, (2) division of labor by journalistic subtask, (3) sharing of the journalistic jurisdictional area without a clear division of labor, (4) advisory control of another profession over certain aspects of journalistic work, and (5) a division of jurisdiction by the nature of journalistic clients and not according to the content of the work. The nature of settlements between journalists and competing groups have varied, depending on the groups and eras under study.[90]

Journalists were involved locally and nationally in jurisdictional disputes throughout the nineteenth century. Such disputes had a significant impact on the development of the journalistic group, its work, and historical and contemporary relationships to other groups and institutions, including patrons, advertisers, politicians, political parties, and government officials and agencies. A resolution follows a jurisdictional contest between journalists and a competitor, and there is a return to a situation of relative equilibrium.

Journalistic Occupational Communication

Occupational communication strategies, as has been noted, play an important role in this process, along with other factors such as political, technological, or social developments. In the case of journalism and political communication, journalists did not attempt to usurp politicians' roles as disseminators of speeches, pamphlets, tracts, political campaign literature, and other forms of nineteenth-century political communication. However, their group by the end of the nineteenth century was to become known as the nation's primary providers of newspaper political news and editorial opinion.

This process involved journalists' construction through occupational communication of flattering public personas, ones that defined them as not only more trustworthy than politicians, but better qualified to provide the public with political news and opinion. To acquire jurisdiction over such work tasks, journalists confronted their occupational "neighbors" in the political communication work sphere, while adapting to events in the environments outside their control. Chief among journalists' political communication "neighbors" were politicians — party leaders and officials, elected and appointed government officials — and any other groups whose members also counted journalistic work among their activities. Especially important to the developing journalistic group in terms of their roles as providers of political communication were changes in the structure of the political party system during the nineteenth century, for by the century's end, the political party system and the work of politicians had also undergone change.[91]

Journalists discursively created occupational boundaries in the political communication work sphere through the issuance of occupational communication. Such communication conveyed occupational messages, both connotative and denotative, about journalistic work. Over time such communication contributed to the social construction of definitions of the nature and roles of journalistic work and assisted the members of the journalistic group in gaining some measure of occupational legitimacy. In addition, such statements, referred to herein as jurisdictional claims, reflected journalists' sensitivities to public concerns about how political information ought to be handled.[92]

An example of such a jurisdictional claim is a pervasive argument across the century that journalists were occupationally independent. Such statements were made in newspaper prospectuses, newspaper mastheads, courtroom testimony, and editorial exposés of the wrongdoing of elected and other public officials. Indeed, historians have long found that journalists' statements about their independence became more common across the nineteenth century. This meaning has largely been interpreted as indicators of growing political independence, rather than as rhetoric that embodies occupational meaning.[93]

Jurisdictional claims are statements that assert an occupational group's legitimate control of a particular kind of work. Such statements are issued in public arenas, including mass media and other settings open to the public. The rhetoric embodied in claims reveals the occupation's terminology and insights and is probably intended to attract public sympathy to its definitions of work tasks and approaches in solving them. In addition, such claims at times embody messages about an occupation's relationships to other important groups in the environment, such as other occupations and patrons.[94] In journalism, jurisdictional claims include any statements issued in public arenas by journalists that discuss their work and their roles in relation to such work.

Like all developing occupational groups, the journalistic group has sought, through dissemination of rhetoric, to create a realm wherein it has complete, established control. Such rhetoric gives both impetus and pattern to journalistic organizational developments, and it serves to further the legitimization of the group. Issuing jurisdictional claims within the public realm is a pervasive activity; for the journalistic occupational group, such activity can do the following:[95]

- Convince the public it has a need that can be met only through journalistic expert help.
- Reveal the journalistic occupation's terminology and insights.
- Attempt to attract public sympathy to its own definition of tasks and its own approach in fulfilling them.
- Provide the public with images of journalistic workers.

Such claims are issued in at least three places: public media, legal sphere, and workplace. Jurisdictional claims have been issued within newspapers, books, pamphlets, and, later in the electronic media; they have been issued orally within various social contexts. Below is a summary and description of some forms of these public jurisdictional claims in journalism.

Newspaper Prospectuses. Newspaper prospectuses are statements introducing new or redesigned newspapers. Eighteenth- and nineteenth-century prospectuses were sometimes issued both in handbill form to test the waters before the newspaper was printed, and the first issue of a new or redesigned newspaper. Written by publishers and/or editors, they included basic information about frequency of issue, subscription and advertising costs, categories of planned content, editorial policies, and standards. Less explicit, often latent, messages and images in these provided definitions of journalism, journalistic work, and journalists.

As sources, prospectuses are particularly valuable for several reasons to those studying occupational development. First, they have been consistently issued since newspapers began in America. Second, compared to many forms of jurisdictional claims just cited, prospectuses are relatively easy to identify and locate. Nearly every first issue of a newspaper includes one, ensuring access to multiple examples if one can obtain first issues. Third, and perhaps most importantly, since the express purpose of prospectuses is to explain the newspapers' and proprietors' editorial policies, they are especially important to studies of occupational messages and meanings.

Claims within Libel Suits. Libel actions against publishers were common in the nineteenth century, both in the criminal and civil court systems.[96] Journalists used the opportunity of trials to issue rhetoric wherein they claimed both the right and duty to expose the wrongdoing of public officials or other citizens involved in defrauding or otherwise betraying the public trust.

Claims in Occupational Associations. The members of various local, regional, state, and national newspaper journalistic occupational associations sometimes published materials articulating their associations' agendas.[97] In the nineteenth century, for example, newspaper articles at times addressed issues pertinent to the journalistic group. Illustrating this is an issue of the *Henderson (Minnesota) Independent* which discussed the problem of politicians expecting editors to print notices as a courtesy, rather than as advertisements for which they could charge a fee.[98] Inherent is a clear notion as to the work and boundaries of newspaper journalists in relation to politicians.

Claims in Portrayals of Heroes. It has been common throughout newspaper history for editors to disseminate occupational messages through published narratives that identify and praise certain journalistic heroes. Accounts of the lives of Benjamin Franklin, John Peter Zenger, and many others have served such purposes.[99] Such potrayals have provided the public with indicators as to what members of the journalistic group consider ideal journalistic behavior. In addition to representing certain members of the group as heroes, nineteenth-century journalists also at times held up to scorn certain journalists who did not abide by contemporary journalistic standards.[100]

Claims in Autobiographies and Biographies. Compared to other occupations, journalism has produced some of the nation's most prolific authors of autobiographies. Many of these also include jurisdictional statements, in which journalists define their work, portray themselves and their fellow journalists as certain types of workers, and define their relationships to other important groups — such as politicians, advertisers, and the public. [101]

Obituaries. By the end of the nineteenth century, obituary writing had evolved into the production of narratives that included more than the pertinent details of one's life; rather, the obituary had evolved into a ritual wherein careers, achievements, and community roles were often explored in depth.[102] In addition to obituaries of local journalists, editors often reprinted obituaries of prominent journalists who had lived elsewhere. An example is the 1894 obituary in the *East Dubuque (Illinois) Register*[103] of George W. Childs, a prominent Philadelphia journalist. Childs's obituary was long and glowing, praising him especially for providing for the best interests of all his employees, including printers. Such portrayals of journalists either introduce, or perpetuate, certain personas, which to some degree contribute to the public's perception of the occupation as a whole.

Other Print Narrative Forms of Journalistic Writing. Throughout the nineteenth century, journalists wrote and disseminated a variety of other narrative forms, including advertisements for newspapers, masthead slogans, poems, essays, and columns. These either explicitly discussed the work of journalists or indirectly provided evidence of the occupational group's roles, work tasks, values, and relationships.

Masthead slogans were common features of newspapers from the beginning. Some consisted of simple platitudes that anyone might abide by. Examples are "May Peace Be Cultivated" and "Virtue Triumphs, and her sons are blest."[104] Others were directed more clearly toward conveying an impression of the newspaper publisher's and editor's roles and political sentiments. For example, "Every American is constitutionally a Democrat and he who is not a Federalist is unwise. — Pasquin."[105]

Some essays that included jurisdictional claims focused primarily on the utility of news and newspapers. For example, editor John Fitzgerald, in a 1819 issue of the *Clarksville (Tennessee) Gazette*,[106] discussed the value of newspaper reading and said subscribers should preserve newspapers in regular files since an accumulation would provide an accurate account of history.

Other columns more explicitly detailed the duties of journalists, such as one published in an 1818 issue of the *Blakeley (Alabama) Sun* titled "Duty of an Editor." According to its author, an editor must "Consult the taste of all his readers, and can never be justified in pleasing one class, to the exclusion of the rest."[107]

A poem, its author unknown, inside a number of the 1802 *Scioto Gazette*, provided the reader with a statement as to the role and relationships of the publisher:

> Here shall the press the people's rights maintain,
> Unaw'd [sic] by influence and unbrib'd by gain;
>
> Here patriot truth its glorious precepts draw,
> Pledg'd to religion, liberty and law.[108]

Such poems and essays were sometimes reprinted in other newspapers by editors who were always looking for material of interest.[109]

Public Oratory. Journalists during the nineteenth century were often asked to speak at local events, such as Fourth of July picnics, or preside over public ceremonies, such as the opening of a new building. A small, but perhaps important group, became well known as orators and members of the various lecture circuits that flourished during the century.[110]

State and Local Histories. Numerous local and state newspaper histories published during the nineteenth century included implicit or explicit information and ideas about journalistic work, occupational values and standards, and the occupational group members' relationships.[111] Additionally, accounts of local and state newspaper presses, which often included biographies of journalists, appear in local and state general histories. For example, a chapter in the *History of Ross and Highland Counties, Ohio,* entitled "The Press of Ross County," provides a history of the county's newspapers, along with biographical sketches of its journalists and publishers.[112]

Discourse in jurisdictional claims portrays occupational groups as if they are homogenous entities with no hierarchical or other differences between members. Thus, journalists would be portrayed in journalistic jurisdictional claims as equals, with no distinctions made between members within the group based on work specialties, training, or skill. Rhetoric in jurisdictional claims might also explicitly discuss the occupational group as a whole. At other times, it might refer only to a single practitioner, although it would have connotative implications for the whole group.[113]

A common discursive strategy of groups seeking legitimacy in a particular area of work is to portray the members of such group as being in opposition to another nearby group. In the case of journalists seeking to construct a boundary surrounding the work terrain of political news, this would mean that they would frequently compare their work to that of politicians in a self-serving way. Because the public in the early nineteenth century generally decried inflammatory political journalism, journalists often compared their brand of journalism to those of politicians in flattering terms, even when, in fact, their own political reports and essays were filled with material that provoked strong reactions.

SUMMARY

Using the model just presented, this book studies an important question in the history of American journalism: How did Americans come to accept journalists, rather than politicians, as their primary providers of political news and editorial opinion? To understand the process that led to the construction of journalists as the nation's political reporters requires studying how the social boundary that would come to differentiate the work of journalists from politicians formed. In other words, what process led to the division of the political communication work sphere into one with differentiated roles for politicians and journalists?

To understand how this boundary was constructed involves development of the following more specific research questions: How, when, and under what conditions did a journalistic occupational group emerge in America? Who did such work? What did their work consist of and what purpose or social need was such work meant to fulfill? Did eighteenth- and nineteenth-century journalists issue occupational rhetoric in public or other arenas that constructed a social boundary around journalistic political communication work? If so, how did this communication represent journalists' relationships to politicians and political bodies? What changes in the broader political environment may have affected the construction of boundaries around journalistic work in the political communication work realm?

To explore these questions, research focused on the eighteenth century, 1704 to 1800, and the earliest and latest periods of the nineteenth century, 1800 to 1830, and 1870 to 1900, looking at journalistic constructions of their political communication work and their personas as political communicators across time in particular historical circumstances. Three major bodies of primary source materials were studied. A first effort entailed gathering newspaper prospectuses issued by establishers of new or renewed newspapers during the three periods.[114] A second stage of research included gathering libel trial transcripts that included testimony of journalists or others who issued statements about the duties of newspaper journalists.[115] A third area of research consisted of amassing biographical profiles of newspaper proprietors, publishers, and/or editors of newspapers in America's towns and cities during the periods studied.[116]

In total, 260 newspaper prospectuses, 14 libel trial transcripts, and 200 biographical profiles were analyzed. Secondary sources provided the basic information about American newspapers, politicians, and political structures in the eighteenth and nineteenth centuries — information integrated throughout the book, especially as appropriate in the presentation of the case studies.[117]

The methodology is primarily qualitative and strongly influenced by the cultural studies approach. While the theoretical framework comes from sociology, the methodology rests on the cultural studies theory that meaning (or reality) is fluid and socially constructed through cultural experiences, primarily language and other communication forms.[118] The underlying argument is that journalists, through statements in newspaper prospectuses and in other public arenas such as courtrooms, were part of the process whereby definitions of the journalistic occupation were socially constructed. Journalistic discourses embodied themes that both reflect and constitute (or construct) perceptions of (1) journalistic work, (2) what journalists should do and how, (3) what the public should depend on journalists for, and, equally importantly for purposes here, (4) what groups should not be depended on for the kind of work journalists claimed as theirs.

Discourse analysis used both in study of newspaper prospectuses and libel trial transcripts sought to ascertain meaning constructed through the dissemination of messages on several levels. The assumption was that because texts have multiple, differentiated, and sometimes even contradictory uses and functions, the analysis of prospectuses and trial transcripts should be conducted on two levels: denotative and connotative. As embodiers of denotative messages, these texts embodied explicit messages about newspaper printers and their publication designs and plans. In addition, they were considered as texts that expressed connotative messages, that is, indirectly implied positive appeals, about newspapers and about printers and publishers and their work. [119] The model's emphasis is not on a linear information process that involved journalists and the public. It is beyond the scope of the research to understand the public's social construction of meaning in terms of journalistic work. However, nonjournalists defined those who produced newspapers in new ways during the two centuries studied, and journalistic occupational discourse would have played some part in this process.

Occupational communication contributed to social construction of occupational work tasks as it differentiated those from tasks in the domain or jurisdiction of an occupational group's chief competitors. Throughout the book, the competing occupational groups under study are journalists and politicians of nineteenth-century America. But since an assumption is that systems affect occupations and professions as they emerge and develop, it was considered important to study the evolving relationship between journalists and politicians during times of major shifts in the political environment.

During the eighteenth and nineteenth centuries, at least five major political shifts could be examined for their impact on the journalistic occupational group, including the American Revolution, the collapse of the Federalist Party and the development of second and third party systems in the early nineteenth century and the Civil War. Case studies of two of these, the American Revolution and the Era of Good Feelings were developed with an eye toward understanding their implications for the development of the journalistic occupation, particularly in the area of political communication.[120] It was thought that the American Revolution's radical transformation of the nation's political communication system would have implications for the developing journalistic occupation. The Era of Good Feelings occurred during the party press era, a time when journalism and politics were closely related. In light of this, it was considered probable that journalistic work and its occupational development would be affected by the radical restructuring of the political party system that took place during this time, 1816 to 1825. Evidence of possible ramifications of changes in America's political systems during the American Revolution and Era of Good Feelings on the journalistic occupational group's work and development were sought in newspaper prospectuses and biographies of those produced newspapers.

Biographical analysis of nineteenth-century newspaper journalists was used to supplement and corroborate evidence found through textual analysis of prospectuses and other journalistic statements. Every occupation has typical careers, and the detection of changes in career structures can reveal insight into how occupational groups can both be affected by and react to fluctuations within broader environments.[121] Such analysis is of special importance in Chapter 5, which provides a case study that explores the possible impact of political change during the Era of Good Feelings. Among the biographical data collected were the kinds of newspaper work these journalists were involved in over their careers and any additional publishing or printing enterprises and other nonprinting or publishing career ventures they may have engaged in.

Chapter 2 examines journalistic work and occupational development in the eighteenth century, a period when journalism underwent its earliest development as a work group. Through study of journalistic occupational communication in newspaper prospectuses and libel courtroom testimony, Chapters 3 and 4 look at the nineteenth century for insight into how newspaper proprietors constructed journalistic work as an occupation with an increasingly important political communication role. Chapter 5 focuses on the history of the developing occupational group during the Era of Good Feelings, asking how newspaper journalists were both affected by and adapted to the challenges with which the period's political events confronted them. Finally, Chapter 6 summarizes the findings and considers the implications of the research.

NOTES

1. For examples of journalists who held political office during the early decades of the nineteenth century, see Milton Hamilton, *The Country Printer: New York State, 1785-1830* (New York: Columbia University Press, 1936); Donald H. Stewart, *The Opposition Press of the Federalist Period* (Albany, NY: State University of New York Press, 1969); Hazel Dicken-Garcia, *Journalistic Standards in Nineteenth-Century America* (Madison, WI: University of Wisconsin Press, 1989); and Thomas C. Leonard, *Power of the Press: The Birth of American Political Reporting* (New York: Oxford University Press, 1986).

2. Wilfred E. Binkley, *American Political Parties: Their Natural History* (New York: Knopf, 1963); Jerry W. Knudson, "Political Journalism in the Age of Jefferson," *Journalism History* 1 (Spring 1974): 20-23; Allan Nevins, *American Press Opinion, Washington to Coolidge* (Boston: Heath, 1928); James E. Pollard, *The Presidents and the Press* (New York: Macmillan, 1947); Carl E. Prince, "The Federalist Party and Creation of a Court Press, 1789-1801," *Journalism Quarterly* 53 (Summer 1976): 238-41; W. David Sloan, "The Early Party Press: The Newspaper Role in National Politics, 1788-1812," *Journalism History* 9 (Spring 1982): 18-24; Stewart, *Opposition Press.*

3. Historians who have studied aspects of this journalistic transformation include Gerald J. Baldasty, *The Commercialization of the News in the Nineteenth Century* (Madison, WI: University of Wisconsin Press, 1992); Dicken-Garcia, *Journalistic Standards*; Michael Schudson, *Discovering the News: The Social History of American Newspapers* (New York: Basic Books, 1978).

4. J. Herbert Altschull, *Agents of Power: The News Media in Human Affairs* (New York: Longman, 1984); Bernard Berelson, Paul F. Lazarsfeld, and William McPhee, *Voting: A Study of Opinion Formation in a Presidential Campaign* (Chicago: University of Chicago Press, 1954); Steven H. Chaffee, ed. *Political Communication: Issues and Strategies for Research* (Beverly Hills, CA: Sage, 1975); Jack Dennis, ed., *Socialization to Politics: A Reader* (New York: Wiley, 1973); Sidney Kraus and Dennis Davis, *The Effects of Mass Communication on Political Behavior* (University Park, PA: Pennsylvania State University Press, 1976); Kathleen Hall Jamieson and Karyl Kohrs Campbell, *The Interplay of Influence: News, Advertising, Politics, and the Mass Media* (Belmont, CA: Wadsworth Publishing, 1997); Maxwell E. McCombs and Donald L. Shaw, *The Emergence of American Political Issues: The Agenda-Setting Function of the Press* (St. Paul, MN: West Publishing, 1977); Thomas E. Patterson, *The Mass Media Election: How Americans Choose Their President* (New York: Praeger, 1980).

5. Examples of general critiques include the following: W. Lance Bennett, *News: The Politics of Illusion* (White Plains, NY: Longman, 1988); Noam Chomsky, *Deterring Democracy* (London: Verso, 1991); Michael Parenti, *Inventing Reality* (New York: St. Martin's Press, 1993); Howard Zinn, *Declarations of Independence: Cross-Examining American Ideology* (New York: HarperCollins, 1990).

The new technologies that have offered nonjournalists opportunities to by-pass or replace journalists are discussed in Jerome Aumente, *New Electronic Pathways* (Beverly Hills, CA: Sage, 1987); Nick Heap, Ray Thomas, Geogg Einan, Robin Masson, and Hughie MacKay, *Information, Technology and Society* (Thousand Oaks, CA: Sage, 1995); John P. Pavlik and Everett E. Dennis, *Demystifying Media Technology* (Mountain View, CA: Mayfield, 1993).

For a discussion and analysis of mainstream journalistic responses to four examples of new media, see Patricia L. Dooley and Paul G. Grosswiler, "'Turf Wars': The New Media and the Struggle for Control of Political News," *The Harvard International Journal of Press/Politics* 2 (Summer 1997): 31-51.

6. This definition is my own, and is inspired by the work of scholars Joan Wallach Scott and Andrew Abbott, among others. In her analysis of gender and feminist history, Scott discusses her view that knowledge and communication play important roles in the construction of fluid concepts such as gender. Acknowledging her intellectual linkages to Michel Foucault and Jacques Derrida, these ideas can be used in studies of occupations and professions. See *Gender and the Politics of History* (New York: Columbia University Press, 1988), 2-8.

Like Scott, Andrew Abbott's theoretical approach is undergirded by the assumption that concepts such as occupation and profession are volatile and constructed at least in part through communication. See Chapter 1 and preface, *The System of Professions: An Essay in the Division of Expert Labor* (Chicago: University of Chicago Press, 1988).

7. Occupational sociology at times has tended to dominate the field of sociology. In *Encyclopedia of the Social Sciences*, 1968 ed., s.v., "Professions," for example, Talcott Parsons wrote that the "professional complex,"

> has already become the most important single component in the structure of modern societies. It has displaced first the "state," in the relatively early modern sense of that term, and, more recently, the "capitalistic" organization of the economy. The massive emergence of the professional complex, not the special status of capitalistic or socialistic modes of organization, is the crucial structural development in the twentieth-century society.

The importance of the professions in society is further attested to by the immense volume of work published by sociologists on various aspects of the professions during the last fifty years. During the period 1953-1959, for example, 45.5 percent of the articles in sociological journals focused on the professions. See George Ritzer, *Man and His Work: Conflict and Change* (New York: Appleton-Century-Crofts, 1972), 5.

8. Other traits that some argue mark professionals from nonprofessionals are concern with fulfillment of certain intrinsic values, such as disinterested service, and universalistic standards based on science or intellect. See Ernest Greenwood, "Attributes of a Profession." *Social Work* 2 (July 1957): 44-55; Geoffrey Millerson, *The Qualifying Associations* (London: Routledge, 1964).

9. (Glencoe, IL.: Free Press, 1958). Hughes also wrote the following works that deal with occupations and professions: *The Sociological Eye: Selected Papers* (Chicago; New York: Aldine-Atherton, 1971); and "The Professions," *Daedalus* 91 (Fall 1963): 655-688. Robert Dingwall's "Introduction" to *The Sociology of the Professions: Lawyers, Doctors and Others*, Dingwall and Philip Lewis, eds. (London: Macmillan Press, 1983), 1-13, discusses the view that much of the sociological literature on the professions is based on the contributions of Talcott Parsons and Everett C. Hughes.

10. See Douglas Klegon, "The Sociology of Professions: An Emerging Perspective," *Work and Occupations* 3 (August 1978): 259-183, for a useful summary of the criticisms and new directions of the sociologists who reject the work of some of the earlier sociologists.

11. These terms are used by Julius A. Roth, "Professionalism: The Sociologist's Decoy," *Sociology of Work and Occupations* 1 (February 1974): 6-23, as well as by other sociologists cited in this section of the chapter.

12. Roth, "Professionalism," 18.

13. See, for example, the following: Philip Abrams, *Historical Sociology* (Ithaca, NY: Cornell University Press, 1982); Peter Burke, *Sociology and History* (London: George Allen and Unwin, 1980); Seymour Martin Lipset, "History and Sociology: Some Methodological Considerations," in *Sociology and History: Methods,* Seymour Martin Lipset and Richard Hofstadter, eds. (New York: Basic Books, 1968); Mildred A. Schwartz, "Historical Sociology in the History of American Sociology," *Social Science History* 11 (Fall 1976): 1-16; Theda Skocpol, ed., *Vision and Method in Historical Sociology* (New York: Cambridge University Press, 1984); Theda Skocpol, "Social History and Historical Sociology: Contrasts and Complementarities," *Social Science History* 11 (Fall 1987): 17-30; Piotr Sztompka, "The Renaissance of Historical Orientation in Sociol-

ogy," *International Sociology* 1 (March 1986): 321-37; Charles Tilly, *As Sociology Meets History* (New York: Academic Press, 1981); B. R. Wilson, "Sociological Methods in the Study of History," *Transactions of the Royal Historical Society* 21 (1972): 101-18.

14. Hughes, *Men and Work,* 133.

15. Thomas Gieryn, George M. Bevins, and Stephen C. Zehr, "Professionalization of American Scientists: Public Science in the Creation/Evolution Trials," *American Sociological Review* 50 (June 1985): 392-409; Carol L. Kronus, "Evolution of Occupational Power: An Historical Study of Task Boundaries Between Physicians and Pharmacists," *Sociology of Work and Occupations* 1 (February 1976): 3-37; John F. Runcie, "Occupational Communication as Boundary Mechanism," *Sociology of Work and Occupations* 1 (November 1974): 419-44.

16. See Table 1.1, Geoffrey Millerson, "Dilemmas of Professionalism," *New Society* 4 (June 1964): 5.

17. Terence J. Johnson, *Professions and Power* (London: Macmillan [British Sociological Association], 1972): 41-86.

18. Ibid.

19. Julius Roth, "Professionalism: The Sociologist's Decoy," *Sociology of Work and Occupations* 1 (February 1974): 6-23.

20. Ibid., 6.

21. Abbott, *System of Professions,* 35.

22. Ibid., 57-58.

23. Magali Sarfatti Larson, *The Rise of Professionalism* (Berkeley, CA: University of California Press, 1977).

24. See Elliott A. Krause's review of Larson's work cited in note 23, for example, where he discusses how her work is based on Weberian assumptions, in *Sociology of Work and Occupations* 6 (May 1979): 251-53.

25. John B. Cullen, *The Structure of Professionalism* (New York; Princeton, NJ: Petrocelli Books, 1978).

26. Abbott, *System of Professions*, 56; Gieryn, Bevins, and Zehr, "Professionalization of American Scientists"; Kronus, "Evolution of Occupational Power"; Runcie, "Occupational Communication."

For example, Gieryn, Bevins, and Zehr, in "Professionalization" study how scientists attempt to establish a professional monopoly over the market for knowledge about nature. They examine rhetoric issued by scientists at two trials about creationism and evolution they were called in to testify within: the famous Scopes trials of 1925, and the McLean trial, a 1981 trial on the creation and evolution issue.

27. Ibid. On licensing, see Magali Sarfatti Larson, "Profession," in *International Encyclopedia of Communication*, s.v., "Profession."

28. Kronus, "Evolution of Occupational Power"; Runcie, "Occupational Communication."

29. Abbott, *System of Professions*; Eliot Freidson, *Profession of Medicine: A Study of the Sociology of Applied Knowledge* (New York: Dodd, Mead, 1970); Larson, *Rise of Professionalism*.

30. In Kenneth S. Lynn, ed., *The Professions in America* (*Daedalus* Library Series. Boston: Houghton-Mifflin Co., 1965).

31. Louis Hodges, "The Journalist and Professionalism," *Journal of Mass Media Ethics* 1 (Spring-Summer 1986): 32-36.

32. Jack McLeod and Searle E. Hawley, "Professionalization Among Newsmen," *Journalism Quarterly* 41 (1964): 583-90; Gaye Tuchman, "Professionalism as an Agent of Legitimation," *Journal of Communication* 28 (Winter 1978): 106-13.

33. As is recommended by Charles Tilly and Hazel Dicken-Garcia, understanding the history of large social structural and institutional development requires large, and long frames of analysis. See Dicken-Garcia, *Journalistic Standards*; Charles Tilly, *Big Structures, Large Processes, Huge Comparisons* (New York: Russell Sage Foundation, 1984).

34. Hanno Hardt and Bonnie Brennen, eds. *Toward a History of the Rank and File* (Minneapolis, MN: University of Minnesota Press, 1995).

35. Scholars who recommend that mass communication historians study the history of mass media work and workers include John D. Stevens and Hazel Dicken-Garcia, *Communication History*, Sage CommText Series, vol. 2. (Beverly Hills, CA: Sage, 1980), 32; David Paul Nord, "Intellectual History, Social History, Cultural History," *Journalism History* 67 (Winter 1990): 645-58.

36. This is, essentially, a variation on an open systems model. See Wayne A. Chess and Julia M. Norlin, *Human Behavior and the Social Environment: A Social Systems Model* (Needham Heights, MA: Allyn and Bacon, Inc., 1988).

37. Abbott, *System of Professions*, 35.

38. The many definitions of news have similarities, including elements of freshness or recency, human interest, and some form of report. But definitions of news can also differ to some extent depending on the purposes and chronological focus the study one is undertaking. Webster's *Third New International Dictionary* defines "news" as "a report of a recent event; new information; fresh tidings." 1966 ed., s.v. "news." Press historians Michael and Edwin Emery, *The Press in America* (7th ed., Englewood Cliffs, NJ: Prentice Hall, 1992), 7, define news as "information of interest to the general public." They also discuss how the word "news" was coined to differentiate between the casual dissemination of information and the deliberate attempt to gather and process the latest intelligence. Mitchell Stephens, *A History of News* (New York: Penguin Books, 1988), 9, defines "news" as "new information about a subject of some public interest that is shared with some portion of the public."

39. Richard D. Brown, *Knowledge Is Power: The Diffusion of Information in Early America, 1700-1865* (New York: Oxford University Press, 1989); Richard D. Brown, *Modernization: The Transformation of American Life, 1600-1865* (New York: Hill and Wang, 1976); William J. Gilmore, *Reading Becomes a Necessity of Life in Rural New England, 1780-1835* (Knoxville, TN: University of Tennessee Press, 1989).

40. Brown, *Knowledge,* and Thomas C. Leonard, *Power of the Press: The Birth of American Political Reporting* (New York: Oxford University Press, 1986), discuss how nineteenth-century journalistic political reporting played a role in creating need among Americans for political news.

41. Studies of the press during the eighteenth century include Arthur M. Schlesinger, *Prelude to Independence: The Newspaper War on Britain, 1764-1776* (New York: Alfred A. Knopf, 1958); William F. Steirer, "Riding 'Everyman's Hobby Horse': Journalists in Philadelphia, 1764-1794," in *Newsletters to Newspapers: Eighteenth-Century Journalism,* Donovan H. Bond and W. Reynolds McLeod, eds. (Morgantown, WV: West Virginia University, 1977), 264-76; Carol Sue Humphrey, *This Popular Engine: New England Newspapers During the American Revolution: 1775-1789* (Newark, DE: University of Delaware Press, 1992). See Dicken-Garcia, *Journalistic Standards*, for infor-

mation on changes in news during the nineteenth century. Her book identifies three emerging models that over that century gained influence in the newspaper industry: political, information, and business.

42. See, for example, the following sources: A. O. Bunnell, comp., *New York Press Association, Authorized History for Fifty Years, 1853-1903* (Dansville, NY: F. A. Owen Publishing Co., 1903); Edwin Emery, *History of the American Newspaper Publishers Association* (Minneapolis, MN: University of Minnesota, 1949); Myra B. Lord, *History of the New England Woman's Press Association* (Newton, MA: Graphic Press, 1932); Alf Pratte, *A Critical History of the American Society of Newspaper Editors 1922-1990* (Washington, D.C.: American Society of Newspaper Editors, 1992).

43. Abbott, *System of Professions,* 53.

44. Joseph Griffin, *History of the Press of Maine* (Brunswick, ME: The Press, 1872), 21.

45. Dicken-Garcia, *Journalistic Standards*, 41, claims that by 1860 this differentiation of the printer-editor role was common. Descriptions of newspaper work in the eighteenth and nineteenth centuries can be found in Charles E. Clark, *The Public Prints: The Newspaper in Anglo-American Culture, 1665-1740* (New York: Oxford University Press, 1994); Lawrence C. Wroth, *The Colonial Printer* (Portland, ME: Southworth-Anthoensen Press, 1938); and in autobiographical reminiscences of newspaper journalists, as well as in state newspaper histories. For example, see the following: Hamilton, *Country Printer*; Isaac C. Pray, *Memoirs of James Gordon Bennett* (New York: Stringer and Townsend, 1866; rpt. Arno Press and the New York Times Company, 1970).

46. Abbott, *System of Professions*, 35-40, 52-57, 86.

47. The act of news gathering in essence depends on gathering observations and information from the community, but how such practices are handled by news people has changed. During the nineteenth century, journalists developed the practice of attributing news to sources. For a history of attribution as a practice, see the following: Lynne Marie Groth, "The Journalistic Standard of Attribution: An Historical Study of the Change in Attribution Practices by Journalists Between 1890-1924," (Master's thesis, University of Minnesota, December 1989).

During the twentieth century, a kind of journalistic knowledge system has been under development in theoretical works on mass communication, particularly those that discuss mass media processes and the functions, roles and effects of journalistic mass media. This differs from systems of knowledge in other professions, such as medicine, where medical scientific knowledge is used in the daily practice of physicians.

48. Ibid, 56, 286, 298.

49. Ibid, 35-40.

50. Abbott, *System of Professions.*, quote on 40; see also 41-52.

51. Accounts of this journalistic process are described by Clark, *The Public Prints*; Wroth, *The Colonial Printer*; Hamilton, *Country Printer*; as well as in numerous state newspaper histories, memoirs of journalists, and in newspaper prospectuses and other statements of journalists to their readers. Leonard, *Power of Press*, also discusses eighteenth- and nineteenth-century political reporting.

52. Dicken-Garcia, *Journalistic Standards*, discusses on page 19, the origins of the reporting role, and on page 61, the era of the reporter. See also the following: Ted Curtis Smythe, "The Reporter, 1880-1900: Working Conditions and Their Influence on the News," *Journalism History* 7 (Spring 1980): 1-10; Richard Kielbowicz, "Newsgathering

by Printers' Exchanges Before the Telegraph," *Journalism History* 9 (Summer 1982): 42-48; Victor Rosewater, *History of Cooperative News Gathering in the United States* (New York: Appleton-Century-Crofts, 1930); Robert E. Drechsel, *News Making in Trial Courts* (New York: Longman, 1983), 35-77.

53. Dicken-Garcia, *Journalistic Standards*, discusses the emergence and implications of the role of editor as decision maker in nineteenth-century journalism. See especially pages 61-62, 133-34.

54. Dicken-Garcia, *Journalistic Standards*; Baldasty, *Commercialization of the News*.

55. See Table 4-1, on page 70, in Humphrey, *This Popular Engine*.

56. Dicken-Garcia, *Journalistic Standards*, on pages 41-42, discusses how during the period from 1830 to 1870, news became more local than it previously had been. See also Baldasty, *Commercialization of News*, 121-34; Donald Shaw, "At the Crossroads: Change and Continuity in American Press News 1820-1860," *Journalism History* 8 (Summer 1981): 38-50; Irene Barnes Taeuber, "Changes in the Content and Presentation of Reading Material in Minnesota Weekly Newspapers 1860-1929," *Journalism Quarterly* 9 (September 1932): 280-89.

57. Scholars who study changes in journalistic news and styles include the following: Baldasty, *Commercialization of the News*, 113-38; Dicken-Garcia, *Journalistic Standards*, 63-69.

58. William G. Bleyer, *Main Currents in the History of American Journalism* (Boston: Houghton Mifflin, 1927); Dicken-Garcia, *Journalistic Standards*, 53; Donald Shaw, "News Bias and the Telegraph: A Study of Historical Change," *Journalism Quarterly* 44 (Spring 1967): 3-12; Stephens, *History of News*, 252-56.

59. Abbott, *System of Professions*, especially 143-50.

60. The formation of America's earliest printing guild, The Company of Printers of Philadelphia, occurred in 1794. See Wroth, *Colonial* Printer, 165-68. For accounts on the development and ratification of the Bill of Rights, see the following: Merrill Jensen, *The New Nation: A History of the United States During the Confederation, 1781-1789* (New York: Knopf, 1950); Gordon S. Wood, *The Creation of the American Republic, 1776-1787* (Chapel Hill, NC: University of North Carolina Press, 1969); Edmund S. Morgan, *The Birth of the Republic, 1763-1789*, 3d ed. (Chicago: University of Chicago Press, 1959).

61. On the development of journalistic standards, see Dicken-Garcia, *Journalistic Standards*. For information on the formation of journalistic associations, see Baldasty, *Commercialization of the News,* 101-04. For histories of journalism education see the following: Forest O'Dell, *The History of Journalism Education in the United States* (New York: Columbia University Teachers College, 1935); Albert A. Sutton, *Education for Journalism in the United States from Its Beginning to 1940* (Evanston, IL: North-western University, 1945).

62. For information on the U.S. Supreme Court's treatment of the First Amendment, see Richard C. Cortner, *The Supreme Court and the Second Bill of Rights* (Madison, WI: University of Wisconsin Press, 1981); John Hart Ely, *Democracy and Distrust: A Theory of Judicial Review* (Cambridge: Harvard University Press, 1980); Paul L. Murphy, *The Meaning of Freedom of Speech: First Amendment Freedoms from Wilson to FDR*, Contributions in American History Series (Westport, CT: Greenwood Press, 1972).

Journalistic occupational associations, education programs, and news councils are discussed in Alfred Balk, *A Free and Responsive Press* (New York: Twentieth Century

Fund, 1973); John A. Ritter and Matthew Leibowitz, "Press Councils: An Answer to Our First Amendment Dilemma," *Duke Law Journal* 24 (December 1974): 845-70; William Rivers, et al., *Backtalk: Press Councils in America* (San Francisco: Canfield Press, 1972); H. Phillip Levy, *The Press Council: History, Procedures and Cases* (New York: St. Martin's Press, 1967).

63. C. A. Gifford, "Ancient Rome's Daily Gazette," *Journalism History* 2 (Winter 1975-1976): 106-09; Richard Claverhouse Jebb, "Ancient Organs of Public Opinion," in *Essays and Addresses* (Cambridge: University Press, 1907); Stephens, *History of News*, 96-99. News ballads were spread by balladeers in the fifteenth century and perhaps even earlier. Little evidence remains for historians with an interest in understanding these workers. For example, it is unclear what balladeers, for example, may have understood to be their social roles.

64. These criteria have been gleaned from analysis of a number of definitions of occupations and work provided by sociologists. Everett C. Hughes, for example, asserts a new occupational group emerges when its people begin to perform work "formerly performed by amateurs, or for pay by people with little or no formal training." See Hughes, *Men and Work*, 133. Eliot Freidson claims an occupation exists when workers perform the same activity and develop common methods that are passed on to new recruits. See *Profession of Medicine*, 71.

Several other definitions include the following: "Specific activity(s) with a market value which an individual continually pursues for the purpose of obtaining a steady flow of income; [which] . . . determines the social position of the individual," Arthur Salz, "Occupation," *Encyclopedia of the Social Sciences*, 3rd ed., s.v., at "Occupation"; and "Relatively continuous patterns of activities that provide workers a livelihood and define their general social status [which] emerge whenever division of labor is associated with a monetary economy and labor and commodity markets," William H. Form, "Occupations and Careers," in *International Encyclopedia of the Social Sciences*, 1968 ed., s.v. at "Occupation and Careers."

Another method for discerning whether an occupational group has emerged is suggested by Terry C. Blum, Paul M. Roman, and Deborah M. Tootle in "The Emergence of an Occupation," *Work and Occupations* 15 (February 1988): 96-114. These researchers suggest that measuring and finding commonalities in work-related variables across a group of workers who come from distinctly different backgrounds indicates the emergence of an occupation.

65. The label "task" is applied here since it conforms to terminology used in Andrew Abbott's theories. Such tasks are also frequently referred to as roles, specialties, or job categories. For example, publishers are often discussed as fulfilling a publishing role, and reporters are often referred to as comprising a separate occupational specialty.

66. Compare descriptions of journalistic work in Clark, *Public Prints*, and Wroth, *Colonial Printer,* to those discussed by Dicken-Garcia, *Journalistic Standards*, and Baldasty, *Commercialization of the News*.

67. Baldasty, *Commercialization of the News*, 83-84.

68. Thurlow Weed, *Autobiography of Thurlow Weed*, Harriet A. Weed, ed. (New York: DaCapo Press, 1970, reprint edition), 70.

69. Dicken-Garcia, *Journalistic Standards*, 41.

70. Ibid. Discusses the emergence and implications of the role of editor as decision maker in nineteenth-century journalism. See especially pages 47, 84, 133-34.

71. Clark, *Public Prints*, 207-14.

72. See the following histories that include discussion of the history of news writing: Clark, *Public Prints;* Dicken-Garcia, *Journalistic Standards,* 63-64, 84-89; Humphrey, *This Popular Engine*; Stephens, *History of News*, 44-47. In addition, the focus of literary journalistic scholars stresses the history of journalistic writing. See, for example: Linda Patterson Miller, "Poe on the Beat: 'Doings of Gotham' as Urban, Penny Press Journalism," *Journal of the Early Republic* 7 (Summer 1987): 164; Thomas B. Connery, "Fusing Fictional Technique and Journalistic Fact: Literary Journalism in the 1890s," (Ph.D. diss., Brown University, 1984). There are also numerous studies of certain traits of journalistic writing, such as sensationalism. See, for example: Mitchell Stephens, "Sensationalism and Moralizing in 16th- and 17th-Century Newsbooks and News Ballads," *Journalism History* 12 (Autumn-Winter 1985): 92-95; John D. Stevens, "Sensationalism in Perspective," *Journalism History* 12 (Autumn-Winter 1985): 78-79.

73. Milton E. Flower, *John Dickinson, Conservative Revolutionary* (Charlottesville, VA: University Press of Virginia, 1983).

74. Dicken-Garcia, *Journalistic Standards,* 61-62, 133-34; Knudson, "Political Journalism," 20-21; Stewart, *Opposition Press,* 61-62, 133-34.

75. See the autobiographies of early journalists such as Benjamin Franklin, Joseph T. Buckingham, and others, for accounts of how, and by whom, eighteenth- and nineteenth-century newspapers were distributed. Obviously, news distribution work varies depending on the medium under discussion. In television news, for example, distribution involves both visual and speech components and has been coalesced into a new subspecialty within the broader journalism field.

76. Hughes, *Men and Work*, 133.

77. This term was coined by Karl Polanyi in *The Great Transformation* (Boston: Beacon, 1957). Polanyi defined it as periods of time in which societies undergo transformations from traditional (local and rural), to more modern (urban and industrialized) forms. According to Larson, *Rise of Professionalism*, 76, the modern American professions are a product of this nation's twin processes of urbanization and industrialization, which were underway early in the early nineteenth century.

78. On America's transformation from a traditional to a modern society, see Brown, *Modernization*. For general theories and interpretations see: Emile Durkheim, *The Division of Labour in Society* (New York: Macmillan, 1933); Karl Marx and F. Engels, *The German Ideology* (London: Lawrence & Wishart, 1965); Polanyi, *Great Transformation*; Max Weber, *Economy and Society*, eds. G. Roth and C. Wittich (New York: Bedminster Press, 1968).

79. Roger Chartier, ed., *The Culture of Print: Power and the Use of Print in Early Modern Europe,* Lydia G. Cochrane, trans. (Princeton, NJ: Princeton University Press, 1989); G. A. Cranfield, *The Press and Society: From Caxton to Northcliffe* (reprinted Westport, CT: Greenwood Press, 1978); Elizabeth Eisenstein, *The Printing Press as an Agent of Change* (Cambridge: Cambridge University Press, 1980); Joseph Frank, *The Beginnings of the English Newspaper* (Cambridge, MA: Harvard University Press, 1961); Walther Heide, *Die aelteste gedruckte Zeitung* (Mainz: Verlag der Gutenberg-gesellschaft, 1931); M. Lindemann, *Deutsche Presse bis 1815* (Berlin: Colloquium Verlag, 1969); Walter J. Ong, *Orality and Literacy: The Technologizing of the World* (London; New York: Methuen, 1982), 117-38; Matthias A. Shaaber, *Some Forerunners of the Newspaper in England, 1476-1776* (Philadelphia: University of Pennsylvania Press, 1929); Anthony Smith, *The Newspaper: An International History* (London: Thames and Hudson, 1979).

80. Abbott, *System of Professions*, 56; Gieryn, Bevins, and Zehr, "Professionalization," 393; Kronus, "Evolution," 4-6; Runcie, "Occupational Communication," 419-23.

81. Gieryn, Bevins, and Zehr, Ibid.; Kronus, Ibid.; Runcie, Ibid.

82. Abbott, *System of Professions*, 86-113.

83. Ibid., 8.

84. Ibid., 59-85.

85. Ibid., 88-89. See Abbott's discussion of the permeability of journalistic work in his chapter on the information occupations, pages 225-26.

86. Printing technological improvements are described in Robert Hoe, *Short History of the Printing Press* (New York: R. Hoe and Company, 1902); Calder M. Pickett, "Technology and the New York Press in the Nineteenth Century," *Journalism Quarterly* 37 (Summer 1960): 398-407; Schudson, *Discovering the News*. For information on the history of crime reporting, see Dreschel, *News Making in the Trial Courts*.

87. W. Newhall Beaumont, *The History of Photography from 1839 to Present* (New York: Museum of Modern Art, 1982); R. Smith Schuneman, "The Photograph in Print: An Examination of New York Daily Newspapers," *Journalism Quarterly* 42 (Winter 1965): 43.

88. Lauren Kessler, *The Dissident Press: Alternative Journalism in American History*, Sage Commtext Series (Beverly Hill, CA: Sage, 1984); Merton L. Dillon, *The Abolitionists: The Growth of a Dissenting Minority* (DeKalb, IL: Northern Illinois University Press, 1974); Russell B. Nye, *Fettered Freedom: Civil Liberties and the Slavery Controversy, 1830-1860* (East Lansing, MI: Michigan State College Press, 1963).

89. Abbott, *System of Professions*, 213-14.

90. Ibid., 69-79.

91. Felice A. Bonadio, ed. *Political Parties in American History (1828-1890)* (New York: G. P. Putnam's Sons, 1974); William Chambers and Walter Burnham, eds. *The American Party Systems: Stages of Political Development* (New York: Oxford University Press, 1967); William H. Chambers and Philip C. Davis, "Party Competition and Mass Participation: The Case of the Democratizing Party System, 1824-1852," in *The History of American Electoral Behavior*, Joel H. Silbey, Allan G. Bogne, and William H. Flanigan, eds. (Princeton, NJ: Princeton University Press, 1978), 174-97; James Chase, *Emergence of the Presidential Nominating Convention, 1789-1832* (Urbana, IL: University of Illinois Press, 1973); Ronald P. Formisano, *The Birth of Mass Political Parties: Michigan, 1827-1861* (Princeton, NJ: Princeton University Press, 1971); Richard P. McCormick, *The Second American Party System: Party Formation in the Jacksonian Era* (Chapel Hill, NC: University of North Carolina Press, 1966); Richard P. McCormick and William N. Chambers, eds., *The American Party Systems* (New York: Oxford University Press, 1975); Gerald W. McFarland, *Mugwumps, Morals and Politics, 1884-1920* (Amherst, MA: University of Massachusetts Press, 1975); Paul L. Murphy, ed., *Political Parties in American History*, vol. 3, 1890-Present, Morton Borden, ed. (New York: G. P. Putnam's Sons, 1974); Roy F. Nichols, *The Invention of the American Political Parties* (New York: Macmillan Company, 1967); Michael Wallace, "Changing Concepts of Party in the United States: New York, 1815-1828," *American Historical Review* 74 (1968): 453-91.

92. Abbott, *System of Professions*, 60-68. Additional categories and examples of public sphere jurisdictional claims will be introduced and discussed in Chapter 2.

93. For studies and statistics on the growth of the nineteenth-century politically independent press, see the following sources: Baldasty, *Commercialization of the News*;

Alfred McClung Lee, *The Daily Newspaper in America: The Evolution of a Social Instrument* (New York: Macmillan, 1937); Jeffrey B. Rutenbeck, "The Rise of Independent Newspapers in the 1870s: A Transformation in American Journalism" (Ph.D. diss., University of Washington, 1990); Schudson, *Discovering the News*.

94. Abbott, *System of Professions*, 60-61.

95. Ibid., 59-69.

96. Margaret A. Blanchard, "Filling the Void: Speech and Press in State Courts Prior to *Gitlow*," in *The First Amendment Reconsidered*, Bill F. Chamberlin and Charlene J. Brown, eds. (New York: Longman, 1982); John Robert Finnegan, Jr., "Defamation, Politics, and the Social Process of Law in New York State, 1776-1860" (Ph.D. diss., University of Minnesota, 1985); Timothy Gleason, *The Watchdog Concept: The Press and the Courts in Nineteenth-Century America* (Ames, IA: Iowa State University Press, 1990); Leonard W. Levy, *Emergence of a Free Press* (New York: Oxford University Press, 1988); Norman Rosenberg, *Protecting the Best Men: An Interpretive History of the Law of Libel* (Chapel Hill, NC: University of North Carolina Press, 1986).

97. Baldasty, *Commercialization of the News*, discusses some of the activities of the various occupational associations. See also: Joseph F. Bradley, *The Role of Trade Associations and Professional Business Societies in America* (University Park, PA: Pennsylvania State University Press, 1965); Bunnell, *New York Press Association*; Kenneth Q. Jennings, "Political and Social Force of the New Jersey Press Association, 1857-1939" (Master's thesis, Columbia University, 1940); Harold K. Schellenger, *An Era of Newspaper Organization: Development of the Buckeye Press Association, 1895-1908* (Columbus, OH: Ohio Historical Society, 1939); Henry H. Ward, "Ninety Years of the National Newspaper Association" (Ph.D. diss., University of Minnesota, 1977).

98. *Henderson (Minnesota) Independent*, 13 July 1872, 1.

99. Franklin was often noted by his journalistic descendants as a hero. See, for example, the introduction to Benjamin Franklin's autobiography written by a nineteenth-century journalist, John Bigelow, in *The Autobiography of Benjamin Franklin, The Unmutilated and Correct Version, Compiled and Edited with Notes by John Bigelow* (New York; London: G. P. Putnam's Sons, Knickerbocker Press, 1927).

100. An example would include the moral war against James Gordon Bennett. See Don C. Seitz, *The James Gordon Bennetts: Father and Son, Proprietors of the "New York Herald"* (Indianapolis, IN: Bobbs-Merrill, 1928), 73-101.

101. For citations of the many published autobiographies of journalists see Louis Kaplan, James T. Cook, Clinton L. Colby, Jr., and Daniel C. Haskell, *A Bibliography of American Autobiographies* (Madison, WI: State Historical Society of Wisconsin, 1962); Warren C. Price, *The Literature of Journalism, An Annotated Bibliography* (Minneapolis, MN: University of Minnesota Press, 1959).

For views on autobiography as a narrative and historical form see William C. Spengemann, *The Forms of Autobiography* (New Haven and London: Yale University Press, 1980); James Olney, ed., *Autobiography: Essays, Theoretical and Critical* (Princeton, NJ: Princeton University Press, 1980); James Olney, *Studies in Autobiography* (New York; Oxford: Oxford University Press, 1988); Norman K. Denzin, *Interpretive Biography*, Sage University Paper Series on Qualitative Research Methods Series, vol. 17 (Beverly Hills, CA: Sage, 1989).

An early example of an autobiography that embodied journalistic jurisdictional claims is that of Benjamin Franklin, cited in note 98. Philip Abbott argues in *In States of Perfect Freedom: Autobiography and American Political Thought* (Amherst, MA: The University of Massachusetts Press, 1987) that Franklin's life story is America's first modern autobiography because of its secular materialistic underpinnings.

102. Many examples of this type of obituary were found in research that this author conducted in a collective biography of more than 140 early twentieth-century journalists. For citations see Patricia L. Dooley, "Minnesota Journalists as Elected Officials, 1923-1938: An Historical Study of an Ethical/Conflict of Interest Question" (Master's thesis, University of Minnesota, 1985).

103. *East Dubuque (Illinois) Register*, 9 February 1894, 2.

104. *Boston Courier*, 13 June 1805; [New York] *Weekly Visitor or Ladies' Miscellany*, 9 October 1802.

105. *[Boston] Democrat*, 4 January 1804.

106. *Clarkesville (Tennesse) Gazette,* 27 November 1819, 4.

107. *Blakely (Alabama) Sun*, 15 December 1818.

108. *History of Ross and Highland Counties, Ohio* (Evansville, IN., Williams Brothers Publishers, 1880), 85, for reference to this and other items included in various issues of the *Gazette*.

109. Clark, *Public Prints*, 122.

110. Donald M. Scott, "The Profession that Vanished: Public Lecturing in Mid-Nineteenth-Century America" in *Professions and Professional Ideologies in America*, Gerald L. Geison, ed. (Chapel Hill, NC: University of North Carolina Press, 1983), 12-28.

111. Just several of the many published include the following: Griffin, *History of the Press of Maine*; George Hage, *Newspapers on the Minnesota Frontier, 1849-1860* (St. Paul, MN: Minnesota Historical Society, 1967); Elma Lawson Johnston, *Trenton's Newspapers, 1778-1932* (Trenton, NJ: Trenton Times Newspapers, 1932).

112. *History of Ross and Highland Courier*, 84-93.

113. Abbott, *System of Professions,* 61. According to Abbott, "Public jurisdiction concerns an abstract space of work, in which there exist clear boundaries between homogeneous groups. Differences of public jurisdiction are differences between archetypes."

114. The group is representative in that it includes examples of both daily and weekly newspapers, as well as examples from most of the states of the nation, towns and cities of all sizes, and newspapers of many different political positions and forms, including religious, labor, literary, and other categories of papers.

115. These were gathered via interlibrary loan from libraries and archives around the country.

116. An attempt has been made to include within these two groups newspaper publishers, conductors and editors from as many of the states of the union as possible, as well as from both major population centers and small towns, and those representing both daily and weekly newspapers.

In the selection of individuals for the study, an effort was made to be as representative as possible so as to learn about the "typical," rather than the "notable," newspaper conductor. The individuals studied within the earlier group was largely selected from the index of newspaper conductors included in Clarence S. Brigham, *History and Bibliography of American Newspapers, 1690-1820* (Worcester, MA: American Antiquarian Society, 1947), and research was conducted at the American Antiquarian Society and other libraries and archives.

Information was sought on these individuals' social and educational backgrounds, apprenticeships, printing and publishing business activities, including all the newspapers and other publishing enterprises they initiated or were otherwise involved in, and their political affiliations and possible office holding, among other things. Files were assembled on each, and brief biographical sketches were prepared.

The amassing of biographies representing careers of journalists within the later period was considerably more difficult, since there were many more journalists working in more communities and states. Especially helpful in this process were various secondary sources and directories, including N. W. Ayer's newspaper directories, state and city general histories, and state newspaper histories.

117. Secondary sources consisted of relevant general histories of journalism, institutional histories, case studies, autobiographies, and other works on journalism, journalists, politicians, and political structure.

118. P. L. Berger and T. Luckmann, *The Social Construction of Reality* (London: Allen Lane, 1966); James Carey, *Communication as Culture: Essays on Media and Society* (Boston: Unwin Hyman, 1989); T. A. van Dijk, *Text and Context: Explorations in the Semantics and Pragmatics of Discourse* (London: Longman, 1977); Stuart Hall, D. Hobson, and P. Willis, eds., *Culture, Media, Language* (London: Hutchinson, 1980); Scott, *Gender and the Politics of History;* Raymond Williams, *Communications* (Harmondsworth, UK: Penguin, 1962).

119. Roger Chartier, "Texts, Printing, Readings," in *The New Cultural History*, Lynn Hunt, ed. (Berkeley: University of California Press, 1989), 154-75.

120. Abbott uses a case study approach in his research. See also Klaus Bruhn Jensen and Nicholas W. Jankowski, eds., *A Handbook of Qualitative Methodologies for Mass Communication Research* (New York: Routledge, 1991).

121. Abbott, *System of Professions*, 129; Malcolm Johnson, "Professional Careers and Biographies," in *The Sociology of the Professions: Lawyers, Doctors and Others*, Robert Dingwall and Philip Lewis, eds. (London: The Macmillan Press, 1983), 242-62.

2

Journalistic Work as Occupation in Eighteenth-Century America

Although news was circulated in seventeenth-century America before newspapers were regularly published in the colonies, it is unlikely that those involved in producing and disseminating journalistic communication began to coalesce into an occupation with much definition during this period of sparse populations and primitive conditions. But news work began to assume occupational dimensions during the eighteenth century after the colonists began to publish newspapers. Those who launched the country's first newspapers established discursive practices and other routines that communicated definitions of journalistic work as occupation with particular tasks and social roles, thus situating the burgeoning group within an emerging broader occupational community. Events that originated outside journalistic workers' immediate environment, particularly clashes between producers of newspapers and colonial authorities, and the American Revolution, also led to further occupational definition of journalistic work, especially that journalistic work associated with political communication.

Although the social and cultural boundaries of the fledgling journalistic occupation would still be only barely discernible during the several decades after the nation won its freedom from England, a group had nevertheless begun to coalesce. To understand journalism's occupational history after 1800, we must first consider these eighteenth-century processes, especially the roles played by journalistic occupational communication and the American Revolution.

EARLY JOURNALISTIC OCCUPATIONAL DEVELOPMENT, PRINTING, AND NEWSPAPERS

Work develops occupationally as it becomes infused with social and cultural organizational meaning, and this involves more than the mere performance of work tasks. Not a fixed or natural process, the course of an occupation's development is affected by the particular historical sociological circumstances of the various eras within which it exists. Forces that may both lead to and be indicators of occupational definition of work tasks include the development of remuneration and training systems for workers, the association of the work tasks with particular work products, the discursive practices of workers such as their dissemination of communication that defines them occupationally, and the gradual assignment of a particular social class to workers. However, situations, events, or processes that originate outside the group's environment can also play roles as reinforcers or obfuscators of group boundaries.

America was a primitive and traditional society during the seventeenth century, a period when indigenous people and English and European immigrants lived in wilderness communities and a few scattered population centers formed along the Eastern seaboard. Those who came to America based their ways of life on the customs and practices of those of their homelands, and this meant that most news was circulated interpersonally, by letter, or by religious or governmental sources.[1]

The arrival of printing in the colonies initially did little to change such news practices. While some news would be published in printed proclamation, handbill, and pamphlet formats after the arrival of the first provincial printing press at Cambridge in 1638, sparse populations and a general lack of commercial enterprise in the earliest British American communities discouraged the emergence of locally produced newspapers.[2] In addition, England's strict regulation of printing presses, especially that starting in the 1660s, must have represented a serious deterrent to anyone thinking of starting a newspaper.[3]

But during the eighteenth century, an environment more conducive to journalistic occupational development emerged. Crucial economic change, including the growth of manufacturing outside the home and money and commerce systems, marked the period, and social changes included population growth, emergence of a colonial class system and distinctive religious patterns, birth of higher education systems, and slow increases in literacy.[4] Together, such changes fostered development of American printing and newspaper industries, the fulcrums out of which journalistic occupational development would ultimately emerge.

In the first half of the eighteenth century, an emerging journalistic group was composed of postmasters, printers, and community members of a literary bent. Postmaster John Campbell hired printer Bartholomew Green to print his *Boston News-Letter* in 1704, and William Brooker hired James Franklin to print the first number of his 1719 *Boston Gazette*.[5] But after printer James Franklin established the colony's third regularly published newspaper, the *New England Courant*, in 1721, the journalistic field, at least up to the War for Independence, was largely occupationally dominated by printers.[6] Of the forty Bostonians recorded in one historian's compilation of that city's printers, booksellers, and publishers as having either published, printed, and/or edited newspapers during the period 1696 to 1775, thirty-one (77 percent) were printers. Seven of the remaining nine were postmasters, and two came from the ranks of Boston's legal, publishing, and bookselling communities.[7]

Most of the era's journalists, referred to herein as printer-journalists, were typically operators of multipurpose publishing and printing establishments. For example, in addition to publishing and printing newspapers, printer-journalists often published books, pamphlets, almanacs, tracts, and other materials under their own imprimaturs; they also did job printing for other publishers and/ or local merchants, served as booksellers and/or bookbinders, operated coffee houses and general stores, and they served in appointed local governmental or quasi-governmental offices. Generally, however, these printer-journalists did not come from politically elite groups, although a few served in higher positions in various branches of government.[8]

Most pre-Revolutionary era journalists were proficient in all of the tasks involved in issuing newspapers, including both abstract tasks, such as rudimentary newsgathering and editing, as well as the technical tasks, such as printing.[9] The earliest newspapers were half- or one-page sheets produced entirely, including their physical printing, by one or two individuals — the printer-journalist and an apprentice or other assistant. Although a few publishers of these early newspapers appointed editors, the early editorial work was done generally by printer-journalists themselves.

The newspaper industry grew slowly during the decades leading up to the American Revolution, and this, along with other factors, likely obscured the boundaries of the emerging journalistic occupation during this period. Campbell had the newspaper field to himself until 1719, when he was replaced by William Brooker as postmaster. When Campbell refused to give up the *News-Letter*, Brooker started the second colonial newspaper, the Boston *Gazette*. Only thirteen papers were issued in the colonies from 1704 to 1750; ten more were issued by 1764; and another fourteen were started by 1775, bringing the total to thirty-seven.[10]

But while the slow growth of newspapers, sparse populations, and other environmental factors may have blurred whatever occupational definition journalistic work tasks were assuming during the period, other developments led to clarification of journalism's occupational boundaries. The payment of wages or other remuneration of workers who completed journalistic tasks, for example, led to the definition of journalistic work as occupation. In colonial America, printers who published newspapers were among the first to receive regular payment for performing journalistic work tasks.[11] Evidence of eighteenth-century newspaper business enterprises suggests that, by the American Revolution, all who published successful newspapers earned at least a portion of their livings doing journalistic work. Printer partners Benjamin Franklin and David Hall, for example, earned almost 60 percent of their cash receipts from the publication of the *Pennsylvania Gazette*, while at Williamsburg, Virginia, the Hunter printing firm in 1764 earned over half of its gross printing revenue from the issuance of the *Virginia Gazette*.[12]

The establishment of a regularly used method for training newcomers also contributed occupational attributes to journalistic work.[13] Since most issuers of newspapers by the War for Independence were printers, it can be assumed that most occupational newcomers learned journalistic work through their printing apprenticeships.[14] Clearly, however, the work routines apprentices were expected to learn would have varied depending on a master printers' printing specialties. For example, those who specialized in publishing religious materials and did not issue newspapers would not have incorporated journalistic training into their apprentices' duties.

In addition, newspapers' periodicity would have led to further occupational definition of journalistic work tasks. A serial designed to transmit intelligence and news in printed form at regular intervals, newspapers must have led to changed conceptions among the reading public of the work and workers involved in producing them. This follows an idea suggested by Milton Mueller, who found that the seventeenth-century invention of periodicity in publications engendered in the population a common sense of immediacy over a geographically dispersed readership.[15]

While the contents of early newspapers to some degree depended on the interests and skills of their proprietors, most were surprisingly similar considering how geographically isolated printer-journalists were from each other. In addition to advertisements, pre-Revolutionary era newspapers consisted largely of items reprinted from other newspapers, essays and letters by members of the community, and notices or other brief narratives prepared by printer-journalists. Among the topics typically addressed were foreign and military affairs, commerce, and religion and philosophy, with some attention to local matters. Thus, early journalistic gathering and editing tasks consisted largely of the perusal and selection of other newspapers for items that might be reprinted and the solicitation and preparation for printing of various nonjournalists' correspondence or essays; the journalistic writing tasks consisted largely of the composition of simple news notices.[16]

The assignment of a particular social class to workers who perform certain tasks can also contribute to the occupational definition of work. The social standing of journalists, however, would be less than clear until the nineteenth century when the more mundane technical tasks involved in journalistic work would be separated from the more intellectual tasks. While the social reputations of many of America's early journalists who came from the printing trades were undoubtedly affected by the lower social status of the artisan classes, there were those involved in journalism who must have been awarded higher status because of their social, education, or literary backgrounds.[17]

Botein, who has studied the trade habits and occupational ideologies of eighteenth-century printers, finds that the diversity of colonial newspaper publishers' pursuits meant newspaper publishers ranked neither as lowly as "meer mechanics" nor as highly as society "principal[s];"[18] and, he continued, the multiplicity of their endeavors meant a printer could become "much more than a printer," adding that "by the sum of his activities, he might well become a prominent man — unavoidably involved in a wide range of local affairs, though not necessarily with effective influence."[19]

OCCUPATIONAL COMMUNICATION AND THE SOCIAL CONSTRUCTION OF THE JOURNALISTIC OCCUPATION

Journalistic work tasks acquired occupational meaning in the eighteenth century from more than their association with newspapers and the printing trades.[20] Also playing an important role in the construction of occupational boundaries in the journalistic field was the widespread adoption by those who performed journalistic work tasks of discursive practices involving occupational communication. Examples of communication forms issued by establishers of newspapers that embodied occupational messages were printed essays or letters, often called prospectuses, that were issued on the establishment of new or re-vamped newspapers, printed advertisements for newspapers, and the ongoing interpersonal oral communications of newspaper proprietors with potential subscribers and advertisers as they sought patrons.

Journalists, then, were involved in the eighteenth century in a second category of communication, that which involved occupational communication. In addition to the type of communication embodied in their newspaper's regular news columns, early producers of newspapers communicated messages that led to the construction of the burgeoning group's work, roles, standards, and values. Furthermore, such reoccurring patterns of everyday practices would further lead to models of journalists as occupational practitioners.[21]

One of these discursive practices was the issuance of prospectuses on the establishment of new or newly designed newspapers, a practice apparently imported from England, since Campbell and other producers of early American newspapers had few but British models to guide them as they started their publishing work.[22] While publishers of new newspapers undoutedly depended on word-of-mouth communication of their business and occupational concerns, they also used this more formal communication method.

Prospectus writing was thus one of the earliest occupational routines established by the members of the burgeoning American journalistic group. From the start of newspaper publishing in the colonies, few journalists failed to issue them. Beyond the obvious fact that their English newspaper cousins generally issued prospectuses, there are a number of plausible explanations as to why they were adopted as a regular practice by colonial publishers. Since newspapers have always been identified with literary undertakings, journalists may have adopted already established routines of book authors and publishers, who often introduced themselves and their book plans in introductory statements. In fact, early newspaper prospectus writers at times mentioned that this custom in more general publishing meant they, too, as authors, were expected to introduce themselves and their literary enterprises.[23]

Additionally, some printers may have believed prospectuses would help them reach those who had not heard of their newspapers via other channels of communication. Or, perhaps some hoped such a published statement would lend their new enterprises a degree of formality that would communicate a sense of purpose, stability, and legitimacy. Since censorship was a concern early in the the eighteenth century, anyone starting a newspaper must have believed it essential to provide some explanation of the undertaking to those who wielded authority.[24]

Although journalists rarely started or revamped a newspaper without publishing prospectuses, they differed in length, style, tone, and prominence of display in the newspaper. Campbell's 1704 prospectus, for example, consisted of a few sentences on the bottom of the back of the one-double-sided page. In contrast, James Franklin's 1721 introductory essay was displayed prominently on the front page of the *New England Courant*. Additionally, some authors' rhetoric was direct, simple, and unaffected, while others' statements were more complex and contained more florid language or tones ranging from obsequious to sarcastic.

The authors of prospectuses devised various methods of circulating them to potential patrons. Journalists nearly always included their prospectuses in the first number of their new newspapers. But some also circulated a prospectus in handbill form to test the waters before issuing their proposed newspapers. In 1728, for example, Samuel Keimer published a two-page handbill titled "Advertisement," before he began publishing the *Pennsylvania Gazette, or the Universal Instructor*.[25] Later, having garnered enough support to begin publication, he reprinted the prospectus in the newly established newspaper.

Prospectuses essentially constructed definitions of journalistic work, since over time they embodied self-serving messages about the work, social utility, and authority of journalists and journalism.[26] A group of prospectuses issued from 1704 to 1770 was analyzed for both connotative and denotative messages about journalistic work for insight into how their authors constructed journalism as occupation during this period. Six themes emerged from a reading of these prospectuses. These themes would play a role in the construction of journalistic work as occupation during the period leading up to the American Revolution.[27]

PRE-REVOLUTIONARY WAR PROSPECTUSES

Newspaper Printer/Publishers Perform Journalistic Tasks

While newspaper printers did not explain the specific tasks they performed, they did inform their potential readers about the contents of their proposed newspapers. Prospectuses often described the topics their newspapers would address, as well as provide information on the literary forms information would take. Embodying occupational communication that ultimately would be part of the process whereby the journalistic occupation has been socially constructed, prospectuses would thus become important discursive strategies of those who practiced newspaper journalism.

Among the topics many journalists said they would treat in such literary forms as "news," "accounts," and "essays" were foreign and domestic events, commerce, science, technology, history, agriculture, religion and morals, and military matters. These statements varied considerably; some include brief sketches of the proposed paper's offerings, and others provided more detailed descriptions of what readers could expect. William Brooker simply stated that the *Boston Gazette* would include "the latest News," including that from "adjacent Provinces," as well as "an Account of the Prices of all Merchandise."[28] A longer statement, issued by Samuel Kneeland as he sought to establish the *New England Weekly Journal* in Boston in 1727, said his proposed newspaper would contain communication about the following:

Remarkable Occurrences of Europe, with a particular Regard from time to time to the present Circumstances of the Publick [sic] Affairs, whether of Church or State [and, whatever was] remarkable . . . in Town or Towns adjacent worthy of the Publick View; whether of Remarkable Judgments, or Singular Mercies, more private or public; preservations and deliverances by Sea or Land; together with some other pieces of history of our own, &c. that may be profitable and entertaining both to the Christian and Historian . . . [and] a weekly account of the number of persons buried, and baptiz'd [sic], in the Town of Boston.[29]

Among the longest of these statements was Keimer's two-page alphabetical listing of the subjects to be covered in the *Pennsylvania Gazette* that started with "Agriculture" and ended with "Zoology."[30]

Journalists Provide Useful Services

Many authors of eighteenth-century prospectuses issued before the American Revolution provided their readers with their reasons for establishing new newspapers. Several said they were starting a newspaper simply because individuals in their communities had urged them to. Others said they were starting newspapers to fulfill an unmet need in the community for a newspaper, or to provide a better newspaper. In 1719, when a new Boston postmaster was appointed, and some of Campbell's rural customers complained about delivery problems, William Brooker issued a prospectus that indicated he would attempt to remedy the situation through issuance of the *Boston Gazette*.[31] In 1728, Samuel Keimer claimed that he was issuing the *Pennsylvania Gazette* to provide a better newspaper, compared to the "wretchedly perform'd" late *Mercury*.[32]

Others took a less competitive approach, simply stressing that their newspaper would provide readers with something from which they would benefit. Kneeland, for example, said he was starting the *New-England Weekly Journal* because he hoped to provide the public with entertainment.[33]

In articulating contents of proposed newspapers, authors of prospectuses frequently issued statements that essentially promoted the idea that newspapers would benefit readers. Examples include claims that newspaper readers would be edified, instructed, entertained, pleased, and provided with useful information. Daniel Fowle's 1756 prospectus, for example, discussed the usefulness of newspapers and further explored this topic in a two-page essay, "Remarks on the Advantage of Printing."[34] Campbell's discussion about how his newspaper could be used as a place for advertisements by those who had something to sell or who sought lost items indirectly implies the usefulness of newspapers.[35]

Journalists Are Authoritative, Linked to Elites

Some prospectuses stated that certain members of the community, frequently referred to as "gentlemen," had expressed willingness to financially support the proposed newspaper. Often, prospectus writers offered thanks to these important patrons.[36]

Such references to "gentlemen" might be construed as intended to give the impression that the newspapers were authoritative. In establishing a link between the newspaper and such socially authoritative individuals, printer-journalists may have sought to elevate the reputations of their medium.

Journalists Depend on Public Support

In addition to statements about those who had already expressed support for, and encouragement to, the publisher, some prospectuses included solicitations for support from additional community members. For example, Fowle's prospectus, issued as he launched the *New-Hampshire Gazette* in 1756 said, "I now publish the first *Weekly Gazette*, for the Province of New-Hampshire; depending on the favour [sic] of all Gentlemen who are Friends to Learning, Religion, and Liberty."[37]

Prospectuses sometimes included pleas for literary assistance. Fowle's prospectus included the statement:

The Publisher will esteem it a great Favour to be well supplied by correspondents of genius and generous Sentiments with such Speculations or Essays as may be pleasing and instructive to the Public, agreeable to the Design of this Paper, and acknowledge himself obliged to any Gentleman who will take the Pains to communicate to him any good Intelligence, provided they be sent free of charge.[38]

Journalists Are Trustworthy

Journalists included messages in prospectuses about their characters and credentials, perhaps in response to early Americans' demand for such information. James Franklin, in a relatively humorous and sarcastic prospectus, commented:

It's a . . . sad case, that a man can't appear in print now a day, unless he'll undergo the mortification of answering to ten thousand . . . impertinent questions like these: Pray Sir

From whence came you? And what age may you be of. May I be so told? Was you bred at Colledge [sic] Sir?"[39]

In discussing his age, Franklin warned his readers:

If they should tell me that I am not yet fit nor worthy to keep company with such illustrious sages, for my beard doesn't reach down to my birdle, I shall . . . [give] them no other answer than . . . *Barba non facit philoshum.*[40]

In such statements, Franklin and others implied they were individuals of character and competence. Many conveyed ideas that they should be trusted because they were well connected, saying, for example, they were supported by local "gentlemen." Campbell twice referred to himself in his prospectus as "reasonable," once in relation to his advertising rates and once in relation to the cost of a subscription.[41]

But some appealed more directly for respect. Samuel Keimer told his readers that he was well informed and well traveled;[42] William Weyman gave his new readers an account of his earlier newspaper publishing experience;[43] and William Bradford claimed he should be considered eminently qualified since he was a member of the well-known and highly successful Bradford printing family.[44]

Journalists Are Rarely Embroiled in Political Matters

Until the 1750s, few newspaper prospectuses singled out politics as a topic that would be treated, and many of those that did were unclear about whether local political matters would be discussed.[45] Of the twenty-one prospectuses studied, only two published before 1750 specifically mentioned politics; one was Kneeland's, which preceded the launching in 1727 of the *New-England Weekly Journal*. Kneeland promised news of "Remarkable occurrences of Europe, with particular regard from time to time to the present circumstances of the Public Affairs [sic], whether of Church or State."[46] A second printer-journalist who wrote that his proposed newspaper would provide political communication was William Bradford, who in 1742 claimed the *Pennsylvania Journal* would include "short essays upon political . . . subjects."[47]

The system of political communication in colonial New England was confined largely to the elite sector until 1721, when James Franklin flaunted the Puritan government's jurisdiction over the issuance of newspapers; until then newspapers had been published only "by authority," that is, by permission of the government.[48] In addition, early printer-journalists depended on government printing contracts for a portion of their income. Although the producers of early colonial newspapers generally published some political communication, they tended to shy away from controversy that was frowned upon by local officials and not generally appreciated by the citizenry.[49] Occasionally, colonial printer-journalists deviated from the norm, choosing to flaunt the authorities

through what some considered to be inflammatory political communication. James Franklin, in 1726, became the first colonial newspaper journalist to record in the public press the votes of individual lawmakers on a bill before the legislature. But such conduct was unusual in colonial America, at least until the mid-1700s.[50]

Such a dearth of political communication in newspapers has led some historians to assume that most of America's printer-journalists lacked political convictions until the 1760s. But another interpretation suggests that pre-Revolutionary War printer-journalists realized, as business-minded entrepreneurs, that the survival of their printing enterprises required them to avoid offending both the authorities and the public.[51] Indeed, when the British authorities loosened their controls on the press, as they did for a time after 1735 when John Peter Zenger won his libel trial, or when political unrest grew into serious confrontations, as happened during the decade before the Revolution, journalists may have believed it safer to engage in partisan rhetoric.[52]

Journalists Hold to Community Values and Standards in Their Handling of Information

Establishers of eighteenth-century newspapers may have sought through prospectuses to instill in potential readers the idea that they were sensitive to their concerns and needs. For example, it was quite common for printer-journalists to state that they would select content in such a way that it would be "accurate" or "authentic," as Samuel Keimer did in the 1728 prospectus that introduced the *Pennsylvania Gazette*.[53] Printers occasionally mentioned during this period that the matters their newspapers treated would be handled in an impartial manner,[54] as well as with "immediate care"[55] and "carefully."[56]

Some prospectuses mentioned particular groups or topics that would be treated judiciously. While Daniel Fowle's prospectus for the *New-Hampshire Gazette* included a statement that he presumed no one would be offended if its columns exhibited the "Spirit of Freedom, which so remarkably prevails in the English Nation,"[57] but he added that he would avoid printing material that would abuse such freedom or "foment divisions in Church or State."[58] James Parker, in his 1753 prospectus for the *Occasional Reverberator*, promised not to expose any of the secrets of his correspondents, a group he must have valued highly since they provided him with important information and patronage.[59]

In sum, pre-Revolutionary War newspaper prospectuses, one of the earliest occupational routines of journalists, included both explicitly stated denotative, as well as less specific connotative, messages that constructed journalistic work tasks occupationally. In the former category was information on mundane and important matters, such as the kinds of content journalists would provide the public and messages of a more commercial nature on frequency of publication, subscription cost, delivery procedures, and advertising rates. In addition, the authors of early newspaper prospectuses also discussed more sensitive occupational matters, such as their societal roles, credentials, and affiliations with others in the community.

But it is also obvious from this reading of pre-Revolutionary War prospectuses that only a few newspaper journalists defined themselves as regular providers of political communication. Despite this, some newspapers did provide political communication, and some newspaper journalists used their newspapers as a tool as they engaged in political controversies. To understand why and how the role of newspaper journalists developed as it would later in the eighteenth and nineteenth centuries, one must look at America's political communication system and the diverse forms and providers of political communication before and after the American Revolution.

POLITICAL COMMUNICATION AND POLITICAL COMMUNICATION SYSTEMS IN EARLY AMERICA

Categories of Political Communication Systems

Political scientists categorize political communication systems around the world as elite, hegemonic, petitionary, and associational. Elite communication systems include those where political communication consists largely of the governed communicating among themselves. Any political communication within such systems, whether in oral, print, broadcast, or electronic forms, is issued and controlled by ruling elites and directed toward other elites within society. Political communication is not directed toward nonelite groups or individuals, since they play no direct role in the negotiation of political power within the political system. Most European countries, England, and colonial America had elite communication systems until they began to develop more representative forms of government. [60]

In hegemonic systems, those who govern regularly address the governed, informing them about various political or other governmental or state-related matters, but the governed are not offered formal opportunities to communicate back. In such one-way communication systems, the governed play a limited role in the negotiation of political power within the system. Hegemonic communication systems developed in England and colonial America when representative governmental forms were established, and when the principle that the voting public had a right to know what the legislature was doing was honored. [61]

In petitionary systems, those who govern regularly address the governed, and the governed are allowed to address those in power, although they have little other access to political power. Colonial New England's town meetings serve as an example of a political culture that permitted the governed opportunities for petitionary political expression. [62]

Associational communication systems include those where the governed play an important role. Not only do the citizens communicate political ideas to the governors, but they communicate among themselves on political questions, ultimately making decisions both through referenda and representational gov-

ernmental systems. Political communication among these people is crucial because it precipitates political consensus or compromise. Twentieth-century
America is an example of a society that has an associational communication
system.[63]

These political communication systems, as they have emerged in various
societies, can be seen as either prohibiting or encouraging the development of
occupations and professions whose work includes political communication.
Printers, publishers, journalists, authors, scholars, social reformers, politicians,
public relations experts, and political consultants fall into this category. As
nations experience profound shifts in their systems of governance, transformations in political communication systems transpire as well. Elite and hegemonic
systems discourage development of professional work systems, since professionals by the nature of their work must be free to acquire and manipulate abstract knowledge. Correspondingly, the more democratic of these systems,
which offer citizens opportunities to communicate with those who govern, provide more fertile ground for the development of professional political communication work systems.

Defining work systems as interrelated sets of work tasks, occupational
groups, and the changing links that bind one to the other, a political communication work system, at any given point in time, includes the following elements:
political communication work tasks and the interrelated occupational groups
whose members compete for jurisdiction over such work tasks. Also strongly
related to the political communication work system are the various publics,
funders, patrons, or other groups or institutions related to the occupational
group and the work.[64] Political communication work tasks are those involving
"any transmission of messages that has or is intended to have an effect on the
distribution or use of power in society."[65]

Political communication can be either prescriptive, providing answers to
political questions, or nonprescriptive, providing the political information the
public can use to evaluate and make decisions about political problems.[66] Much
political communication throughout its history has been prescriptive, intended
to provide the public with direction. But at times, political communication
takes on nonprescriptive characteristics. During periods of political repression,
for example, certain providers of political information must be careful in their
handling of potentially sensitive material. As a result, political information
becomes less partisan or is written in code to discourage the scrutiny of
authorities. Certain periods in the history of colonial America would fit this
description.

Forms and Providers of Early American Political Communication

Newspapers were but one of several important providers of political information during America's formative years. A number of participatory and printed
forms of political communication were prominent during the eighteenth and
nineteenth centuries.

Participatory Forms. Much of America's early political communication was greatly restricted, at least in public. A prominent form of political information was participatory activity in which people were allowed to play subordinate roles in "rituals of authority." Examples included early Americans' attendance at court sessions, public executions, and other manifestations of governmental authority.[67] Voting sometimes fell into this category, since in some places, such as Virginia, casting ballots was typically an act of deference since there were no secret ballots. Local sheriffs would ask voters whom they favored in the presence of the candidates, who would then offer their thanks.[68]

New England's political culture allowed for a more petitionary brand of political expression in the form of town meetings. New Englanders, for example, were able to voice their objections to the Stamp Act of 1765 at town meetings.[69]

As the nation developed after the American Revolution, the citizenry learned how to govern themselves by experimenting with various forms of participatory activities involving rhetoric, as well as more symbolic activities, where individuals could express their political sentiments through action.[70] For example, during the height of the controversy that generated the Alien and Sedition Acts, Americans expressed pro- and anti-French sentiments by wearing hats of particular colors.[71] Parades, festivals, picnics, and other public festivities also became forums for dissemination of political rhetoric from people representing many social and political backgrounds. At such events, the public experienced, listened, and sometimes responded to speeches and other forms of spoken or sung political rhetoric.[72]

Oratory was strongly related to public participatory activities, since it was so often included in public ceremonies and celebrations. Defined as "the art of using speech effectively in addressing an audience within political, legal, ceremonial, or religious settings," oratory has been counted as an important form of political communication in many countries, including America.[73] It often has been used as a starting point by those seeking political power in America, whether they are interested in winning political office or in effecting social reforms through political activism from outside the inner circles of government.[74]

Before the emergence of democracy in America, oratory was largely an activity carried on by elites for other elites. But later, speechmaking became popularized and political and other causes were espoused by all sorts of people in all kinds of settings, including formal political occasions and informal events like picnics or Chautauqua meetings.[75]

Printed Forms of Political Communication. In addition to nonprint forms, early Americans developed several printed forms of political communication. Until at least the 1720s, many were elite, since they were published primarily by those who governed for others in the privileged classes. But this began to change by the 1750s, as the colonies moved slowly toward a more democratic form of government. During this period, printed forms of political information began to reach more people and were at times read aloud at the polls.[76]

The various printed forms of political communication included books, pamphlets, broadsides, magazines, and newspapers. Among the providers of these forms were printers, postmasters, politicians, scholars, social activists, and members of the clergy.[77]

Pamphlets, for example, are considered by historians as one of the more important forms of political communication, since their function has largely been to persuade and rouse readers to action.[78] Defined as nonserial publications written for a general audience and not originally intended for permanent preservation, pamphlets, like newspapers, have roots that go back earlier than printing. The term was used as early as 1344 to refer to short manuscript works, but pamphlets have largely consisted of published texts since the invention of printing.[79]

Wars and political controversies inspired early pamphlets, and as a result, they have long been considered as largely polemical. However, pamphlets did not play a role in large-scale public controversy until the Protestant Reformation. The pamphlet remained the leading medium for religious and political controversies throughout the next three centuries. Events such as the Thirty Years' War, the English Revolution, the wars of Louis XIV, the French Revolution, and the American Revolution, were occasions when societies were flooded with pamphlet literature.[80]

The authors of pamphlets have historically represented diverse groups, including philosophers, theologians, teachers, and social reformers. Among the most important pamphlet writers of the past five centuries were Martin Luther, John Milton, Jonathan Swift, Voltaire, Karl Marx, and Thomas Paine. Not all pamphlet texts originated as printed works; some were transcriptions of political speeches and sermons. Pamphlets remained the primary choices for reaching audiences until the magazine and newspaper began to develop, especially during the eighteenth and nineteenth centuries.

The literary products of political communicators, in addition to being categorized by medium, can be grouped according to literary type, genre, and style. Examples of literary genres that have included political communication are essays, speeches, tracts, novels, poems, plays, news stories, and editorials. The forms and styles have varied, depending on the time period and needs of politicians, the public, and emerging occupational groups — such as eighteenth-century newspaper journalists.

Roles of Political Controversy and the American Revolution

Before the American colonies won independence, the political communication system was an elite hybrid, since the English governors had permitted representative forms of government in the colonies since the 1600s. But political communication was not created in such a system for the benefit of the general public, and, in fact, much political knowledge was considered secret. Printers or publishers who were thought responsible for the dissemination of censored political knowledge could, at the whim of authorities, be punished.[81]

While most early eighteenth-century journalists avoided political entanglements, a few notable journalists did not shy away from controversy. Printer James Franklin's thwarting of the authorities in the innoculation controversy, for example, and John Peter Zenger's imprisonment and trial on libel charges fall into the latter category. While the roles of controversial printers such as Franklin and Zenger have largely been studied within the broader historical context of press freedom, they can also be conceived of as struggles over occupation, that is, disputes over who ought to be doing what and for what purpose.

This clash, or intersection, between newspaper printers and the authorities would become an important part of the process where journalistic work began to acquire occupational meaning during the eighteenth century. But any effects such skirmishes between the authorities and the emerging journalistic group's members pale in comparison to the occupational ramifications of the American Revolution — perhaps the century's most potent occupational delineator of journalistic work.

After Franklin and Zenger won their battles, the colonial rulers loosened their hold on printers and other political communicators. But the relaxed atmosphere dissipated with the British government's passage of the Stamp Act, the symbolic beginning of the American Revolutionary War period. The American Revolution and its shift to a democratic government free from English control brought a corresponding structural shift in the nation's system of governance, accompanied by a host of other changes. It was not just America's system of government that was transformed; the country's political communication changed from an elite to a more democratic one. Along with this came changes in the political information issued in America and in the printed forms that issued it, including newspapers. In his 1803 *Retrospect of the Eighteenth Century*, Reverend Dr. Samuel Miller discussed how the American Revolution affected the country's newspapers. According to Miller, newspapers were fundamentally altered:

It is worthy of remark that newspapers have almost entirely changed their form and character within the period under review. For a long time after they were first adopted as a medium of communication to the public, they were confined, in general, to the mere statement of facts. But they have gradually assumed an office more extensive, and risen to a more important station in society. They have become the vehicles of discussion, in which the principles of government, the interests of nations, the spirit and tendency of public measures, and the public and private characters of individuals, are all arraigned, tried, and decided. Instead, therefore, of being considered now, as they once were, of small moment in society, they have become immense moral and political engines, closely connected with the welfare of the state, and deeply involving both its peace and prosperity.[82]

But the effects of the Revolution went well beyond transforming the contents and characters of newspapers, for it would also affect those who produced them. Examination of newspaper prospectuses reveals that not only did the Revolution usher in an era of a more openly politicized newspaper, but it brought about a change in the occupational ideology of the burgeoning journalistic group.

Two groups of newspaper prospectuses were studied, one group whose issues were published between 1704 and 1778 and another after the Revolution from 1783 to 1800.[83] Particular attention was paid to how their authors defined their roles as political communicators and their relationships to politicians, politics, and other political matters; whether the authors of prospectuses published after the revolution specifically discussed any ramifications of the American Revolution; and finally, whether prospectuses included statements about the power, usefulness, or benefits of newspapers in the provision of political information. The following sections discuss three important themes that emerged in the reading of the pre- and post-Revolutionary war prospectuses.

Journalists' Enhanced Role as Providers of Political Information

Some journalists' post-Revolutionary War prospectus statements reflect a possible understanding that they played an enhanced role as providers of political information in America. Few establishers of newspapers before the 1760s specifically mention that they would provide political information or discuss themselves as being important providers of such information. Of the twenty-one early prospectuses, six specifically mentioned political information, and within this group of six, two statements were issued after the Stamp Act crisis, a time recognized by many historians as the symbolic start of the Revolution.[84] In contrast, a larger proportion of the post-Revolutionary War prospectuses, twenty-three out of twenty-nine, specifically discussed the various ways the newspapers would serve their communities as providers of various categories of political information.[85]

One of this group of twenty-three, newspaper journalist Alden Spooner promised readers on his establishment of the *Vermont Journal*, in 1783, to provide them with essays and editorial statements on political subjects. In his words, the *Journal* would include "the productions of the Literarti, on political or moral subjects . . . decent remarks on public measures, candidly stated, and calculated to reform government."[86]

A second example included a prospectus issued in 1784 by William Warden and Benjamin Russell as they set out to launch the *Massachusetts Centinel and Republican Journal*. Accordingly, they promised: "The Publishers engage to use every effort to obtain, and the most serutinous [sic] circumspection in collecting and adjusting whatever may be thought of publick benefit, or private amusement; variety shall be courted in all its shapes, in the importance of political information."[87]

Another such statement was issued by George Kline and George Reynolds, who in 1785 sought to establish a paper titled *Gazette, and the Western Repository of Knowledge* in Carlisle, Pennsylvania. According to these publishers:

The press at this place promises every possible public advantage. Through this channel — the communication of knowledge is facilitated, — every member of the community has it in his power to scrutinize, with candour [sic], the characters of men in office, and to examine, with . . . the measures of government — to detect fraud and . . . and to expose them, stripped of their meretricious covering, to public view.[88]

The larger number of journalists who stressed their role as providers of such political information indicates some recognition that they were playing a more decidedly political communication role than they had before the Revolution.

Journalistic Relationships to Politics and Politicians

In addition to an increase in their articulations of roles as providers of political communication, post-Revolution journalists also increasingly discussed their political positions, affiliations, and politically related editorial policies. Of the twenty-one pre-Revolutionary War newspaper prospectuses studied, four discussed the newspaper's political sentiments (all but one during the period following the 1765 Stamp Act). But of the twenty-nine postwar prospectuses examined, seventeen discussed relationships to politicians, politics, and/or editorial policies in relation to political matters.

Several examples included the *Newport (Rhode Island) Gazette's* new proprietor, Peter Edes, a printer who had earlier started papers in Boston and Haverhill, Massachusetts, and in Augusta and Bangor, Maine.[89] Expressing his political independence, on the first day of March 1787, Edes described how he would treat political content: "While the personal invectives of man against man will be always excluded, his paper shall ever be open to the different politicians of the day."

A second journalist who discussed the standards that he would use in handling political material was Andrew Brown, who on his establishment of Philadelphia's *Federal Gazette*, in 1788, said his paper would be "open to writers on both sides of every political or other question, so long as they are governed by decency."[90]

While explanations concerning newspaper publishers' had before been included in prospectuses by journalists, after the Revolution, it appears possible that journalists increasingly felt the need to explain their positions. Although the members of both groups were involved in the tasks of issuing political information in newspapers before, during, and after the Revolution, there likely was an increase in demand for the services of both groups throughout that period. Considering Americans' distrust of politics and politicians, such closeness likely needed explaining.

Power and Utility of Newspaper Journalists and Their Newspapers

That the American Revolution contributed to a shift in newspaper journalists' thinking about their occupation is also evident in the increased number of prospectuses issued after the war that included explicit references to the benefits brought to Americans by newspapers and journalists. Before the American Revolution, such statements were rare. In twenty-one prewar prospectuses examined, one journalistic author, Samuel Hall, mentioned the press's utility, as he sought to establish the *Essex Gazette* in Salem, Massachusetts in 1768.[91]

However, such statements appeared more frequently in post-Revolution prospectuses. Of the twenty-nine examined, thirteen included statements about the utility of newspapers. William Warden and Benjamin Russell, in proposals to publish the *Massachusetts Centinel* in Boston in 1784, commented on how important the press was to the preservation of democracy: "The Liberty of the Press is the surest bulwark of the people's rights, a privilege to mankind which tyrannical monarchs have beheld with horror and often attempted to annihilate."[92]

Josiah Meigs commented at length about the benefits of newspapers as he cooperated with Moses H. Woodward and Thomas Green in their establishment in 1785 of Middletown, Connecticut's *Middlesex Gazette*.[93] According to Meigs, newspapers provided citizens with more benefits than other forms of political communication:

The advantages of newspapers are too well known to need a particular recital: it may be said in general, that a well regulated News Paper [sic] furnishes a rational Entertainment for the Moments of Relaxation from Business or Labour; that it facilitates and cultivates Commerce; that it is beneficial to agriculture and manufacturers, that it is favourable to Morals, Virtue and Literature, and, as the greatest of its Excellencies, that it is absolutely necessary for the Preservation of Freedom in a Republican Government, such a paper supplying precisely the place of the censorial power in ancient Rome, an office of the highest Dignity in that glorious Republic, the execution of which required the integrity and wisdom of Cato. In a word, the excellent Art of printing enables the publisher of such a paper to entertain or interest, at once, greater multitudes than those which heard the Orators of Greece or Rome.[94]

One of the prospectuses studied mentioned the role of the press in the American Revolution specifically. On their establishment in 1793 of the *Massachusetts Mercury*, publishers Alexander Young and Samuel Etheridge printed the following statement:

At no period, since the discovery of printing, has there ever been so interesting an era as the present . . . . And while the historian is . . . employed to delineate her progress in Arms and Arts, the Printer of a weekly Paper, if faithful to his trust, furnishes in the minutiae of successive detail, events less splendid than those which adorn the historic page, but vastly more interesting to the present actors in the theater of existence. Newspapers, originally fanned that favored flame of Liberty, which first was kindled on the Columbian Altar, and from thence with unexampled rapidity has spread to the furthest bourne [sic] of Europe, illuminating the universe of Man in its progress, and giving freedom to myriads of lives.[95]

Studying the emergence of the journalistic occupation during the eighteenth century reveals much that is important to our understanding of the group's subsequent development in the nineteenth century. While news and other information was conveyed by town criers and others who made it their business to do so, little evidence exists that such work assumed occupational dimensions during the years before the establishment of newspapers. But as printing and newspapers grew as industries during the eighteenth century, a complex process would engender journalistic work tasks with occupational meaning.

While the attachment of eighteenth-century journalism to newspapers and the development of remunerative and training programs for journalistic work were important aspects of this process, also crucial were the various discursive strategies developed by members of the developing group. Occupational communication within prospectus statements imbued journalistic work with social purpose and position.

While such definition early on rarely stressed the political importance of the group's work and members, this would change as the country moved toward a break with England. As is revealed in the writings of newspaper proprietors, the more democratic political communication system ushered in by the American Revolution fueled the first significant wave of journalistic occupational development, although journalists were not yet widely acknowledged as a group with clear-cut duties and occupational authority. By the end of the century, those who produced America's newspapers had been transformed from isolated printers and others who performed journalistic work tasks into a more printer-dominated loose-knit but discernible group whose members considered themselves crucial actors in the new nation's experiment with democracy.

One of the profound transformations rendered by the Revolution was the citizenry's establishment of a more open and democratic political communication system based on a different set of ideals than those that dominated in the previous, more restricted system. The country's more open system, however, did not necessarily automatically lead to an environment wherein journalists, rather than politicians, would be accepted as the proper purveyors of political information. In fact, while the Revolution may have led printer-journalists to believe they had a special calling to serve Americans as crucial providers of certain categories of political communication, the decades following the war are more often recognized as an era wherein they were to be dominated by politicians. If printer-journalists were to attain a position of prominence, they would need to differentiate themselves from politicians.

While the First Amendment offered printer-journalists a rhetorical weapon to use when attacked, the lessons of the Alien and Sedition Acts at the end of the eighteenth century were that it would take more than such a formal constitutional structure for them to attain full jurisdiction over their work. Only when the people of the country recognized a need for political communication that they believed journalists, rather than politicians, ought to fulfill, could those who performed journalistic work achieve some measure of jurisdiction over such work. While the Revolution afforded journalists a measure of occupational identity and authority they did not have earlier, they would still need to carve out a niche for themselves as gatherers, writers, and editors of political information in the form of news stories, editorials, and political analysis. During the nineteenth century, journalists would construct journalistic discourses that assigned them roles as the nation's legitimate providers of political news and opinion.

NOTES

1. Benjamin Franklin discusses in his autobiography how he wrote and disseminated news ballads as a young boy. See *The Autobiography of Benjamin Franklin, The Unmutilated and Correct Version, Compiled and Edited with Notes by John Bigelow* (New York; London: G. P. Putnam's Sons, Knickerbocker Press, 1927), 14. For information on news dissemination, as well as other communication in early America, see: Charles E. Clark, *The Public Prints: The Newspaper in Anglo-American Culture, 1665-1740* (New York: Oxford University Press, 1994); Elizabeth C. Cook, *Literary Influences in Colonial Newspapers, 1704-1750* (New York: Columbia University Press, 1912); Donovan H. Bond and W. Reynolds McLeod, eds., *Newsletters to Newspapers: Eighteenth-Century Journalism* (Morgantown, WV: West Virginia University, 1977); Richard D. Brown, *Knowledge is Power: The Diffusion of Information in Early America, 1700-1865* (New York: Oxford University Press, 1989); Mitchell Stephens, *A History of News* (New York: Penguin Books, 1988); Victor Von Klarwill, ed., *The Fugger News Letters*, 2 vols. (New York: G. P. Putnam's & Sons, 1924-1926).

2. Carl Bridenbaugh, *Cities in the Wilderness: The First Century of Urban Life in America, 1625-1742* (New York: Knopf, 1955); Merle Curti, *The Growth of American Thought* (New York: Harper & Row, 1964); Michael Kammen, *People of Paradox: An Inquiry Concerning the Origins of American Civilization* (New York: Oxford University Press, 1972); Perry Miller, *The New England Mind: The Seventeenth Century* (New York: Macmillan, 1939); Perry Miller, *The New England Mind: From Colony to Province* (Cambridge: Harvard University Press, 1953); Vernon L. Parrington, *Main Currents in American Thought*, vol. 1 (New York: Harcourt Brace Jovanovich, 1927); William Appleman Williams, *The Contours of American History* (Cleveland, OH: World Publishing, 1961).

3. Clyde A. Duniway, *The Development of Freedom of the Press in Massachusetts* (New York: Longmans, Green & Company, 1906).

4. For general accounts of colonial life and culture see Clarence L. Ver Steeg, *The Formative Years, 1607-1763* (New York: Hill and Wang, 1964). On seventeenth-century developments in New England, see Edmund S. Morgan, *The Puritan Dilemma: The Story of John Winthrop* (Boston: Little, Brown, 1958), and Miller, *The New England Mind: The Seventeenth Century.*

Aspects of life in the expanding settlements of the eighteenth century are treated in Richard B. Morris, *Government and Labor in Early America* (New York: Columbia University Press, 1946); Winthrop D. Jordan, *White over Black: American Attitudes Toward the Negro, 1550-1812* (Chapel Hill, NC: University of North Carolina Press, 1968); Eugene Genovese, *The World the Slaveholders Made* (New York: Pantheon Books, 1969); James T. Lemon, *The Best Poor Man's Country* (Baltimore, MD: Johns

Hopkins University Press, 1972); and Wilbur R. Jacobs, *Dispossessing the American Indian* (Norman, OK: University of Oklahoma Press, 1972).

5. Richard Kielbowicz, *News in the Mail: The Press, Post Office and Public Information* (Westport, CT: Greenwood Press, 1989).

6. Clark, *Public Prints*, 193.

7. This demographic data was compiled from a study of the biographies of Boston booksellers, publishers, and printers included in Benjamin Franklin, *Boston Printers, Publishers and Booksellers: 1640-1800* (Boston: G. K. Hall & Co., 1980).

8. Stephen Botein, "'Meer Mechanics' and an Open Press: The Business and Political Strategies of Colonial American Printers," *Perspectives in American History* 9 (1975): 127-225; Patricia Bradley, "No 'Meer Mechanic': William Bradford and the Search for Legitimacy," paper presented at the annual meeting of the American Journalism Historians Association, Philadelphia, PA, 1991; Clark, *Public Prints*; Kielbowicz, *News in the Mail*.

9. Descriptive accounts of early newspapers and the work involved in publishing them are provided by Clark, *Public Prints*, 193-207; Lawrence C. Wroth, *The Colonial Printer*. (Portland, Maine: Southworth-Anthoensen Press, 1938).

10. See the following for figures on the establishment of newspapers in colonial America: Isaiah Thomas, *The History of Printing, With a Biography of Printers*, 2d ed. (New York: B. Franklin, 1967); Clarence S. Brigham, *History and Bibliography of American Newspapers, 1690-1820* (Worcester, MA: American Antiquarian Society, 1947); William Adelbert Dill, *Growth of Newspapers in the United States* (Lawrence, KS: University of Kansas, 1928); Clark, *Public Prints*. Clark, for example, says that Charles Wetherell, in a study of colonial American printers, counted forty-eight newspapers begun in the thirteen colonies from 1690 to 1760, and another forty-six through 1775.

Also see sections on the newspaper press in Ian K. Steele, *The English Atlantic, 1675-1740: An Exploration of Communication and Community* (New York: Oxford University Press, 1986); Charles E. Clark and Charles Wetherell, "The Measure of Maturity: The Pennsylvania Gazette, 1728-1765," *William and Mary Quarterly* 3rd series, 61 (1989): 279-303; David Paul Nord, "Teleology and News: The Religious Roots of American Journalism, 1630-1730," *Journal of American History* 77 (1990): 9-38; and the following three articles by Charles E. Clark: "'Metropolis' and 'Province' in Eighteenth-Century Press Relations: The Case of Boston," *Journal of Newspaper and Periodical History* 5 (Autumn 1989): 2-16; "The Newspapers of Provincial America," *Proceedings of the American Antiquarian Society* 100 (1990): 367-89; and "Boston and the Nurturing of Newspapers: Dimensions of the Cradle," *New England Quarterly* 64 (1991): 243-71.

11. Arthur Salz, *Encyclopaedia of the Social Sciences* 1933-1935 ed., s.v., "Occupation."

12. Botein, "Meer Mechanics," 141-42; Mary Ann Yodelis Smith, "Who Paid the Piper? Publishing Economics in Boston, 1763-1775," *Journalism Monographs* 38 (February 1975).

13. Everett C. Hughes, *Men and Their Work* (Glencoe, Ill: Free Press, 1958), 133; Eliot Freidson, *Profession of Medicine: A Study of the Sociology of Applied Knowledge* (New York: Dodd, Mead, 1970), 71.

14. For accounts of early newspaper printing apprenticeships, see Wroth, *The Colonial Printer*; Carol Sue Humphrey, *This Popular Engine: New England Newspapers*

During the American Revolution: 1775-1789 (Newark: University of Delaware Press, 1992); Milton W. Hamilton, *The Country Printer: New York State, 1785-1830* (New York: Columbia University Press, 1936), as well as in autobiographies of early newspaper journalists like Benjamin Franklin.

15. Milton Mueller, "The Currency of the Word: War, Revolution and the Temporal Coordination of Literate Media in England, 1608-1655" (Ph.D. diss., University of Pennsylvania, 1986).

16. Clark, *Public Prints*, 207-14; Edwin Emery and Michael Emery, *The Press in America* (7th ed. Englewood Cliffs, NJ: Prentice Hall, 1992), 21-32; Frank Luther Mott, *American Journalism* (3d ed. New York: Macmillan Co., 1962), 15-6; Stephens, *History of News*, 184; Thomas, *History of Printing*, 8-21.

17. Bradley, "No Meer Mechanics," 2, as does Botein, "'Meer Mechanics,'" 140-47.

18. Botein, "'Meer Mechanics,'" 140.

19. Ibid.

20. Terry C. Blum, Paul M. Roman, and Deborah M. Tootle, "The Emergence of an Occupation," *Work and Occupation* 15 (February 1988): 96-114.

21. Thomas F. Gieryn, George M. Bevins, and Stephen C. Zehr, "Professionalization of American Scientists: Public Science in the Creation/Evolution Trials," *American Sociological Review* 50 (June 1985): 392-409; Carol L. Kronus, "The Evolution of Occupational Power: An Historical Study of Task Boundaries Between Physicians and Pharmacists," *Sociology of Work and Occupations* 1 (February 1976): 3-37; John F. Runcie, "Occupational Communication as Boundary Mechanism," *Sociology of Work and Occupations* 1 (November 1974): 419-44."

22. On the influence of the colonials' British printer/journalist cousins, see Clark, *Public Prints*. While they may have had examples of English news sheets, as well as earlier print forms such as books, to look to, magazines were only just beginning to be issued in London.

23. James Franklin, for example, said this as he established the *New England Courant*, in Boston, in 1721.

24. Since no statements of early printers and publishers about why they chose to print prospectuses have been uncovered in archives or other collections of letters or other materials, one can only surmise as to the various reasons why they were developed.

25. Such a practice was at times discussed in the prospectuses published in newspapers and appears to have been common from the start. It is doubtful that many of these early handbills have survived, although several were included in the microfilm editions of these newspapers. Other surviving examples of handbill-type prospectuses from the nineteenth century are found in the broadsides collection of the American Antiquarian Society, located at Worcester, Massachusetts.

26. In an examination of more than 300 newspapers established from 1704 to the early-twentieth century, only several have failed to include some form of an introductory statement to the newspaper's potential readers.

27. A group of twenty-one prospectuses, published between 1704 and 1765, were examined. Recognizing that print forms have multiple, differentiated, and sometimes even contradictory uses and functions, the research analyzed prospectuses on two levels: (1) as texts that provided denotative messages to their readers — denotative messages are defined as explicitly expressed information about newspaper printers and their publication designs, plans, and so on; (2) as texts that also expressed connotative messages to readers — connotative messages are defined as indirectly implied positive appeals

about newspapers, as well as about newspaper printers and publishers and their work. See the following, which provided guidance on the qualitative textual analysis completed in the research: Richard R. Beringer, *Historical Analysis: Contemporary Approaches to Clio's Craft* (New York: Wiley, 1978); Karlyn Kohrs Campbell, *The Rhetorical Act* (Belmont, CA: Wadsworth, 1982); Roger Chartier, "Texts, Printing, Readings," in *The New Cultural History*, Lynn Hunt, ed. (Berkeley: University of California Press, 1989), 154-75; T. A. van Dijk, *Text and Context: Explorations in the Semantics and Pragmatics of Discourse* (London: Longman, 1977); Klaus Bruhn Jensen and Nicholas W. Jankowski, eds., *A Handbook of Qualitative Methodologies for Mass Communication Research* (London; New York: Routledge, 1991).

28. *Boston Gazette*, 21 December 1719, 1.

29. Ibid.

30. *New England Weekly Journal*, 1 October 1728, 1.

31. Thomas, *History of Printing*, 220.

32. *Pennsylvania Gazette,* 1 October 1728, 1.

33. *New England Weekly Journal*, 20 March 1727, 1.

34. *New-Hampshire Gazette*, 7 October 1756, 1; the essay was printed in his volume's second number, on 14 October, 1756, 1-2.

35. *Boston News-Letter*, 17 April 1704.

36. Such as Samuel Keimer when he established, in Philadelphia, the *Pennsylvania Gazette.*

37. *New-Hampshire Gazette,* 7 October 1756, 1.

38. Ibid, 2.

39. *New England Courant,* 7 August 1721, 1.

40. Ibid.

41. *Boston News-Letter,* 17 April 1704.

42. *Pennsylvania Gazette*, 1 October 1728, 1.

43. *New York Gazette*, 16 February 1759, 1.

44. *Weekly Advertiser/Pennsylvania Journal*, 2 December 1742, 1.

45. On the contrary, the launchers of the *New England Courant*, in a rather tongue-in-cheek prospectus, promised they would *not* publish information about government. Printer James Franklin, along with co-owners John Checkley and William Douglass, sought to use the new paper for their now famous anti-innoculation campaign. In Franklin's words: "The undertaker promiseth, that nothing shall be inserted, reflecting on the Clergy (or such) of whatever Denomination, nor relating to the affairs of government, and no tresspass against decency or good manners."

For biographical information about Franklin that discusses his rebellious style of newspaper journalism, see Clark, *Public Prints*, 123-40; Joseph P. McKerns, ed. *Biographical Dictionary of American Journalism* (Westport, CT: Greenwood Press, 1989), 239-41.

46. *New England Weekly Journal*, 20 March 1717, 1. See Thomas, *History of Printing*, 242-45, for further information.

47. *Pennsylvania Journal*, 2 December 1742, 1.

48. The first British American newspaper, *Public Occurrences*, for example, published by Benjamin Harris, in Boston, in 1690, only lasted one issue since it was not published "by authority" of the English rulers. On Franklin and the role of the *Courant*, see: Clark, *Public Prints*, 123-24, 132; Duniway, *Development of Freedom of the Press*; Emery and Emery, *Press in America*, 25.

49. Botein, "Meer Mechanics." Although society's more elite members may have had some interest in, or need for, political information, it is not clear whether society had as yet begun to develop a strong belief that every individual's ability to function as a responsible citizen depended on the receipt of a regular supply of political news and other related information. Such an attitude may have been a result of the predominant governmental system the colonies were part of, which did not encourage the growth of newspapers or other media that might inspire a thirst among the subjects of the Crown for political knowledge.

50. Ibid.; Clark, *Public Prints*; Leonard W. Levy, ed., *Freedom of the Press from Zenger to Jefferson* (Indianapolis, IN: Bobbs-Merrill, 1966); Vincent Buranelli, ed., *The Trial of Peter Zenger* (New York: New York University Press, 1957). Scholars who stress the role of printers as espousers of press freedom in the first half of the eighteenth century include Gary Nash, *The Urban Crucible: Social Change, Political Consciousness, and the Origins of the American Revolution* (Cambridge: Harvard University Press, 1979); Jeffery A. Smith, *Printers and Press Freedom: The Ideology of Early American Journalism* (New York: Oxford University Press, 1988).

51. Botein, "Meer Mechanics"; Clark, *Public Prints*.

52. Buranelli, *Trial*; Arthur M. Schlesinger, *Prelude to Independence: The Newspaper War on Britain, 1764-1776* (New York: Alfred A. Knopf, 1958); Michael Schudson, "Political Communication," in *International Encyclopedia of Communications*, 1992 ed., s.v. "Political Communication," 305.

53. *Pennsylvania Gazette,* 1 October 1728, 1.

54. Andrew Bradford, in the prospectus for the *American Weekly Mercury*, 22 December 1719, 2; see also William Goddard's prospectus for the *Providence Gazette & Country Journal*, a prepublication statement dated 31 August 1762.

55. Samuel Kneeland, in the prospectus of the *New England Weekly Journal*, 20 March 1727, 1.

56. William Goddard, in his *Providence Gazette*'s prospectus, 20 October 1762, 1.

57. *New-Hampshire Gazette,* 7 October 1756, 1.

58. Ibid.

59. *Occasional Reverberator,* 7 September 1753, 1.

60. These categories are identified and discussed as they apply to various countries by Schudson in "Political Communication," 303-13. See also Karl Deutsch, *The Nerves of Government* (New York: Free Press, 1966); James A. Leith, *Media and Revolution: Moulding a New Citizenry in France During the Revolution* (Toronto: Canadian Broadcasting Corporation, 1968); George F. E. Rude, *Ideology and Popular Protest* (New York: Pantheon Books, 1980); Charles Tilly, "Collective Action in England and America, 1765-1775," in *Tradition, Conflict, and Modernization: Perspectives on the American Revolution*, Richard Maxwell Brown and Don E. Fehrenbacher, eds. (New York: Academic Press, 1977); Raymond Williams, *The Long Revolution* (New York: Columbia University Press, 1961) and "The Press and Popular Culture: An Historical Perspective," in *Newspaper History from the Seventeenth Century to the Present Day,* George Boyce, James Curran, and Pauline Wingate, eds. (Beverly Hills, CA: Sage, 1978).

61. Schudson, "Political Communication," 304-05.

62. Ibid., 305.

63. Ibid., 309.

64. This definition of the political communication work system is adapted from Abbott, *System,* 86.

65. Schudson, "Political Communication," 304. The term is usually applied to that communication which is related to government, but it also can refer to communication in a variety of settings, such as church, school, family, or any site where power is negotiated.

66. Abbott, *System of Professions,* 216-17.

67. Schudson, "Political Communication," 305, and Dirk Hoerder, *Crowd Action in Revolutionary Massachusetts, 1765-1780* (New York: Atlantic Press, 1977); Pauline Maier, *From Resistance to Revolution: Colonial Radicals and the Development of American Opposition to Britain, 1765-1776* (New York: Knopf, 1973); Tilly, "Collective Action."

68. Schudson, "Political Communication," 305.

69. Ibid.

70. Maurice Bloch, *Political Language and Oratory in Traditional Society* (London; New York: Academic Press, 1975); Robert Paine, ed., *Politically Speaking: Cross-Cultural Studies in Rhetoric* (Philadelphia, PA: Institute for the Study of Human Issues, 1981); Donald M. Scott, "The Profession that Vanished: Public Lecturing in Mid-Nineteenth-Century America," in *Ideologies in America*, Gerald L. Geison, ed. (Chapel Hill, NC: University of North Carolina Press, 1983), 12-28.

71. James M. Smith, *Freedom's Fetters: The Alien and Sedition Laws and American Civil Liberties* (Ithaca, NY: Cornell University Press, 1956); John C. Miller, *Crisis in Freedom: The Alien and Sedition Acts* (Boston: Little, Brown, 1951).

72. Mary Ryan, "The American Parade: Representations of the Nineteenth-Century Social Order," in *The New Cultural History*, Lynn Hunt, ed. (Berkeley, CA: University of California Press, 1989), 131-53. Even mob violence is considered by some historians to be a ritualized form of political communication. One historian wrote that, in Europe and England, food riots were "generally an assertion of the local community's right to consume available food at a fair price." Schudson, "Political Communication," 305; Hoerder, *Crowd Action*; Maier, *From Resistance;* Tilly, "Collective Action."

73. Alessandro Duranti, "Oratory," *International Encyclopedia of Communication*, s.v., "Oratory."

74. Bloch, *Political Language*; Paine, *Politically Speaking.*

75. Scott, "The Profession That Vanished."

76. Schudson, "Political Communication," 305.

77. For information on books, see John W. Tebbel, *A History of Book Publishing in the United States,* vol. 1. (New York: Bowker, 1972); Brown, *Knowledge*; David D. Hall, "The World of Print and Collective Mentality in Seventeenth-Century New England," in *New Directions in American Intellectual History*, John Higham and Paul K. Conkin, eds. (Baltimore, MD: Johns Hopkins University Press, 1979), 166-95; David D. Hall and John B. Hench, eds. *Needs and Opportunities in the History of the Book: America, 1639-1876* (Worcester, MA: American Antiquarian Society, 1987). On pamphlets see Bailyn, *Ideological Origins*; Lester Condit, *A Pamphlet about Pamphlets* (Chicago: University of Chicago Press, 1939). For broadsides see Schudson, "Political Communication," 305. For magazines see Elliott Anderson and Mary Kinzie, eds. *The Little Magazine in America: A Modern Documentary History* (Yonkers, NY: Pushcart, 1978); Frank Luther Mott, *A History of American Magazines,* 5 vols. (Cambridge: Harvard University Press, 1938-1968). For newspapers see Clark, *Public Prints*; Michael

Schudson, *Discovering the News: A Social History of American Newspapers* (New York: Basic Books, 1978); George Boyce, James Curran, and Pauline Wingate, eds. *Newspaper History: From the Seventeenth Century to the Present Day* (Beverly Hills, CA: Sage, 1978).

78. Bailyn, *Ideological Origins*.

79. Schudson, "Political Communication," 305.

80. Ibid.

81. Clark, *Public Prints;* Duniway, *Development*; Leonard W. Levy, ed. *Freedom of the Press from Zenger to Jefferson* (Indianapolis: Bobbs-Merrill, 1966); Schudson, "Political Communication," 304-09; Frederick Siebert, *Four Theories of the Press* (Urbana, IL: University of Illinois Press, 1956).

82. Thomas, *The History of Printing in America*, 251-55.

83. The year 1783 was when the Treaty of Paris was signed. The group studied consisted of twenty-nine prospectuses issued in Massachusetts, Vermont, Connecticut, New York, New Hampshire, Pennsylvania, Rhode Island, Maryland, Ohio, South Carolina, Maine, and New Jersey between 1783 and 1800.

84. Such included newspapers first issued in 1727, 1742, 1756, 1764, 1767, and 1772.

85. Samuel L. Boardman, *Peter Edes, Pioneer Printer in Maine* (Bangor, ME: Printed for the DeBurians, 1901).

86. *Vermont Journal,* 7 August 1783, 1.

87. *Massachusetts Sentinel and Republican Journal,* 11 March 1784, 1.

88. *Gazette and Western Repository of Knowledge,* 17 August 1785, 1.

89. Thomas, *History of Printing*, 136-37, 293-94. See also Boardman, *Peter Edes*.

90. *Federal Gazette,* 16 October 1788, 1.

91. See *Essex Gazette,* 2 August 1768, 1. Hall said: "Although the Printing Business [sic] is but just introduced into this town and county, and consequently this paper is the first publication of the kind that has been printed here; yet there can be no doubt but that every inhabitant is sufficiently sensible that the exercise of this art is of the utmost importance to every community; and that newspapers, in particular, are of great public utility."

92. Issued on 1 March 1784 within Warden's and Russell's separately printed and disseminated "Proposals for publishing . . . a free, uninfluenced newspaper."

93. For more on Meigs, see Humphrey, *This Popular Engine*, and Franklin B. Dexter, *Biographical Sketches of the Graduates of Yale College With Annals of the College History* 6 vols. (New York: H. Holt and Company, 1885-1912) 4: 43-47.

94. *Middlesex Gazette.* 8 November 1785, 1.

95. *Massachusetts Mercury,* 1 January 1793, 1.

3

Discursive Construction of Journalists as Political Communicators in Nineteenth-Century Newspaper Prospectuses

In 1820, Maine printer and publisher Ephraim Fellowes began issuing the *Belfast Gazette* in a new format. To introduce this new periodical, renamed the *Waldo Democrat*, and to persuade the community that it would be worth the price of a subscription, he published this statement in the first issue:

We this day present the public with No. 1 of a new series of our paper . . . in an enlarged and improved form, with new hopes and prospects. . . . From the want of an editor on whom might rest the responsibility, the publishers . . . have been aware that their paper has heretofore wanted that strong and decided political character which is required to gain the confidence of the community, and to give a proper tone to public sentiment. . . . The political character of this paper is to be, as its name purports, Democratic, heartily and entirely Democratic.[1]

Long before Fellowes issued this statement in 1820, the practice of introducing newspapers with published statements on the work, relationships, and responsibilities of journalists was a pervasive one in American journalism — rarely was a newspaper established without one.[2] But since the American Revolution, the emphasis in prospectuses was on politics. Not only had newspapers become vehicles for the provision of crucial political communication during this period, but journalistic work was transformed occupationally as well. As the eighteenth century drew to a close, increasing numbers of Americans started newspapers for expressly political purposes. From the Revolution to 1800, the number of newspapers published in the country increased more than fivefold, from 37 to 200, and many of them were political papers.[3] The heightened sense of journalistic political importance that the American Revolution induced in those who produced its newspapers may be one factor that would help explain why their numbers began to grow at a faster rate.

Editors like Fellowes undoubtedly wrote prospectuses that would help them as they confronted local challenges. Not only did those who were starting newspapers in the early nineteenth century need to attract enough readers to sustain their newspapers financially, but they also needed to cater to politicians, factions, or others in their community who wielded influence. But the fact that editors were focused on local concerns as they developed and published prospectuses does not mean that they and their essays would not be part of another communication process, one central to the development of the American journalistic occupational group.

Looking at the development of journalistic work within a broader political communication work system, this chapter continues the analysis of newspaper prospectuses begun in the previous chapter by focusing on the nineteenth century. Research consisted of gathering and analyzing 206 newspaper prospectuses issued across America by nineteenth-century newspaper publishers and editors, most of whom were printers who operated diverse businesses including more than newspaper publishing.[4] The prospectuses studied were issued in two periods: the first group, totaling 120, was issued between 1800 and 1830, and the second, which numbered 86, appeared between 1870 and 1900.[5] One of a number of journalistic practices that imparted occupational meaning to journalistic work, prospectuses contributed to the process whereby a link was established between the journalistic occupational group and the work tasks involved in providing political information.

JOURNALISTS AND THEIR NEWSPAPERS DURING THE NINETEENTH CENTURY

The newspaper press from 1800 to 1830 can best be characterized as a political institution, although its earliest clear-cut development as a social institution also began during this period. As newspapers grew in number, they moved west and south into the nation's frontiers. The dominant concept of the press's role in the first half of the nineteenth century was political, and such a press model is clearest during these three early decades. For instance, most of the period's newspapers were partisan in nature, published largely for, and in many cases directed by, the nation's political party officials and governmental elected and appointed officials. The contents of newspapers during the first decades of the century have been described as idea-centered, largely composed of political essays, debates, or editorials. Much of this material, when judged by contemporary standards, was scurrilous.[6]

Many newspaper journalists served in government and party positions, and conversely, many politicians served as newspaper publishers and editors. America's attention during the period was focused primarily on government, and other newspapers were scattered and lacking regular reporters in centers of government; thus, newspapers published in seats of government on both national and state levels became especially powerful. Examples include the *National Intelligencer* in Washington, D.C., and certain state and territorial capital newspapers.[7]

Newspaper publishers struggled financially to maintain their businesses. Advertising did not develop as an industry and solid source of funding for newspapers until later in the century, and subscription collections rarely provided enough sustenance. This led newspaper publishers to become dependent on politicians and government officials who could help sustain them with printing contracts and other forms of patronage.[8]

But the dominance of the political model did not prevent the press from experiencing early development as a social institution. In 1800, few people experienced the press as a regular part of their lives, but by 1830, the press had grown more integral to society. Part of this was due to the continued proliferation of newspapers. From 1800 to 1820, their numbers grew from about 200 to 512.[9] But the purposes and contents of newspapers changed, and new forms emerged, including those serving the needs of religious institutions, laborers, Native Americans, African Americans, pacifists, and women.[10] The period also saw growing awareness among editors and publishers that timelier newspapers and cooperative news gathering enterprises could help them better serve both their own and the public's needs.[11]

The close relationship between newspaper proprietors and controversial politics that developed in the decades following the American Revolution did more than encourage the proliferation of newspapers, for it placed those who issued them in an awkward position, one that necessitated a discursive solution. While Americans seemed to increasingly appreciate newspapers as important political vehicles, they simultaneously felt disdain for those who produced highly partisan or scurrilous newspapers, since they had not entirely gotten over their pre-Revolutionary War dislike for political controversy.

Occasionally newspaper editors would publish essays that discussed the pernicious effects of publicly aired political disputes. In 1794, for example, the editor of the *Hartford Courant* included a column titled "On Parties." Its author wrote, "A party spirit is as great a curse to society as can befall it. It makes honest men hate each other, and destroys good neighbourhoods."[12] Admitting that political disagreements are superior to the "awful and death-like calm of despotism, where the discontented . . . are obliged to seal their lips," a Boston columnist in 1809 complained that the negative effects of party spirit go well beyond public affairs: "It enters into their local as well as public concerns, and stamps the features of their social transactions with a strange inconsistency. It perverts the judgement of the wife, and renders men, in regard to reason and truth, as deaf as an adder, and blind as a mole."[13]

The public's strong feelings against party rancorousness placed editors in an awkward position. Because they and the rest of the country's citizens were grappling with important political questions, they must have felt compelled to print essays on hotly disputed public issues. But at the same time, they knew that publishing inflammatory materials would deeply offend at least some of their readers. As one editor put it, he was worried about feeling "exposed . . . to the indiscriminate censure of the whole community."[14]

Two newspaper printers in such a position were Matthias Day and Jacob Mann. Strong supporters of President Thomas Jefferson's political philosophies, they wrote of their backgrounds, political creeds, and publishing plans as they set out in 1801 to establish the *True American* in Trenton, New Jersey.[15] Identifying themselves as fervent republicans seeking to play important political communication roles through the publication of a newspaper, they also attempted to assure their readers that their political principles would not prevent them from providing the public with the kind of journalism they desired. In addition, in comparing themselves to other editors, they implied that they were holders of work standards that would enable them to provide a more edifying and less scurrilous brand of political information than those of their more politically self-interested competitors. Accordingly, they stated:

[To] conduct a press in support of original republic principles, in opposition to a powerful combination, with hostile sentiments and clashing interests . . . requires a degree of firmness, perseverance, and talent, which perhaps few are independently possessed of. We'll leave it to other editors to heat themselves and the public by unprofitable disputes.

Day and Mann thus constructed a discourse of journalism that defined them as members of a work group with a special calling, a calling that differentiated them from others in the political communication work sphere. Admitting that they were devoted to a particular set of political principles, they simultaneously portrayed themselves as political communicators who were more independent than "other editors" in the community who lacked their "degree of firmness, perseverance, and talent."[16] Such statements essentially placed a discursive boundary between legitimate journalists and other, more politically partisan ones who could not be trusted to serve the general public's needs above all others in the community.

Throughout the nineteenth century, editors like Mann and Day constructed newspaper prospectuses as central sites for discursive negotiation of political communication work roles as they established new newspapers, renamed old ones, celebrated important anniversaries, and acquired new partners. [17] After the Civil War, revolutions in American society affected virtually every aspect of national life. Industrialization, urbanization, new technologies, and the emergence of progressivism profoundly affected newspapers. One of the most noticeable developments from 1870 to 1900 was a tremendous acceleration of growth in the number of newspapers published. Daily newspapers increased from 574 in 1870 to 2,226 in 1900, while the number of copies sold each day rose from 2.6 million copies to 15 million.[18]

The press also developed commercially during this period. Important aspects of this were the development of advertising as an industry in America and the establishment of advertising as a crucial source of newspaper income. While they still served politicians, news began to more accurately reflect the needs of advertisers as well.[19]

Another aspect of commercialization was the development of what some later called the "New Journalism."[20] News became thought of as a commodity, and events and personalities were stressed over political issues and questions. Newspapers were low-priced and easy to read; their contents were popularized, stressing human interest themes; they were sensationalized through use of exaggeration, drama, and other emotional appeals; journalists readily manufactured news and used stunts and crusades to attract and keep readers; and they increasingly used these techniques and seized upon developments in photography, oversized headlines, and other devices to boost circulations.[21]

A trend toward concentration of ownership that started before the Civil War was more clearly defined by the 1880s. Competition between publishers fostered diversification beyond the newspaper into a larger journalistic structure. Agencies and bureaus developed to sell news, and city news bureaus and press associations proliferated. This all led to the creation of media barons, with Joseph Pulitzer and William Randolph Hearst exemplifying how financially successful journalists could become.[22]

By the end of the century, however, a less sensational, more responsible journalism had begun to develop. Journalists like Adolph Ochs, who took control of the *New York Times*, promising "All the News That's Fit to Print," believed journalism should be more dignified. At about the same time, the muckraking era emerged and enhanced the more positive role of journalism — at least for the long term.[23]

All through these decades, as the newspaper grew and changed, journalists continued issuing newspaper prospectuses that embodied occupational communication. Indeed, such practices became a pervasive aspect of the practice of newspaper journalism in America and would be especially pronounced in communities that by the end of the century often had competing dailies and weeklies.

Within newspaper prospectuses were claims that journalists would perform specific political journalistic work tasks, provide political journalistic products, and be guided by special standards in their handling of political information. In addition, they contained arguments that journalists were needed as powerful, but deferent political protectors and educators. While some of the authors of prospectuses admitted to having more than a casual interest in politics, they wrote as if their special journalistic calling, with its standards for handling information, would enable them to overcome any conflicts with which such relationships presented them. Such a discourse would come to play an important role in the process that clarified journalism's occupational boundaries by the end of the century. Essentially, journalists, rather than politicians, would be discursively defined in prospectuses as the group the public should trust to serve as their primary providers of political news and editorial opinion.

JOURNALISTS AS POLITICAL COMMUNICATORS

American newspaper publishers and editors across the nineteenth century issued prospectuses that constructed the journalistic occupation as a body whose members played a central role in America's political communication process. Such a discourse was most clearly articulated in prospectuses during the early decades of the century. As is evident in Table 3.1, nearly all authors of prospectuses explicitly or implicitly referred to their general role as one of disseminating political information.[24]

Table 3.1
Claims to a Political Journalistic Role by Authors of Newspaper Prospectuses

1800-1830	90% (108 of 120 prospectuses)
1870-1900	67% (58 of 86 prospectuses)

Among the many early nineteenth-century newspaper proprietors who issued such a claim was Alden Spooner, a Vermont native born into a well-known printing and publishing family.[25] Spooner was named after his father, publisher of at least three of the state's newspapers, including *Spooner's Vermont Journal*, and Spooner's uncle was Judah Spooner, founder of Vermont's first newspaper, the *Vermont Gazette*. After apprenticing as a printer in his father's shop, Spooner began a newspaper and printing career of his own that took him to New York and Connecticut. He finally established himself permanently in New York City, where in 1817 he established *The New-York Columbian*. Throughout these publishing endeavors, he sought to serve the public through his adoption of a political communication role. For example, on the establishment of the *True American*, in New London, Connecticut, he wrote, "Political communication shall receive early attention."[26]

Printer John A. Stevens also related similar intentions to his public. Seeking to start a paper in 1806 named the *Genessee Messenger* in Canandaigua, New York, after operating a printing and publishing business in Bennington, Vermont, Stevens wrote to his potential patrons: "The *Messenger* will be occasionally, if not principally, devoted to the local interests and politics of the western part of the state . . . [and newspapers] are the only convenient medium through which subjects for the aggrandizement of the country can be proposed to the people."[27]

While this theme of the journalist as political communicator was nearly always embodied in the prospectuses of the early century, they were only slightly less prevalent at its end. Two-thirds of the 1870-1900 prospectuses examined included such claims, and they were strikingly similar qualitatively to those issued in the early decades of the century. Indeed, if it were not known that the following statement was published in 1900, one might guess it was published a century earlier. As W. N. Miller and John E. Lewis sought to establish their newspaper *The Searchlight*, in Wichita, Kansas, in 1900, they pledged: "We will speak on political questions and not fail to use our *Searchlight*, and probe all matters that concerns our people and the public to its fullest extent, and then speak of things as we find them, without reserve."[28]

JOURNALISTS AS PERFORMERS OF POLITICAL JOURNALISTIC TASKS AND PROVIDERS OF JOURNALISTIC POLITICAL PRODUCTS

In addition to claiming that they fulfilled important political communication roles in their communities, newspaper publishers and editors also delineated specific categories of journalist tasks and products that they would perform and provide. The political journalistic tasks prospectus authors claimed they would perform included reporting, as well as producing and disseminating certain political journalistic products. While it was more common for the authors of prospectuses to stress products more than work tasks, at times they were explicit in their delineation of work tasks. Examples include authors of prospectuses who stated that they would "do political reporting,"[29] "investigate" political matters, [30] "record" political facts,[31] "give facts" to their readers,[32] "provide information on the transactions of their state and national governments,"[33] "diffuse information on political subjects,"[34] and "present a view" of government and important political measures.[35]

The forms of political journalism authors of prospectuses pledged to their readers across the country included political reports; editorial discussions and exposes; reprints of laws, state and federal official legislative or other proceedings, and speeches; and essays and/or letters submitted by members of the public.[36] As is shown in Table 3.2, authors of 1800-1830 prospectuses appear to have been more concerned than those in the later period about delineating for their readers the forms of political journalism they would include in newspapers. That authors of prospectuses in the last three decades of the nineteenth century seemed less concerned with identifying such products could be the result of the public's increased familiarity with newspapers during that period.

Within both periods studied, editorials and political reports were the political work products most often specified by prospectus writers. Editorials were rarely identified specifically as such. Instead, they were referred to in less specific terms such as general discussion, debate, and provision of opinions on political questions and the evaluation or canvassing and exposure of the character of public functionaries, political factions, or parties.[37]

Table 3.2
Claims to Provision of Journalistic Work Products in Prospectuses

	1800-1830	1870-1900
Editorial essays or exposés	48% (57)	35% (30)
Political reports	38% (45)	9% (8)
Reprints of laws, proceedings, speeches	14% (17)	< 1% (1)
The public's letters and essays	13% (15)	< 1% (1)
	n=120	n=86

IMAGES OF JOURNALISTS

Especially in the early decades of the century, the authors of prospectuses often expanded their journalistic claims well beyond mere statements of their general political roles, tasks, and products. Within the 206 nineteenth-century prospectuses examined were statements about the power and utility of political journalists and, more specifically, their power as the nation's protectors and political educators. Such statements, which essentially constructed journalists as powerful political protectors and educators, were more prevalent in the early decades of the century as seen in Table 3.3.

The Power of Political Journalists

Embodied within prospectuses was the idea that journalists were among the nation's most powerful political communicators. An example of a particularly richly descriptive prospectus statement was issued by printer and publisher Benjamin True as he sought to establish the Boston *Courier* in 1805. A prolific journalist who established at least seven newspapers during his printing and

Table 3.3
Journalists as Political Protectors and Educators

1800-1830	49% (59 of 120 prospectuses)
1870-1900	15% (14 of 86 prospectuses)

publishing career, True's prospectus revealed an expansive pride in the power of his work:[38]

The American press is now generally acknowledged to be an engine of great influence. Under the superintendence of skilled hands and judiciously conducted, it is calculated to disseminate useful information; to keep the public mind awake and active, to confirm and extend the love of freedom; to correct the mistakes of the ignorant, and the impositions of the crafty; to tear off the mask from corrupt and designing politicians; and finally, to promote union of spirit and action among the most distant members of an extended community.[39]

The author of an 1809 prospectus compared the political power of American newspapers and journalists to their counterparts in other nations, attributing the proliferation of American newspapers to such power:

Newspapers probably have a greater influence upon the political affairs of the United States, than upon those of any other nation. Hence they are multiplied in this country, beyond all example. Forming a constant, and at the same time a cheap source of information and amusement, they are naturally sought after with eagerness, and encouraged with liberality. As they are in every man's hands, they will in greater or less degrees, influence the opinions and conduct of every man.[40]

While the idea that journalists are powerful political communicators was not as frequently discussed by the establishers of 1870-1900 newspapers, some did incorporate notions of journalistic potency into their prospectuses. For example, in 1881, the proprietor of the *Los Angeles Daily Times* wrote that journalists are powerful forces in the political realm and even beyond, claiming "a free and enlightened people enjoy but few blessings that are greater . . . [and with] higher influence" than an independent and reliable public press.[41] In 1895, the editor of the *National Reflector*, a paper published for the African American community in Wichita, Kansas, wrote that newspaper journalists offer knowledge, and knowledge is "power and light."[42]

Journalists as the Nation's Protectors

In addition to their construction of journalists as powerful political communicators, authors of prospectuses also sought to create the impression that they should be looked to by the nation as vigilant soldiers who, much as they had done during the American Revolution, would fight for the nation, protecting it from those who would threaten it. In such a fashion, Cincinnati's James H. Looker wrote of the duty of journalists to protect the public and nation from harm. As he sought, in 1823, to establish the *National Republican and Ohio Political Register,* Looker argued that newspaper editors should use their independence and protection under free press law as a "weapon of attack" against political intrigue, and as a "shield of defense" to protect the innocent and meritorious. "The office [of editor] is important and the responsibility of no ordinary character," he added.[43]

Timothy B. Crowell was also one of those who promised to protect the nation from any threats that might come its way. As he established Goshen, New York's *Orange County Patriot,* in 1809, Crowell claimed he would "keep a watchful and jealous eye out" for any who might threaten democracy.[44]

In Concord, New Hampshire, printer William Holt claimed, in 1808, in a prospectus published to start the *American Patriot,* that he would serve the nation as "a perpetual Monitor [sic] to our Citizens to keep in remembrance those sacred principles, for which a Jefferson wrote, a Washington fought, and a Warren and Montgomery died."[45]

In addition to promising to defend the nation from enemies within its border, authors of newspaper prospectuses also promised to save it from foreign threats. In his 1809 letter to the community as he sought to establish the *Columbian* in New York City, in 1809, Charles Holt wrote about his journalistic goals: "To maintain and vindicate the rights and immunities of the United States, as a free, sovereign and independent nation, against the pretensions, the violations, and the aggressions of any and every foreign power."[46]

Journalists as the Nation's Political Educators

Not only did authors of prospectuses construct the image of the political journalist as an important protector, but they sought to convey the impression that journalists were crucial political educators. As he sought to establish the *True Republican* in New London, Connecticut, for example, during July 1807, Alden Spooner wrote, "No citizen of our representative government should be without correct information on the state of public affairs."[47]

Spooner's words were echoed in many other prospectuses published during the early decades of the century. For example, in Belfast, Maine, in 1820, printers Ephraim Fellowes and William Simpson sought to establish a new paper they would name the *Hancock Gazette.* In introducing themselves, they wrote of their project's educative value:

In this enlightened period of the world it were [sic] superfluous [sic] to descant [sic] on the importance of education; but, among the various methods of diffusing practical knowledge, that great teacher, experience, has shown that 'none stands so high in the rank of utility and pleasure, as a periodical paper.' To disseminate political information, to communicate discoveries in the arts and the sciences, to impress moral instruction.[48]

Another statement, issued by the establisher of the *Fredonian* in Boston in 1810, argued that journalists provide the public with indispensable supplements to their classical educations:

The existence of a free government essentially depends on the diffusion of knowledge and virtue among every class of citizens. The rudiments of knowledge may be undoubtedly best acquired from classic authors; but the great body of the people no sooner find themselves liberated from the restraints of their instructors, than they demand that a variety of new and interesting information should be interspersed with what they have been taught to esteem useful. A question then arises, how can a variety of interesting knowledge be presented to the Public, so blended with what may be useful, as to insure their present gratification, as well as future improvement? To this important query, a practical answer will be attempted in *The Fredonian*.[49]

Another example of a journalistic statement that asserted that the nation's voters were thoroughly dependent on journalists for their political knowledge was published in an 1803 prospectus introducing the *Charleston (South Carolina) Courier*:

The management of public journals has become in every free state a subject of important consideration. A very large portion of the people derive the whole of their knowledge from them; and, exclusive of the effect which they thus necessarily produce on the mind, the manners, and the conduct of a commonwealth, the fabric of its liberty may, in a great measure, be supported or endangered by their influence, more especially in states where, as in this free and flourishing republic, all political authority is conferred by the suffrages of the people; and where frequent elections permit them to rectify or repeat an erroneous choice.[50]

Cincinnati's James H. Looker, who portrayed himself in 1823 as one of the nation's journalistic protectors, also included statements in his prospectus on the responsibilities of those undertaking newspaper vocations. In an essay titled "To the Public," Looker discussed the contributions of newspaper journalism to the nation. According to Looker, by circulating political journalistic reports and essays to the most remote reaches of the country, newspaper journalists can help create a more intelligent public, one with a "uniform tone and character."[51]

Journalists as Responsible and Deferent Public Servants

Throughout the nineteenth century, perhaps to counteract any negative impressions the expressions of journalistic political power might engender in their readers, a theme of responsibility and subservience to the public ran through prospectus statements. Such statements took both denotative and connotative forms. In the former category were statements that spoke plainly of the author's devotion to the public. In other, less explicit statements, authors of prospectuses connoted a sense of deference to the public through articulations of the idea that they held great responsibilities as newspaper journalists. As editor of the *Charleston Mercury*, a new paper established in South Carolina in 1822, Edmund Morford wrote:

The direction and management of the press is an undertaking of high responsibility. . . . As public patronage and favour [sic] are the sole support of a Gazette, the community has a right to exact of its publisher all the advantages that are to be expected, from his assumption of the character of one acting as the dispenser of intelligence. . . . That confidence . . . holds him by solemn ties, as pledged to consecrate it to the public good, to make it subservient to the prosperity and happiness of the country.[52]

THE CONSTRUCTION OF A BOUNDARY BETWEEN POLITICAL
JOURNALISTS AND POLITICIANS

Before journalism would be recognized as an occupation with special duties, responsibilities, and legitimacy in the political communication work sphere, the public had to believe that journalists were a different breed of political communicator, one who, unlike politicians, would not put political ambition and partisan creed above the needs of the more general public. Thus, authors of prospectuses throughout the century would not only issue declarations of journalistic independence from politics and politicians, but they would forward the idea that journalists held special standards that enabled them to handle political information in a way that would please the public.

Such a discourse was necessitated by at least two factors: Not only did the public have little tolerance for those who engaged in politically inflammatory journalism practices, but those who issued newspapers had to distract the public from the reality that many of them in fact were personally involved in politics.

Professions of Journalistic Political Independence

As is shown in Table 3.4, during both periods, about half of the authors of newspaper prospectuses issued declarations of independence. Among the 120 journalistic statements studied in the early group, issued from 1800-1830, 53 percent represented themselves as being independent, whereas in the 1870-1900 group, 49 percent did so. Two types of independence claims were issued by journalists: a group who wrote that, while they were affiliated with a particular political group or partisan creed, they were independent, and a second group who claimed to be totally free from attachments to party and politicians.

Table 3.4
Political Positions of Prospectus Authors vis-à-vis Journalistic Independence

	1800-1830	1870-1900
Openly partisan	36% (43)	19% (16)
Affiliated, but independent	24% (29)	16% (14)
Independent, with no party affiliation	29% (35)	33% (28)
No reference to political stance	11% (13)	33% (28)
	n=120	n=86

An early nineteenth-century printer who fell into the "Affiliated, but independent" category was James Jefferson Wilson. A native of Essex County, New Jersey, Wilson was invited in 1801 by *True American* publishers Matthias Day and Jacob Mann to join them in publishing and editing their Trenton paper. According to one of his biographers, Wilson was "fiery, energetic and certainly one of the most picturesque figures in Trenton journalism."[53] Upon joining Day and Mann on the paper's masthead, Wilson wrote of his passionate devotion to republican political sentiments. But then, perhaps to counterbalance such assertions, he promised: "No local pursuit, no personal concern, shall ever interfere with my public duty, or divert my attention from the general interest."[54]

Wilson eventually took control of the *True American*, serving as its publisher and editor until 1824. Moving from his journalistic position directly into politics, Wilson was elected and appointed to political and governmental positions on both the state and federal levels. Not only would he serve as Trenton's postmaster, but he was elected to the New Jersey state legislature and United States Senate.[55] The attainment of these public offices, and his fulfillment of his responsibilities once he got there, must have made it more difficult for him to fulfill his promises to his public to put them first. Yet, Wilson's self-portrayal did not reveal such complexities. While such conflicting allegiances were commonplace during this period of history, they nevertheless required creative discursive remedies, ones that were embodied in prospectuses and other essays published in newspapers.

A second example of a newspaper proprietor who was allied with a political faction, but who claimed to be independent from party, is Peter Bertrand, a printer from the Alabama Territory. As Bertrand sought to establish a weekly paper titled the *Florence Gazette,* in 1819, he wrote:

Custom has made it requisite for the editor, or publisher, of a newspaper to make a declaration of the feelings and principles by which he will be actuated and governed. Upon this subject, the person who now solicits the patronage of the public, will boldly observe, that his feelings are in unison with all well wishers to their country's cause. His principles are what they ever have been, and, he trusts, ever will be, Republican. His exertions will ever be directed to support the American Constitution. No blind devotion to party, shall ever divert him from the path of truth and candor, or induce him to stain his columns with personal abuse.[56]

An example of a newspaper proprietor who claimed total independence from political parties and factions, was Andrew Marschalk, who established the *Washington (Mississippi) Republican.*[57] In explaining his intentions, Marschalk wrote in 1813:

As to his political opinions, he claims the right of a free born American — to have them — and to express them (with decency) — but he claims for himself, no greater privilege in the columns of his paper, than he is ready and willing to grant to every individual in his community. With one positive promise he concludes — viz., that as his press has not been purchased by any party or set of men — no control, except his own shall be exercised over it.[58]

As already discussed, of the eighty-six prospectuses studied from the 1870-1900 period, nearly half of their authors claimed they were either affiliated but independent, or totally independent, from politicians and political parties. A prospectus that contained an example of the former type of statement was published in 1882 by the establishers of the Burlington, Iowa, *Saturday Evening Post*:

In politics, *The Saturday Evening Post* will endeavor to maintain an independent republican position. There will be times when it will declare itself to be in favor of certain men or certain measures, but that will be solely with a view to the public good, and its action on such occasions will be free from party lines.[59]

An especially cogent example of a politically independent stance was found in the introductory address of the Menominee, Wisconsin, *Journal*, published in 1893:

We are under no obligation to any party or creed, hence we are not compelled to follow or uphold every theory or pet measure, however bad, or such, simply because the leading spirits within the party may so dictate in order to keep their organization or party together. Good traits are to be found in all parties, as well as in all men; but it does not therefore follow that the less acceptable or the bad traits in men or party should be adhered to and all their suggestions followed simply because they emanate from the party in question. We are of the opinion that the orthodox party people are sufficiently represented in this city.[60]

Journalistic Standards for the Handling of Political Information

The construction of work jurisdictions involves more than the members of an aspiring occupational group foisting their own definitions of their work on the public. Any occupational group seeking to win jurisdiction over work has to cope with public reluctance to accept it as the expert provider of certain services. To win jurisdiction over political communication-related work, journalists could not assume that they could simply impose their own definitions of work on the public without responding to the citizenry's concerns about how political information ought to be handled.

During the eighteenth and nineteenth centuries, journalists had to contend with public ambivalence about partisanism, scurrility, and licentiousness.[61] That journalists felt a need to respond to such public sentiment is evidenced by the number of prospectus statements in the nineteenth century in which journalists contrast themselves with politicians in their handling of political information. The standards touted by nineteenth-century prospectus writers are included in Table 3.5.

Table 3.5
Claims to Political Journalistic Standards in Nineteenth-Century Prospectuses

Specific Standards Claimed	1800-1830	1870-1900
Coverage of all sides of political questions	48% (58)	55% (47)
No politically inflammatory materials or ideas	49% (59)	9% (8)
Accurate reports	10% (12)	6% (5)
Guided by truth and dignity	12% (14)	14% (12)

Nearly half of the issuers of the 120 early prospectuses promised that they would be guided by the principle that they should cover all sides of political questions in a fair, impartial, neutral, or independent manner. More specifically, journalists issued statements that promised they would carefully handle politically sensitive materials in such a way that they would be presented in an impartial and independent manner; open their columns to individuals representing all political parties and philosophies; refuse to be bought by partisan interests; seek a middle course in political concerns in their newspaper columns; and accept essays and letters representing all political perspectives, as long as authors wrote in a decent, nonbiased manner.[62]

As discussed, when James Jefferson Wilson in 1801 joined Jacob Mann and Matthias Day on the masthead of Trenton, New Jersey's *True American,* he looked for the public's approval in an essay addressed to the paper's readers. Not only did he portray himself as a protector of the nation who would guard its republican institutions against "open or insidious violation," he explained further that he would serve the public by handling political information in such a manner that it would be accurate, impartial, and free from licentiousness and scurrility.[63]

Some of those who issued prospectuses stated a belief that professions of independence from political parties were folly. But despite this, they still claimed it was possible for them to treat political material impartially. A journalist who discussed this in a prospectus was the establisher, in 1802, of Litchfield, Connecticut's *Gazette*:

On the subject of politics, no man, who duly regards the best interests of the country can, in times like these, stand on neutral ground. To profess neutrality on such a subject, at such a season as the present, would be not only to incur suspicion, but to deserve it. On this point, therefore, the editors wish to be explicit: their political principles are decidedly Federal. And if an adherence to these principles necessarily disqualifies them to deal impartially between the great political parties, into which the citizens of the United States are divided, they must acknowledge that an impartial view of public affairs is not to be expected from their press. In their opinion, however, true practical impartiality in politics consists, not in equally respecting, or equally confiding in, all parties, but in doing equal justice to all. This the editors will scrupulously endeavor to do.[64]

In addition to claims that they would handle political material in an impartial manner, about half of the authors of early prospectuses claimed they would not publish inflammatory, licentious, or scurrilous political material. One way to ensure this, according to some journalists, was to avoid discussing political personalities and focus instead on political principles. Such a standard was much less frequently touted by prospectus writers of the 1870-1900 period. Only 9 percent of those authors claimed they would not publish inflammatory materials in political reports.

Among those in the early nineteenth century who pledged that his newspaper would not include political materials that would stir up political passions was Joseph Cushing, who, in 1802, sought to establish *The Farmer's Cabinet*, in Amherst, New Hampshire. According to Cushing:

It is evident that party animosity has already too long marred the fair fabric of American freedom, disturbed the friendly intercourse of societies and neighbourhoods [sic], and introduced discord even into families and among nearest connections. Whoever, then, continues to encourage it, must be considered inimical to his country's welfare, to social order, harmony and happiness. Viewing the subject in this light, and wishing to make his paper as extensively useful as possible, the Editor pledges himself, that those base insinuations, and that virulent abuse and personal calumny, which disgrace so many of the publications of the present day, shall not find a place in the *Cabinet*.[65]

Prospectuses would become an important occupational practices of nineteenth-century journalists. Through their prominent placement in public media, their repetitiveness, rhetorical structures, and journalistic occupational discourses related to politics and political relationships, they situated journalists more prominently in the nation's political communication work system. Not only did they impart meaning to journalistic work tasks, but they negotiated the occupational and broader social positions of journalists, strategically placing them where they could meet not only their own needs, but those of the public and the politicians they were often involved with. While portraying themselves in opposition to politicians, in reality, journalists were often heavily involved in politics and with politicians. Many journalists, in fact, were politicians themselves. But such realities were commonly obscured in prospectuses, since they would not serve the journalists' needs to cater to the interests of the citizenry.

Prospectuses constructed a public need for political news and information in newspapers, one that was said to be required by the public's need to participate in the democratic process. As a cultural form within a developing print culture, eighteenth- and nineteenth-century newspaper prospectuses helped journalists in a process wherein they sought power, identity, and a legitimate position in the occupational and broader social structure.

NOTES

1. Joseph Griffin, *History of the Press of Maine* (Brunswick, ME: The Press, 1872), 159.

2. Research that examined about 300 eighteenth- and nineteenth-century newly established newspapers revealed that only several were not introduced with some sort of prospectus.

3. Statistics on publication of newspapers in this early period are available in Clarence Brigham, *History and Bibliography of American Newspapers, 1690-1820* (Worcester, MA: American Antiquarian Society, 1947); W. T. Coggeshall, *The Newspaper Record, Containing a Complete List of Newspapers and Periodicals in the United States, Canada and Great Britain* (Philadelphia, PA: Lay and Brother, 1856).

4. This group of 205 prospectuses was gathered by examining 206 newly established newspapers. The prospectuses differed in title, length, form, and style.

5. An effort was made to select and examine prospectuses representing each of the years during the decades studied, all regions of the country, and as many categories of types of newspapers meant for general readership as possible. The 1800 to 1830 group represents the following twenty-one states and territories: Alabama, Arkansas, Connecticut, District of Columbia, Illinois, Kentucky, Massachusetts, Maryland, Maine, Mississippi, Missouri, North Carolina, New York, New Jersey, Ohio, Pennsylvania, Rhode Island, South Carolina, Tennessee, Virginia, and Vermont. The 1870 to 1900 group were issued within the following twenty-five states and territories: Alabama, Alaska, California, Colorado, District of Columbia, Hawaii, Illinois, Iowa, Indiana, Oklahoma Indian Territory, Kentucky, Kansas, Louisiana, Massachusetts, Michigan, Minnesota, North Carolina, North Dakota, New Hampshire, New York, Ohio, Texas, Utah, Virginia, and Wisconsin.

6. Gerald J. Baldasty, "The Political Press in the Second American Party System: The 1832 Election" (Ph.D. diss., University of Washington, 1978); Hazel Dicken-Garcia, *Journalistic Standards in Nineteenth-Century America* (Madison, WI: University of Wisconsin Press, 1989), 30, 71-82.

7. William E. Ames, *A History of the National Intelligencer* (Chapel Hill, NC: University of North Carolina Press, 1972). Examples of newspapers financially supported by state-level legislatures are discussed in Culver H. Smith, *The Press, Politics and Patronage* (Athens, GA: University of Georgia Press, 1977).

8. Ames, *National Intelligencer*, 111-12, 153, 281-83; Smith, *Press, Politics and Patronage*.

9. Edwin Emery and Michael Emery *The Press in America* (7th ed. Englewood Cliffs, NJ: Prentice Hall, 1992), 77.

10. Dicken-Garcia, *Journalistic Standards*, 40; Emery and Emery, *Press in America*, 73-94, 98-99; Lauren Kessler, *The Dissident Press: Alternative Journalism in American History*, Sage Commtext Series (Beverly Hills, CA: Sage, 1984).

11. For example, newspaper editors realized how faster reporting would have helped the business community, whose membership was worried about the loss of New Orleans, an important maritime port, to the British. See the following: Dicken-Garcia,

Journalistic Standards, 25; Richard A. Schwarzlose, "Harbor News Association: Formal Origin of the AP," *Journalism Quarterly* 45 (Summer 1968): 253-60; Victor Rosewater, *History of Cooperative News-Gathering in the United States* (New York: D. Appleton, 1930), 57.

12. *Hartford Courant,* 13 January 1794, 2.

13. *Boston Daily Advertiser,* 6 June 1809, 4.

14. James H. Looker, "To the Public," *The National Republican and Ohio Political Register*, 1 January 1823.

15. Their prospectus was published on 10 March 1801, on page 1. For further information on them, see an essay titled "True American" in John O. Raum, *History of the City of Trenton, New Jersey* (Trenton, NJ: W. T. Nicholson and Co., printers, 1871), 23.

16. *True American*, 10 March 1801, 1.

17. Very few newspapers were established without some sort of statement issued by the publisher or editor meant to introduce the proprietors and the paper to its potential readers. Research for this chapter examined 207 new newspapers; only one of which failed to include such a statement. At times they were titled salutatories, introductory addresses, and letters, among other things.

The newspapers studied in the research were established to serve the needs of the general public. Of the group of 206 examined, 120 represented the period 1800 to 1830 and 86 represented the period 1870 to 1900. Nearly every year of these two thirty-year periods was represented in the group, and an effort was made to select prospectuses that represented all regions of the country. Categories of newspapers excluded from the research were foreign language newspapers, as well as special purpose newspapers such as labor and social reform papers.

The 1800 to 1830 group represented the following twenty-one states and territories: Alabama, Arkansas, Connecticut, District of Columbia, Illinois, Kentucky, Massachusetts, Maryland, Maine, Mississippi, Missouri, North Carolina, New York, New Jersey, Ohio, Pennsylvania, Rhode Island, South Carolina, Tennessee, Virginia, and Vermont. The 1870 to 1900 group were issued within twenty-five states and territories, including: Alabama, Alaska, California, Colorado, District of Columbia, Hawaii, Illinois, Iowa, Indiana, Oklahoma Indian Territory, Kentucky, Kansas, Louisiana, Massachusetts, Michigan, Minnesota, North Carolina, North Dakota, New Hampshire, New York, Ohio, Texas, Utah, Virginia, and Wisconsin.

18. Emery and Emery, *Press in America*, 155, endnote 15.

19. Baldasty, *Commercialization of the News*, 6-7.

20. Dicken-Garcia, *Journalistic Standards*, 52-62; Emery and Emery, *Press in America*, 161; Michael Schudson, *Discovering the News: A Social History of American Newspapers* (New York: Basic Books, 1978).

21. Dicken-Garcia, *Journalistic Standards*, 89-96.

22. Ibid., 61-62; Hudson, *Journalism*, 536-38, 656-66, 703-04; Frank Luther Mott, *American Journalism* (3d ed. New York: Macmillan Co., 1962), 443-44.

23. Emery and Emery, *Press in America*, 227-37.

24. Of the few journalists in the early period who did not either explicitly, or implicitly, include in their prospectus a definition of the political communication content that their newspaper would include, six appear to have been issued with special groups in mind. For example, three appear to have been issued primarily with women readers in mind, although they were still billed as newspapers; one for farmers; one on behalf of

America's workers; and another was primarily a religious newspaper. Such include the following: the *Weekly Visitor or Ladies' Miscellany* (New York City; 1802); *Weekly Visitor and Ladies' Museum* (New York City, 1817); *Ladies' Port Folio* (Boston, 1828); *Patron of Industry* (New York City, 1820); *American Farmer* (Baltimore, 1820); *Christian Watchman* (Boston, 1819).

Biographical research was conducted on two groups of newspaper editors and publishers. Of the first group, composed of 108 newspaper publishers and editors who practiced journalism between 1800 and 1830 eighty-four (77 percent) were printers, while twenty-four came from other fields including literature, commerce, religion, and law. Research on the later group revealed only a few printers. Most of those studied entered the ranks of journalism from reporting or editing or by purchasing an interest in the paper.

25. The American Antiquarian Society maintains printer files on all the Spooners discussed here. In addition, for information on the elder Spooners, see Isaiah Thomas, *The History of Printing in America, with a Biography of Printers* (2d ed. rprt. New York: B. Franklin, 1967), 302, 586-87, and for information on Alden Spooner's son, also named Alden, see James Grant Wilson and John Fiske, eds., *Appleton's Cyclopedia of American Biography*, vol. 5 (New York: D. Appleton, 1988-1891), 634.

26. *True American*, 1 July 1807, 3.

27. *Genessee Messenger*, 25 November 1806, 3. A biographical sketch of Stevens can be developed from the printer file on Stevens maintained at the American Antiquarian Society, at Worcester, Massachusetts.

28. *The Searchlight*, 2 June 1900, 1.

29. *The (Hanover, New Hampshire) American*, 7 February 1816, 1.

30. *Charleston (South Carolina) Courier*, 10 January 1803, 1.

31. *Spirit of Pennsylvania*, Easton, 6 June 1815.

32. *Orange Farmer*, 5 February 1820, 1.

33. *Lancaster (Pennsylvania) True American*, 12 June 1805.

34. *New York Evening Journal*, 16 November 1801, 1.

35. *Maine Intelligencer*, Brunswick, 23 September 1820, 1.

36. For example, the following newspaper prospectuses promised to provide these forms of political information: political coverage — *Lancaster (Pennsylvania) True American*, 12 June 1805; *Carthage (Tennessee) Gazette*, 30 January 1808, 1; *Topeka (Kansas) Tribune*, 24 June 1880, 1; *Rockbridge County News*, Lexington, Virginia, 7 November 1884, 2; editorials or exposés — *New York Evening Journal*, 16 November 1801, 1; *Saratoga Advertiser*, Ballston Spa, New York, 12 November 1804; *Schoolcraft County Pioneer*, Manisque, Michigan, 29 April 1880, 2; *Saturday Evening Post*, Burlington, Iowa, 19 August 1882, 4; reprinting of laws, speeches of legislative bodies, and so on — prospectus of the *(Jackson) Missouri Herald*, published in the *Edwardsville (Illinois) Spectator*, 12 June 1819, 2; *Columbian Advocate and Franklin Chronicle*, Worthington, Ohio, 7 January 1820, 1; *The (Newberry, Michigan) News*, 10 June 1886, 1); letters or essays from the public — *Lancaster (Pennsylvania) True American*, 12 June 1805; *The Grit*, Washington, D.C., 21 December 1883, 4.

37. For example, the wording used included the following: *National Intelligencer*, Washington, D.C., 3 November 1800, 1 — "include political ideas"; *New York Evening Journal*, 16 November 1801, 1 — "discussion . . . [will] inculcate just principles in politics"; *Saratoga Advertiser*, Ballston Spa, New York, 12 November 1804 —

"dissemination of just principles"; *Genesee Messenger,* Canandaigua, New York; 25 November 1806, 3 — "discuss characters of public functionaries of government"; *Orange County Patriot,* Goshen, New York, 9 March 1809, 2 — "We'll keep a jealous eye out"; *Evening Transcript,* Boston, 24 July 1830, 1 — "[We'll] express our own opinions."

38. True's printing and publishing enterprises took him from New Hampshire, where he started what may have been his first newspaper publishing venture, the *Eagle* (1795-1799), to Boston, where he established and operated six more newspapers from 1804 to 1840. For additional information on his life, consult the printer file at the American Antiquarian Society.

39. *(Boston) Courier,* 13 June 1805, 3.

40. Publisher Charles Hosmer and editor Theodore Dwight, *Connecticut Mirror,* Hartford, 10 July 1809, 1.

41. *Los Angeles Daily Times,* 4 December 1881, 1.

42. *National Reflector,* 8 December 1895, 1.

43. *National Republican and Ohio Political Register,* 1 January 1823, 1.

44. *Orange County Patriot,* 9 March 1809, 2.

45. *American Patriot,* 18 October 1808, 1.

46. A proposal for a paper published in the *American Monitor* in Plattsburgh, New York, on 14 October 1809.

47. *True Republican,* 1 July 1807, 1.

48. *Hancock Gazette,* 6 July 1820, 1.

49. *Fredonian,* 20 February 1810, 1.

50. *Courier,* 10 January 1803, 1.

51. *National Republican,* 1 January 1823, 1. For information on Looker, see his printer file at the American Antiquarian Society.

52. *Charleston Mercury,* 1 January 1822, 1, 3.

53. Raum, *History of the City of Trenton,* 23.

54. *True American,* 23 June 1801, 2.

55. Raum, *History of the City of Trenton,* 23-24.

56. Prospectus published in 27 November 1819 issue of the *Clarksville (Tennessee) Gazette.*

57. Marschalk has been revered by some Mississippians as the "Benjamin Franklin of Mississippi." Having probably learned printing in England, he is said to have brought a printing press with him to America, which he then carried to Mississippi, where he used it to print the territory's first set of laws in 1798. For more information on Marschalk see Charles S. Sydnor,"The Beginning of Printing in Mississippi," *Journal of Southern History* 1 (February 1935): 49-55.

58. *Washington (Mississippi) Republican,* 13 April 1813, 1.

59. *Saturday Evening Post,* 19 August 1882, 4.

60. *Journal,* 16 August 1893, 1.

61. While some mass communication historians for this reason have called this period the dark ages of journalism, historian W. David Sloan, in "Scurrility and the Party Press, 1789-1816," *American Journalism* 5 (1988): 98-112 has discussed how style of journalism ought to be considered less severely, since it simply reflected the character and mood of the period within which it was issued.

62. For examples, see the following: *National Intelligencer,* Washington, D.C., 3

November 1800, 1; *The Farmer's Cabinet,* Amherst, New Hampshire, 11 November 1802, 1; *Washington (Tennessee) Republican,* 12 February 1813, 1; *Franklin Monitor,* Charlestown, Massachusetts, 3 January 1819, 1; *Metropolitan and Georgetown Commercial Advertiser,* 26 January, 1820; *Northern Intelligencer,* Plattsburgh, New York, 7 May 1822, 3; *Greensborough (North Carolina) Patriot,* 23 May 1829; *Evening Transcript,* Boston, 24 July 1830, 2.

63. *True American,* 23 June 1801, 2.

64. *Gazette,* 16 March 1802, 1.

65. *The Farmer's Cabinet,* 11 November 1802, 1.

4

Discursive Construction of Journalists as Political Communicators in Nineteenth-Century Libel Courtrooms

The birth of a democratic nation in the American Revolution certainly did not rule out libel disputes between political authorities and those who issued newspapers and the authorities. Especially after the turn of the nineteenth century, particularly in states where party rivalry was especially virulent, journalists faced the threat of libel suits. James Cheetham was brought to court thirteen times during his first two years as editor of the *American Citizen*. Editor William Duane was sued for libel so often that one lawyer claimed that no matter how slanderous his writings might be, they could not injure those they targeted because his own reputation was so soiled. While few nineteenth-century journalists spent this much time in court, libel nevertheless must have been a concern throughout much of the century.[1]

The law can be seen as a complex communication process, one that constructs cultural and social meanings that have ramifications beyond the confines of the courtroom. Such an idea, coupled with the suggestion that discursive strategies play important parts in the emergence and development of occupational and professional groups, encouraged speculation that libel courtroom statements constructed occupational, as well as legal meanings. In addition, it was considered that such arguments might have extended beyond courtroom walls through dissemination in newspapers, pamphlets, or other print forms of mass media.[2]

As discussed in Chapter 1, to understand the history of any occupational group, historians must identify and study as many forms of occupational communication as possible. While prospectuses were an important part of the process whereby occupational boundaries demarcating journalistic work tasks would emerge, competitive struggles between journalists and others who sought to control journalistic work took place not only in public media, but in legal and workplace settings.[3] This chapter describes and discusses nineteenth-century libel disputes as sites where disputes between journalists and politicians led to dissemination of a journalistic discourse on the group's occupational duties, roles, and relationships.

LIBEL IN NINETEENTH-CENTURY AMERICAN PRESS HISTORY

Throughout the nineteenth century, in both civil and criminal libel suits, American politicians and government officials continually threatened, and imposed financial burdens on, the nation's more outspoken journalists. Especially prevalent during the early and late decades, such suits occurred throughout the century.[4] In their examination of these cases, most scholars have studied libel suits primarily for what they can tell them about the history of the First Amendment as it pertains to the communication rights of individual journalists.[5] But recently, some scholars have adopted an approach that views libel more broadly as a communication process with relationships to social, cultural, political, and economic environments. Among them is historian Norman Rosenberg, who contends that legal materials and phenomena ought to be viewed as historically contingent.[6] Rosenberg argues that during certain times, such as during the politically explosive period of the 1790s, libel suits become "prominent instruments in social-political struggles."[7] In addition, he maintains: "Libel law should be conceptualized as a legal manifestation of fundamental battles over the nature of social and political power relationships in United States history."[8]

Such an idea was borne out in an examination of courtroom transcripts printed after verdicts were issued in nineteenth-century libel trials. In each of the trials studied, politicians, specifically elected or appointed government officials, sued journalists for libel. Occupational communication is defined in this chapter to include statements that explicitly discuss the work or tasks of the newspaper journalistic group. It was assumed that occupational rhetoric could have both led to, and been indicative of, development in the work system in which journalists and politicians coexisted. Additionally, it was thought that such communication, along with other rhetoric issued during these legal disputes by journalists and politicians concerning political communication-related work, constructed a discourse that was meant to contribute to the public's understanding of, and sentiments about, journalists' work tasks, duties, and societal roles.[9]

Transcripts and other published materials representing fourteen libel disputes between politicians and journalists during the period 1805 to 1875 were studied. Additional libel suits involving journalists discovered in preliminary research were excluded because the plaintiffs were not politicians or government officials and because the focus here is on the occupational relationship between journalists and politicians and public officials.[10]

In addition to offering glimpses into nineteenth-century occupational life, each of the fourteen libel cases provides a colorful picture of the period's more general social and cultural milieu. While many of these trials relate to corruption in politics and government, they also tell stories that touch on various nineteenth-century American social, political, economic, and cultural customs.

NINETEENTH-CENTURY COURTROOM DISPUTES OVER JOURNALISTIC OCCUPATIONAL DUTY

Fourteen libel trial transcripts were examined to learn whether nineteenth-century courtrooms were places where debates concerning the political communication-related duties of journalists were engaged in, and, if so, whether occupational meaning was embedded within such discourse. A reading of the fourteen libel trial transcripts revealed that twelve of the trials embodied discourse that assigned journalists special occupational duties in the area of political communication, while eight statements disputed this idea (the frequency of such occupational statements for and against this idea is tabulated by year in Table 4.1). A slightly higher incidence of these discussions occurred after the middle of the century.[11]

Typically issued by plaintiff's or defendants' lawyers in opening and closing statements, courtroom debates over the duties and societal positions and roles of journalists largely centered on two questions: (1) Do journalists have a special duty to monitor, report on, and critically evaluate the conduct of politicians or others who seek or hold public office? and (2) Does the health of America's democratic political system depend on the citizenry's acquisition of such political information from journalists.

Journalists' "Watchful Eye" Duty

In the earliest of the libel suits studied, attorneys for both plaintiff and defendant clashed over whether journalists have special duties as reporters to watch over the conduct of public officials. In the 1807 dispute, Federalist editor William Coleman was accused of libeling Philip R. Arcularius, New York City's almshouse superintendent, in the *Evening Post*.[12] Coleman's newspaper report claimed Arcularius had mistreated a homeless black woman about to give birth by refusing to give her shelter, forcing her to have her baby in a vacant lot. The courtroom arguments of Coleman's lawyer included statements on the newspaper editor's right to print such a story because of the liberty of the press. But his case did not rest solely on this fundamental concept, for he added a second defense, one which related not to the rights of editors, but to their public duties. A passage from his courtroom speech illustrates this:

I do not mean to take up your time by declaiming upon the importance of the liberty of the press. But I do insist that it is the object of an editor of a public paper to make true observations upon the conduct of the officers intrusted by the people with the management of their affairs. It is his duty to keep a watchful eye over them, and to call the attention of the public to any of their acts, which in his opinion are neglectful or criminal. If you shall be of opinion from the evidence, that Mr. Coleman has done no more in this case than exercise his right as an editor, and his duty to the public, it is impossible that you should find a verdict against him.[13]

But plaintiff Arcularius and his attorney strongly disagreed with the notion that the role of newspaper editors ought to encompass such a "watchful eye" duty, as is clear in the attorney's statement:

When an editor undertakes to print, he does it at the peril of the law. He has no rights, nor duties, nor privileges, but as every other man. There is no peculiar protection accruing from the circumstances of having assumed that office. He is to see that his news is faithful, and his intelligence pure; otherwise, he must abide the legal consequences.[14]

At the trial's conclusion, the jury, apparently finding Coleman's plea the more persuasive of the two, exonerated him. Perhaps to gain sympathy for his plight, Arcularius published a pamphlet that included an account of the entire trial proceedings. Aside from that, the incident has been all but forgotten by most historians.[15]

Another courtroom statement that embodied claims that journalists have special duties to watch over the conduct of public officials involved New York City newspaper publisher Charles N. Baldwin. Indicted in 1818 by the City of New York for statements in the *Republican Chronicle*, which alleged that the city's lottery officials were guilty of mismanagement and fraud, Baldwin's lawyer argued that his client was a "champion of the people's rights":

I hope no apology is necessary for the daring, the noble, the exalted course which Mr. Baldwin has pursued. No subject is so generally interesting to the people of the United States, as the faithful, upright, and correct management of our lottery wheels. . . . He therefore who sees any evidence of a fraud about a lottery wheel, and winks at it, or passes it over in silence, no matter from what motive, whether of hope or fear, merits public censure. . . . The evils which he has already remedied, and which his exposure will continue to remedy to the remotest time, entitle him to the name of public benefactor.[16]

Baldwin was exonerated by the jury.

In an 1822 case, defendant and *Connecticut Journal* editor Sherman Converse was sued by politician and public official Joshua Stow. According to Stow, Converse libeled him when he ran for the Connecticut state legislature. Converse had printed statements in the *Journal* that accused Stow of cheating in his collection of taxes, failing to properly fulfill his responsibilities as postmaster, and being guilty of fraud in his capacity as director of the local bank. In Converse's trial, which he lost, his attorney declaimed on the roles of public editors:

To these allegations, the Defendant replies, that he made the publication in the course of his duty as the Editor and publisher of a public Journal, and . . . that the Plaintiff was then a candidate for the important office of senator in the State legislature; that as a candidate for that office, the Defendant had not only a right but it was his duty, as the

Table 4.1
Statements About Journalists' Occupational Duties in Libel Trials

U =   Unclear, since only a partial transcript is available

X =   Present

− =   Absent

	Plaintiff	*Defendant*
1807 (Arcularius-Coleman)	X	X
1807	X	−
1818	−	X
1822	X	X
1829	U	X
1830	−	X
1833	−	X
1836	X	−
1851	U	X
1861	X	X
1865	X	X
1866	X	X
1870	X	X
1875	−	X

editor of a public journal, to investigate his character, and make known his pretensions.[17]

Another strong statement on the public duties of journalists was issued in a
South Carolina courtroom in 1875. Arrested and sued under criminal libel law
by the State of South Carolina, publisher and editor Captain F. W. Dawson
allegedly unfairly ruined the reputation of Sheriff, and former United States
Congressman, Christopher Columbus Bowen, when he accused him of induc-
ing, threatening, and instigating a murder that had occurred a decade earlier, in
1864.

According to Dawson's attorney, if the members of the press are silent when
they have information that will benefit the public, they are abandoning their
responsibilties:

When it is silent, it betrays its trust; but when, for private advantage, it shrinks from its
duty and dares not publish that which is should publish, lest it draw down upon its own
head the wrath of the wrong-doer, it forfeits all right to public confidence, and deserves
to perish for lack of support. It holds its tenure by its boldness, its independence, its
truth.[18]

The case ended in a mistrial. A week after the trial ended, a warrant was
issued that ordered Bowen's arrest for the murder that Dawson had accused
him of instigating.

Journalistic Work as a Crucial Component of Democracy

A second theme embodied in nineteenth-century courtroom debates on the
occupational roles of journalists centered on questions of the importance of
journalistic services to the American polity. Illustrating this is a libel suit
brought in 1830 by Timothy Upham, a U.S. Custom's Office Collector and
candidate for New Hampshire's governor.[19] Upham asked for $10,000 in dam-
ages for the loss of his reputation, which allegedly occurred at the hands of
journalists Horatio Hill and Cyrus Barton, owners of the *New Hampshire Patriot and Star Gazette*. In the end, the trial resulted in a hung jury.

The dispute arose out of a political battle being waged in the *Patriot and
Star,* where Hill and Barton published three statements accusing Upham, who
resided in Portsmouth, of corruption, smuggling, cowardice, and misappropria-
tion of custom funds for the purpose of financing a partisan newspaper. In response, Upham sued them for libel.

Hill and Barton's attorney said that his clients published the statements because, being involved in a political campaign, they believed it their duty to
publish what information they had about Upham. He said they published such
statements "without any malevolence against the plaintiff — but merely to
prove his unfitness for the office to which he was then aspiring."[20]

After accusing Upham of trying to muzzle the press, in their final arguments,

Hill and Barton's lawyer claimed that the work of journalists is crucial, especially during political campaigns:

When a man is a candidate for a public office, depending on the suffrages of the people, he invites an examination into his character and qualifications; and agrees that, if he is deficient in either, it may be made known to the electors. If the defendants had good reasons to believe the plaintiff had been guilty of violating the laws of his country, it was their duty to inform the public. . . . How is the necessary information to be given but by means of the press? It can be given in no other way.[21]

The great importance of journalistic work was also discussed in a 1865 trial that came out of a libel suit filed by former New York City Mayor George Opdyke. Claiming his reputation was ruined by publisher and editor Thurlow Weed in a series of articles published in the Albany *Evening Journal*, Opdyke sought $50,000 in damages. From June 18 to 24, 1864, Weed published material that accused the former mayor of being a swindler, speculator, and seller of public offices. The trial, which lasted nearly a month and attracted a great deal of public attention, ended with a deadlocked jury.

Weed did not testify at his trial, but his attorney spoke eloquently on his behalf. Among his speeches were statements on both the rights, and the responsibilities, of journalists. In addition, journalistic work was portrayed as being of great public import:

This is a public question. Is it not right to expose the frauds of men in public places? If it is right to expose them, then it is wrong that Mr. Weed should be punished for exposing them. He ought to have a monument rather. The only tribunal before whom such offenders can be brought is that of public opinion; and the only instrument we can use is the public press. Will you destroy that?[22]

The idea that the public is highly dependent on journalists for political information was not always disputed in court. Instead, plaintiffs' lawyers at times argued that journalists had not performed these special responsibilities in an acceptable manner. For example, when New York City Recorder Maturin Livingston successfully sued journalist James Cheetham in 1807 over a statement that accused him of cheating in cards, his attorney claimed in court that he had failed in his responsibility as a guardian of the public. He stated:

The defendant has forced the press to become the disturber of domestic quiet — the assassin of private reputation. Our press, gentlemen, was destined for other purposes. It was destined not to violate, but to protect the sanctity of human rights. It was kindly ordained by a beneficient providence to inform, expand and dignify the public mind. It was ordained the watchful guardian, the undaunted champion of liberty — not the syren [sic] word liberty, which is sometimes used as an *ignis fatuus* to allure mankind through the mire and swamps and mountains and precipices of revolution; — but that liberty which spreads the banners of its protection over man in the walks of private life, and gives him the proud consciousness of security in the enjoyment of property, person and character. It is for these high purposes that our press was ordained; but the defen-

dant has rendered it the degraded vehicle of foul defamation. . . . There was a time
when the press of our country had an exalted character. . . . But now our press has lost
its character for veracity. The demon of party has forced it to become a prostitute in the
service of licentiousness.[23]

Cheetham was a prolific and controversial journalist. Born in England, and
briefly imprisoned there for his political activities, in 1798 he immigrated to
New York City, where he launched a career as a newspaper journalist and political pamphleteer. His sharply barbed rhetoric quickly earned him a reputation
in America; among his enemies was Aaron Burr and among his friends was
Thomas Paine.[24] Cheetham was sued for libel more than a dozen times during
his first two years in America.[25]

Among Cheetham's various newspaper projects was the *American Watchman*, which, in 1807, included an article that said that one of his political opponents, Maturin Livingston, had cheated while playing cards. Livingston sued
him for libel, claiming that his reputation had been ruined.

Instead of making lofty speeches about freedom of the press, or about the
duties of journalists, Cheetham's lawyer seemed to apologize for the press. In
doing so, he asked for leniency:

Suppose that he had committed great faults, that like all the rest of the printers he has
assailed the reputations of those most cherished in the hearts of their fellow citizens.
Yet still, gentlemen, humanity will revolt against persecution, and when the punishment
is too great it turns itself to an offence. And so will the threatened ruin of this defendant
be thought too terrible a vengeance.[26]

He also told the jury that, in his opinion, upstanding citizens could not be
libeled by newspapers' columns:

I will ask you whether any man in this country loses his reputation by newspapers. I do
not believe it. I know as far as my experience goes that a character in itself good cannot
suffer from such attacks. Without prying into your individual opinions, gentlemen, of
one or other party, I could single out some who have been high in political standing, and
ask you if newspapers could ever injure them. Whatever our difference of public opinion
may be, did the fame of General Hamilton ever suffer, does that of Mr. Jefferson now
suffer from newspaper attacks. Certainly if Mr. Livingston has had hitherto an unsullied
reputation, nothing in that obscure paragraph could injure him.[27]

The jury awarded Livingston $1,000 in damages.

In several of the cases, defendants' counsel argued that their journalistic clients, in exposing the wrongdoing of public officials and candidates for public
office, were simply doing what all citizens ought to do. But at the same time,
they praised the journalists for their important services to the public. One such
statement is found in *Commonwealth of Boston vs. Snelling*,[28] a case that arose
in 1833 to 1834 out of a dispute over the conduct of Boston Police Court Judge
Benjamin Whitman. The libel suit commenced after journalist William J. Snelling began investigating illegal gambling in Boston. Ultimately, the state won
its case against Snelling, but only after an appeal of his conviction in the lower

court trial.

During the course of his investigations, having been threatened by one of the parties whose actions he questioned, Snelling went to the Boston police court to complain. On arriving in the court, Snelling was apparently treated disrespectfully by Judge Benjamin Whitman. In response, he inserted the following statement in the *New England Galaxy*:

We accuse him of disgracing his office, of perverting law — which, bad as it is, is yet worse in such hands — of doing injustice on his seat, of descending from his official dignity, of suffering personal feeling to interfere with the discharge of his functions. . . . These, bitter as they are, are not the words of passion, but the deliberate expression of our conviction, respecting the duty we owe to ourself and our country. We think we shall do service to God and man by removing this unjust magistrate from the seat he disgraces.[29]

Snelling filed fourteen indictments against the judge, one accusing him of habitual drunkenness, the others relating to specific instances where Whitman had allegedly acted improperly in the handling of cases brought to his court. On losing the case at the lower court level, Snelling appealed his conviction to the Supreme Judicial Court of Massachusetts.

At Snelling's second trial, the state's prosecuting attorney opened the trial by discussing his views on the law of libel. For example, he stated his dissatisfaction with a law recently enacted in Massachusetts that allowed libel defendants to use truth as a defense. In addition, he also claimed that punishment for libeling public officials should be more severe than for libeling ordinary citizens, warning of the dangers that threatened public officials in communities that permitted the press to have certain powers: "The press is the most powerful of political enemies, and may be used for good and important purposes, and it may also be so perverted as to produce great evils. It is for courts of law to guard against such perversion."[30]

During both trials, Snelling's lawyers discussed the importance of freedom of the press but did not make statements that assigned any special occupational duty to journalists. Instead, they lumped journalists together with all citizens, who they said ought to be watching out for corrupt public officials:

Mr. Snelling is no vagrant or felon; he is not the associate or abettor of thieves or rogues. He stands before you a fellow citizen, and an equal, entitled to all the privileges and indulgence the law allows to such. . . . Mr. S. [sic] has preferred charges against this magistrate, which we say are true, and were published with good motives. If they be so, Mr. S. is a public benefactor, and ought rather to be rewarded than punished; for a judge has more opportunity to injure the public than a private individual, and it is, therefore, doing the public a most importance service, to expose his misdemeanors.[31]

Although the lawyers argued that journalists' responsibilities to expose corrupt officials emanates from their citizenry, their reference to Snelling as a "public benefactor" who had provided an important public service differentiated journalists from politicians.

POLITICAL AFFILIATIONS OF PLAINTIFFS AND DEFENDANTS

It might be claimed that arguments that journalists are bound by occupational duty to expose unscrupulous politicians would be weightier if they were willing to expose the wrongdoing of all corrupt politicians and officials, not just those of an opposing political party. As illustrated in Table 4.2, some of the journalists accused of libel in the latter half of the time period studied did expose the wrongdoing of members of their own parties.

For example, in 1866, New York State Senator Demas Strong sued George C. Bennett, publisher of the Brooklyn *Daily Times*, a member of his own political party.[32] Strong's suit was prompted by Bennett's publication of a newspaper article alleging that the senator was guilty of corruption, bribery, and receiving money for votes. Concerned that the reputation of the state legislature was at stake in this trial, Bennett's counsel contended it was his journalistic duty to expose the plaintiff's wrongdoing:

Every man who hears me feels and knows that if Mr. Bennett believed that statement to be true, it was not only his clear duty to publish it, but it was a duty that it would have been mean and criminal to decline. It was a matter in which every good citizen, every patriot, was bound to feel in interest, and lend a hand to drive the miscreant from the seat he had disgraced. . . . But it was peculiarly the duty of a journalist to sound the alarm — to call the public attention to the facts. It is what he professes to do by his very calling. He stands upon the outer wall — a sort of watchman — guarding the interests of the State, while you repose from the fatigue of more private toil and labor. It is time you buy a copy of his journal. If he fails thus to discharge his duty, he cheats you of your money — he obtains a sale of his property by false pretenses. He is faithless to his high public trust.[33]

Plaintiff's counsel did not attempt to refute the idea that journalists had a special calling but argued instead that the court should not extend its protection to sensational journalists:

In all pursuits, in every profession, and in every business, there are different classes, and in the Newspaper Press, if you turn it over in your recollections, you will fasten upon some newspaper that has been dragging out a miserable existence not by the honorable legitimate course of a public journal, but by gathering together the dirt and filth of society, and making what are called sensational sheets. Such liberty of the Press is not to be protected or defended.[34]

While the jury found the defendant guilty, the plaintiff, who asked for $10,000 in damages, was awarded six cents.

A second example, illustrating that some journalists were willing to expose members of their own political parties, was a libel trial in the 1870s. Defendants James N. Matthews and James D. Warren were accused of libel by David S. Bennett, a Buffalo, New York, businessman who was a member of the United States House of Representatives.[35] Publishers and editors of Buffalo's *Commercial Advertiser*, Matthews and Warren had earlier supported Bennett in his bid for election to Congress. But despite this earlier allegiance, they exposed him in their newspaper when they became convinced he was guilty of defrauding the members of the Buffalo Elevator Association of a large sum of money. Matthews and Bennett's attorneys argued that the two journalists had a right, as well as a special occupational responsibility, to print information about the wrongdoing of elected and appointed public officials and corrupt businesspeople:

The defendants are gentlemen well known in this community. They have for many years been engaged in publishing, as the counsel has been pleased to say, a conservative and respectable newspaper. As such, it has been their duty to hold up to the public the character of individuals who are engaged in public business. Because I hold it to be equally

Table 4.2
Political Affiliations of Libel Plaintiffs and Defendants

Year	Political Opponents	Political Allies	Unclear
1807	X		
1807	X		
1818		X	
1822	X		
1829	X		
1830	X		
1833			X
1836	X		
1851			X
1861	X		
1865		X	
1866		X	
1870		X	
1875			X

the duty of a public newspaper to give information to the public in regard to the merchant engaged in great and general transactions as in regard to the man who holds an office of public trust and honor at the voice of the people. Such men are in a certain sense public property. . . . Hence, then, gentlemen, it is the duty of the public newspaper — and it was the duty of these defendants in view of the two-fold position occupied by the plaintiff here as a public merchant and as a public servant — to denounce his actions if he was guilty of corruption and improper or dishonest practices.[36]

Apparently this was persuasive, since the jury found them not guilty. Such a position might have reflected a more general trend in journalism during the later nineteenth century, which led journalists to distance themselves, at least on the surface, from politicians and members of their local business communities.[37]

AMPLIFICATION OF JOURNALISTIC OCCUPATIONAL DISCOURSE OUTSIDE COURTROOM WALLS

It is important to consider whether the jurisdictional contests waged within legal settings between members of the journalistic and political groups may have extended into the public sphere, thus possibly amplifying the impact on the groups' occupational development. Research revealed that the debates did reach the broader public via the print medium in several forms: (1) full and partial texts of the trials and the occupational statements they embodied were printed and disseminated by both plaintiffs and defendants; (2) some of the pamphlets published after verdicts were rendered included posttrial claims of journalists to occupational duty; and (3) news reports and editorials concerning the trials were published in area newspapers both by plaintiffs as well as their journalistic associates.

From a careful reading of the trial transcripts, it is apparent that many of these cases were controversial, having become the topics of intense, widely dispersed public scrutiny. Among media that circulated information about these trials were newspapers. Some of the libel trials, for example, were the subjects of in-depth news coverage and verbatim reproductions of the trial proceedings. In the *State vs. Bowen*[38] and *Bennett vs. Matthews*[39] cases, for example, the verbatim transcripts of important courtroom speeches were reproduced on the front pages of local daily newspapers, along with other pertinent trial-related information, throughout the trial.

Another example involves a pamphlet newspaper journalist David Lee Child published after being found guilty in 1829 of libeling Massachusetts State Senator John Keyes. Child's pamphlet not only included the entire trial proceedings, but reiterated the occupational claims issued at the trial by his lawyer. In Child's words:

In exposing the two great corruptions of the State Prison and the State Printing — the defendant has doubtless expended many hundreds of dollars — endured great labor — and incurred much personal abuse — but let him not be discouraged. — He discharges well, the duty of a faithful sentinel upon the walls of the Republic. Let him persevere: — the public will finally reward him. The people will not — cannot — must not forget him.[40]

Sympathetic newspaper editors published editorials that strongly supported the plight of their beleaguered peers.[41] Child's conviction precipitated at least ten sympathetic editorial responses, some of which echoed the defendant's occupationally charged rhetoric. In response to Child's conviction, for example, the editor of the Boston *Daily Advertiser* argued on behalf of his editorial colleague: "It is evident that Mr. Child was influenced from no other motives than the desire to discharge his duties faithfully to the public, by making known what he considered material to forming a correct judgment of the conduct of public officers."[42]

In another case, in response to New York City journalist George Wilkes's battering at the hands of judge and jury in a libel suit brought by New York's former attorney general Ambrose L. Jordan, at least forty supportive editorials appeared on Wilkes's behalf. While many of these were issued within the northeastern United States, several were published as far west and south as Ohio and Tennessee.[43]

SUMMARY

Nineteenth-century courtrooms were places where more than legal meaning was constructed. An examination of trial transcripts of libel proceedings revealed that libel courtrooms were among the sites where the contents and legitimacy of journalistic work in the area of political communication were contested and debated.

Within twelve of the fourteen libel trial transcripts examined were statements by the legal representatives of either one or both of the parties on the occupational duties of journalists. Common themes centered on questions pertaining to whether journalists have a duty to watch out for and report on politicians' misconduct and on the utility of journalistic work to the American polity. Especially toward the end of the century, journalists were sued for libel by members of their own political parties in newspaper articles, meaning that not all such disputes were the result of nothing but rampant political partisanism. Finally, debates between journalists and politicians over occupational duties and their societal value extended beyond the walls of courthouses into the towns and cities surrounding them through publication of trial transcripts, news reports, and editorial pieces on the legal disputes of journalists and politicians.

Initially, it was assumed that the courtroom arguments would directly involve journalists and the politicians who had sued them. However, in only several of the cases did the accused journalists actually testify, and when they did appear on witness stands, they did not issue general statements about what they perceived their occupational roles to be. Thus the trial statements examined were largely issued by defense and plaintiff attorneys, a situation that does not necessarily diminish the weight of the statements on journalistic duty. Indeed, it might be argued that the courtroom arguments of attorneys might carry more weight in the community than those of plaintiffs or defendants.

NOTES

1. Norman L. Rosenberg discusses this and libel more generally during the early decades of the nineteenth century in *Protecting the Best Men: An Interpretive History of the Law of Libel* (Chapel Hill: University of North Carolina Press, 1986), 107. On Cheetham, see Frank Luther Mott, *American Journalism* (3d ed. New York: Macmillan Co., 1962), 183. On Duane, see *Portsmouth (New Hampshire) Oracle,* 10 December 1801. Duane admits to having been a defendant in about sixty defamation suits. *Aurora,* 12 August 1806.

2. Press historians often discuss examples of journalists who were involved in politics. For evidence of the many who held elective offices during the nineteenth century, see Milton W. Hamilton, *The Country Printer: New York State, 1785-1830* (New York: Columbia University Press, 1936), who lists and discusses state senators and journalistic members of the United States Senate and House of Representatives. In addition, see Donald H. Stewart, *The Opposition Press of the Federalist Period* (Albany: State University of New York Press, 1969), who identifies in note 42 of Chapter 1, thirty printers who were affiliated with political societies in nine states in the 1790s.

3. Andrew Abbott, *The System of Professions: An Essay on the Division of Expert Labor* (Chicago: University of Chicago Press, 1988), 62-63.

4. Rosenberg, *Protecting the Best Men,* 107, 130-31, 133-34, 136-40, 197.

5. Jeremy Cohen and Timothy Gleason analyze scholarship on libel in *Social Research in Communication and Law,* vol. 23, Sage CommText Series (Newbury, CA: Sage, 1990), finding that studies of libel can be broken into the following categories: First Amendment theory, torts, sociology of litigation, sociology of libel, and communication. Among these, the last best fits the research conducted for this chapter.

Among the many scholars who study the history of press freedom and libel are the following: Timothy Gleason, *The Watchdog Concept: The Press and the Courts in Nineteenth-Century America* (Ames: Iowa State University Press, 1990); Leonard Levy, *Emergence of a Free Press* (New York: Oxford University Press, 1985); Jeffery A. Smith, *Printers and Press Freedom: The Ideology of Early American Journalism* (New York: Oxford University Press, 1988); Rosenberg, *Protecting the Best Men*; Margaret A. Blanchard, "Filling the Void: Speech and Press in State Courts Prior to *Gitlow,*" in *The First Amendment Reconsidered,* eds. Bill F. Chamberlin and Charlene J. Brown (New York: Longman, 1982); John Robert Finnegan, Jr., "Defamation, Politics, and the Social Process of Law in New York State, 1776-1860" (Ph.D. diss., University of Minnesota, 1985); Mary Ann Yodelis and Gerald J. Baldasty, "Criticism of Public Officials and Government in the New Nation," *Journal of Communication Inquiry* 4 (Winter 1979): 53-74

6. See Rosenberg, *Protecting the Best Men,* as well as the following: Cohen and Gleason, *Social Research*; Finnegan, "Defamation, Politics, and Social Process of Law"; David Kairys, "Freedom of Speech," in *The Politics of Law: A Progressive Critique,* David Kairys, ed. (New York: Pantheon Books, 1990).

7. Rosenberg, *Protecting the Best Men,* 259.

8. Ibid.

9. The method used in the analysis of printed courtroom statements was qualitative. For more information, see Klaus Bruhn Jensen and Nicholas W. Jankowski, eds. *A Handbook of Qualitative Methodologies for Mass Communication Research* (London; New York: Routledge, 1991), 18-36; T. A. van Dijk, *Text and Context: Explorations in the Semantics and Pragmatics of Discourse* (London: Longman, 1977).

10. Compared to the number of libel trials that have been held in American history, relatively few trial courtroom transcripts have been transcribed and printed for public distribution. Of this group, only a few have found their way into archives and libraries for use by historians.

Forty trial transcripts were received via interlibrary loan and, of this group, fourteen fit the research design that examined libel trials involving journalists and politicians. The twenty-six not used in the research involved journalists and individuals representing other walks of life.

11. It was found that in some cases, judges also made references to occupational duties in their statements, but these are excluded from this analysis.

12. *A Faithful Report of the Trial of the Cause of Philip R. Arcularius* (New York: Kirk for Dornin, 1807).

13. Ibid, 30.

14. Ibid., 43.

15. Research did not reveal any additional information about this incident, the ensuing libel trial, or its aftermath.

16. *Report of the Trial of Charles N. Baldwin for a Libel* (New York: C. N. Baldwin, 1818).

17. *Report of the Case of Joshua Stow vs. Sherman Converse, for a Libel.* (New Haven: S. Converse, 1822), 73.

18. *The Great Libel Case. Report of the Criminal Prosecution of the News and Courier for Libelling Sheriff and Ex-Congressman C. C. Bowen* (*News and Courier*, Charleston, SC, 1875).

19. *Report of the Case of Timothy Upham Against Hill and Barton* (Dover, DE: George. W. Ela, 1830).

20. Ibid., 22-23.

21. Ibid., 126.

22. *The Great Libel Case. Geo. Opdyke agt. Thurlow Weed. A Full Report of the Speeches of Counsel, Testimony, Etc., Etc.* (New York: The American News Company, 1865), 128.

23. Ibid., 41-42.

24. Eventually, he would publish pamphlets on both of these figures. He described Burr as "vindictive," and Paine as "distorted." See Dan Morris, *Who Was Who in American Politics* (New York: Hawthorn), 146; and *Who Was Who in America*, (Historical Volume. Chicago: Marquis, 1975), 172.

25. Rosenberg, *Protecting the Best Men*, 105.

26. *Trial of the Hon. Maturin Livingston Against James Cheetham for a Libel* (New York: S. Gould, 1807), 32.

27. Ibid., 34-35.

28. *Trial of William J. Snelling* (Boston: Printed for the Reporter, 1834).

29. Ibid., 3.

30. Ibid., 6.

31. Ibid., 26.

32. *The Strong-Bennett Libel Suit* (Brooklyn, New York, 1866).

33. Ibid., 4.

34. Ibid.

35. *The Great Libel Suit; David S. Bennett v. James N. Matthews and James D. Warren* (Buffalo, NY: Matthews and Warren, 1870).

36. Ibid., 150-51.

37. Evidence of this was found in a number of the late nineteenth-century newspaper prospectuses, which stated that those who produced newspapers were not under the control of certain business interests. But research conducted by Dicken-Garcia shows that the late nineteenth-century press was largely dominated by a business model, and Baldasty found that advertisers had a tremendous impact on newspaper journalism. Perhaps a plausible explanation for this journalistic rhetoric is that those who issued it felt a need to distance themselves from business interests. See Hazel Dicken-Garcia, *Journalistic Standards in Nineteenth Century America* (Madison, WI: University of Wisconsin Press, 1989), 51, 62, 229; and Gerald J. Baldasty, *The Commercialization of the News in the Nineteenth Century* (Madison, WI: University of Wisconsin Press, 1992), 137-46.

38. *Great Libel Case. Report.*

39. *Great Libel Suit.*

40. *Review of the Report of the Case of the Commonwealth versus David Lee Child, for Publishing in the Massachusetts Journal a Libel on the Honorable John Keyes* (Boston: J.H. Eastburn, Printer, 1829), 8.

41. Not all newspapers supported journalists such as Wilkes, for there was some division based on the political affiliations of editors.

42. Ibid., 12.

43. *To the Press of the United States, and Especially To the Press of State of New York* (Hoboken, NJ: George Wilkes, 1851), 14-32.

5

Discursive Construction of Journalistic Occupational Roles During the Era of Good Feelings

On July 12, 1817, one of Boston's most rabidly Federalist papers, the *Columbian Centinel*, noted a change in America's political climate:

Era of Good Feelings

During the late Presidential Jubilee many persons have met at festive boards, in pleasant converse, whom party politics had long severed. We recur with pleasure to all the circumstances which attended the demonstration of good feelings.

During the previous year's elections, James Monroe's ascendancy to the presidency brought the official death of the Federalist Party, which had mustered only enough strength to carry the states of Massachusetts, Connecticut, and Delaware. The old party essentially ceased to exist, although it "clung, in a rather fungoid manner, to certain localities."[1] Americans previously split along party lines thus merged into a single political family. Almost everyone called themselves Jeffersonian Republicans, and national political conflicts tended to be arguments between personalities rather than about principles or programs.[2]

The collapse of the country's nascent multiparty system signaled by the Era of Good Feelings was an important turning point in the development of the nation's political structure. But while historians have avidly studied the newspaper press during the early national period, they have rarely mentioned the calmer years, let alone probed whether it may have brought change to a newspaper press with a predominantly political role and strong ties to politicians, political parties, and patronage.[3]

Throughout the decades since the American Revolution, the nation's newspaper proprietors had sought to carve out a special role for journalists in the political communication system, one that differentiated them from politicians. Not only did newspaper editors construct a discourse in prospectuses that defined them and their newspapers as crucial political communicators, but they portrayed themselves as holders of special standards for the handling of political information. The public, who had no taste for the rampant partisanism of day, needed to be convinced that journalists, rather than other political communicators, could be trusted to provide them with the kind of newspaper they desired.

But when the *Centinel's* editor dubbed the period the Era of Good Feelings in 1817, the previous generation's party divisions were gone, as were the partisan disputes that had so often made their way into the country's newspapers despite their proprietors' promises to remain above petty political squabbles.[4] This, coupled with the suggestion that when confronted with changes in broader environments, occupational groups must renegotiate their positions if they are to remain viable, encouraged exploration of the work situations of journalists during the Era of Good Feelings. While the political changes wrought by the period would not be as profound as those ushered in by the American Revolution, it was thought that the collapse of the Federalist party would have presented newspaper proprietors with a significant challenge, one that may have called for remedies that included the reconstruction of discursive strategies, career lines, and trade practices that had been common for the past thirty years.

Such assumptions led to research that explored the following more specific questions: Did Federalist newspapers die as a result of the Era of Good Feelings, driving home the point that journalists, if they were to survive as a viable group, should redefine their work and position with the political work system and society? Among those newspapers that were established anew, or survived the period, is there evidence that the period's altered political climate encouraged newspaper proprietors to adjust their political affiliation or alter them in some other way? Finally, did any of the period's newspaper proprietors leave newspaper work as a result of the period's changed political environment or did some adjust their trade practices or careers in reaction to it?

Using both primary and secondary sources, three bodies of data were gathered in research that explored these questions. First, the starting and ending dates of clearly Federalist newspapers were compiled with an eye toward learning whether any died as a result of the collapse of the Federalist party.[5]

Second, biographies of more than ninety newspaper proprietors, publishers, and/or editors involved in the issuance of newspapers in America's towns and cities during the period encompassing the Era of Good Feelings were compiled and studied.[6] Every occupation has typical careers, and the detection of changes in career structures can reveal insight into how occupational groups can both be affected by and react to fluctuations within broader environments.[7] Three types of information was sought in this research: (1) the categories of newspapers, such as political, mercantile, labor, or religious, that early nineteenth-century journalists were involved with over the course of their careers; (2) the publishing and printing enterprises beyond newspapers that journalists engaged in;

and (3) the nonprinting or publishing career pursuits of journalists.

Third, a group of newspaper prospectuses, fifty-six in number, issued by the hopeful establishers of new or renewed newspapers during the Era of Good Feelings, were examined and compared to prospectuses published before the era, from 1800 to 1815.[8]

The calmer period represented by the Era of Good Feelings lasted from about 1816 until 1825, although stresses, just beneath the surface, such as the economic panic of 1819, at times threatened the peace. Its demise was ultimately brought by shifting economic interests, sectional rivalries and bitter personal conflicts that resulted in a very close 1824 presidential election and the rebirth of a multiparty system.[9] While the era would prove in the end to offer only a short-lived respite from the early national period's widespread political strife, it nevertheless posed a challenge that was addressed by the members of the journalistic community.

A SYMBOL OF CHANGE: DEATHS OF FEDERALIST NEWSPAPERS

The demise of Federalist newspapers during the Era of Good Feelings must have served as a powerful symbol of what could happen to newspaper proprietors who failed to adjust their newspapers' publishing plans and trade practices to the new environment. While the overall growth rate of the newspaper industry continued to be positive throughout the Era of Good Feelings, an examination of the histories of newspapers with the words "Federal" or "Federalist" in their titles shows that at least ten died from 1816 to 1825. At least three papers folded in 1816, for example, including Georgetown's *Daily and Weekly Federal Republican*, Cumberland, Maryland's *Alleghany Federalist*, and Fredericktown, Maryland's *Federalism*. Additional papers closed between 1817 and 1825 in West Chester, Pennsylvania, Greenfield, Massachusetts, New Bern, North Carolina, St. Clairsville, Ohio, and in Baltimore and Fredricktown, Maryland.[10]

While this number is small, it is undoubtedly only a portion of the number of Federalist papers that died during the period for lack of a party. Also of interest are papers that folded for similar reasons but whose political affiliations are less obvious, but these are more difficult to identify. One example is the *American Advocate*, a newspaper started by Seth Alden Abbey[11] and his brother Dorephus, in Watertown, New York. The *Advocate* lasted just two years, from 1818 to 1819. According to a historian of Jefferson County, New York, Abbey harbored Federalist leanings, which made it difficult for this newspaper, as well as the one he established immediately after its demise, to survive:

When the Abbeys came into possession of the *American Advocate*, there was very little party feeling. Mr. Monroe had been chosen President the previous year, and there was little opposition to the Democratic, then styled Republican party. It was therefore up-hill work for a purely party paper, and their paper stopped at the end of two years.[12]

Journalists and those who patronized America's newspapers during the early days of the Republic were certainly used to newspapers coming and going rather quickly, since many lasted but a year or two for reasons that had nothing to do politics. Economic panics, such as the one suffered by the nation in 1819, the deaths of publishers or other principals, fires or other natural disasters are some of the reasons that newspapers closed during the early decades of the nineteenth century.

But the deaths of Federalist papers certainly did not go unnoticed in the newspaper community, especially since most editors routinely exchanged papers with their fellow newspaper proprietors. At least, the demise of even a few Federalist party papers must have added a new dimension to the chronic insecurity experienced by newspaper proprietors who published newspapers during the early decades of the century. This was, after all, the first time newspaper closures were caused by the collapse of the nation's multiparty system, and while such collapses have been rare in American history, those who practiced journalism in American in during this period did not know that.[13] Although it is impossible to gauge just how much stress this political event added to the work lives of newspaper proprietors, it is clear from a reading of Era of Good Feelings newspaper prospectuses, that some journalists felt compelled to respond to its challenges by redefining their political-related work roles and newspapers contents.

OCCUPATIONAL COMMUNICATION IN ERA OF GOOD FEELINGS PROSPECTUSES

For at least a generation, nearly all of America's newspaper proprietors had written prospectuses that assigned them and the members of the burgeoning journalistic occupational group political communication roles as the nation's political saviors and educators. While some claimed that they were completely independent from politics and politicians, others pledged their allegiance to a party. But even the most politically fervent among them said they would handle political information in such a way that it not be scurrilous or licentious. While the editors often failed to hold to this last pledge, they did fulfill at least one of their promises: They provided their readers with a steady diet of political reports, essays, proceedings and speeches, and letters.

The political climate these editors worked within as they produced the nation's newspapers during the generation preceding the Era of Good Feelings was normally one of extreme discord and unrest. The nation faced a number of great challenges that required political solutions, and this meant that the members of differing political camps would squabble over a wide range of issues and events.

In light of the important parts newspaper editors often played in these debates, it was thought that the starkly different political environment that they were greeted with in 1816 would have been a topic of discussion in journalistic discourse in prospectuses, and an examination of a group of such statements bore this out. A reading of fifty-six newspaper prospectus statements issued from 1816 to 1825 revealed fourteen clearly stated references to the Era of Good Feelings, as well as evidence of altered political stances and statements on how newspapers would be changed to meet the period's challenges. The examples below show that at least some of the period's newspaper conductors, like Benjamin Russell, publisher of the Boston *Centinel* and coiner of the term "Era of Good Feelings," were aware that they must adjust to the changes the period had forced on them.

A Different *Centinel*

Well known for a generation as one of Masschusett's most stridently Federalist editors, Benjamin Russell turned away from his old party toward republicanism with the coming of the Era of Good Feelings. Joseph T. Buckingham, in his classic *Specimens of Newspaper Literature*,[14] recalled how Russell brought trouble on himself and his newspaper when it began to take on such an uncharacteristic Republican-friendly stance toward President Monroe's visit and subsequent tour. Some of Russell's Federalist friends, who had been important correspondents for years, said they would no longer accept delivery of the *Centinel* nor serve as correspondents. From this point on, the *Centinel*'s circulation began to decline, and, losing its former political clout, it soon was disregarded as an authority in political circles.

As time passed, the *Centinel* began to more openly support Republican candidates. Eventually, the paper's proprietor abandoned the secondary title "Massachusetts Federalist," which had been printed on the masthead for more than twenty years. But Russell's approach was only one of several adopted by newspaper editors.

The Era's Political Tranquility Will Not Be Upset

Some of the era's issuers of prospectuses commented favorably on the peaceful spirit of the times and promised that their newspapers would not publish material that would dredge up old political arguments. Editorial promises to refrain from publishing politically inflammatory material were nothing new, since newspaper publishers had long displayed an awareness of the public's deeply felt ambivalence toward party spirit.[15] But with the coming of the calmer political period, such rhetoric took on a new twist, as its issuers claimed that with the trouble-making political cliques and factions gone, they could be even more effective in fulfilling their roles as the citizenry's chief political educators.

In their first issue, Philadelphia newspaper proprietors John Norvell and Richard Bache,[16] in 1819, issued a statement introducing the *Franklin Gazette*. Insisting the state was in good hands and that they would do nothing to upset the calm, they wrote: "[We hope you will not be] allured from that quiet path of harmony and good will. . . . By this we mean we shall avoid the wretched personal broils which discontent and faction engender; we shall enjoy the present and look forward with pleasure to the future." [17]

A second example is in a prospectus by printers Elisha Bellamy and Thomas Green in 1819,[18] as they sought to establish the *Franklin Monitor* in Charlestown, Massachusetts. The two enterprising publishers had not failed to notice that Charlestown, the county's largest town, had no newspaper, a situation they hoped to correct. Their prospectus outlined the kinds of material the *Monitor* would include, such as essays on literary and moral subjects; hints on agriculture; poetry; the news of the day, both foreign and domestic; and lastly, communications on political subjects. In expanding further on the last point, they revealed an awareness of the newer political environment:

The *Monitor* will not have a tendency to destroy the happy union which at present prevails. . . . But it will ever be their aim to discourage all party asperity, and whatever may tend to revive that political rancour, from which, happily, we are in a great measure free. In short, the *Monitor* is not intended, neither shall it be, a party paper.[19]

We are Americans, not Federalists or Republicans

Another group abandoned old party names altogether and announced in their prospectuses and choices of newspaper titles that, rather than being of party, they were first and foremost Americans. Such tactics had long been practiced by newspaper proprietors, especially by those who had chosen to proclaim they were not aligned with any political party. But there was an increase in such rhetoric during the Era of Good Feelings.[20]

Illustrating this is an 1819 essay announcing that the *Journal of the Times* was being renamed the *Morning Chronicle and Baltimore Advertiser*. Publishers Thomas Martin Maund and Frederick G. Schaeffer[21] had started the *Journal* the year before to provide their friend Paul Allen with an editorial position. In their introduction to the *Chronicle*, they described the political times, as well as their own brand of political sentiments:

The *Chronicle* makes its first entry into the public, when the storms of political vengeance have ceased to beat; when the season so happily denominated the 'Era of Good Feelings' has arrived. . . . With regard to the politics of this paper, it becomes necessary to state, that we shall endeavor to be exclusively American . . . [a pledge that some might say] includes everything and means nothing. . . . [But] we mean by the term American, what the term American strictly imparts — an ardent attachment to our native country.[22]

Another example of this use of Americanism in lieu of a party affiliation is evident when comparing two prospectuses issued by newspaper proprietor David Watson, one issued before the Era, and a second after its beginning. The career of printer and publisher Watson began in Boston in 1810 and took him to towns in New Hampshire, Vermont, Massachusetts, and New York before he died in 1867.[23] He published newspapers through much of the Era, including the *American* in Hanover, New Hampshire, from 1816 to 1817, and the Woodstock, Vermont, *Observer*, from 1820 to 1823. In addition to newspapers, Watson also published books, pamphlets, and other nonnewspaper materials.

When Watson sought to establish the *American* in 1816, he issued a prospectus in which he explained his political position:

The good people of this country have been so long accustomed to considering party politics as an essential characteristic of Newspapers, that the main question cannot be waived. What are to be the politics of *The American*? The question is a reasonable one, and we are not disposed to give a deceptive reply. The name of our paper is intended as indicative of its politics and principles. Its politics shall be purely American. The ground we shall take will be American ground, from which, we flatter ourselves, we shall neither be enticed nor driven.[24]

Watson was soon lured from Hanover to Woodstock, Vermont, in about 1819, by the publishers of a Christian hymnbook, and after becoming established there, he decided to start a second newspaper, the *Woodstock Observer*, in January 1820. His second prospectus reflected the new political times in which he was publishing and restated his "American" approach:

Since the political elements of our government have ceased to war with each other; and since those of the European world are generally marked with the same character — no political animadversions [sic] shall be admitted into our paper, tainted, in the slightest degree, with the acrimony of party. Its character shall be purely American—a supporter of the rights and liberties of the people, and the constitution upon which those rights are predicated.[25]

Other Variations on Party Themes

Some die-hard Federalists could not completely give up the cause and adopted such labels as "Federal Republican." A few, such as Peter Hardt, harkened back to earlier times: He explained his position as he took over the *York Recorder*, a York, Pennsylvania, weekly, from its former proprietor Charles T. Melsheimer:

As to the political sentiments of the editor — he frankly avows himself a Federal Republican. . . . The *Recorder* will support the policy of those happy times when integrity, principles, and impartiality enabled the Father of his country to give us a character highly respectable among the nations of the earth, and to lay a solid foundation for our future eminence and prosperity.[26]

Old Federalists such as Seth A. Abbey, the Watertown, New York, publisher discussed in the previous section, also sometimes chose to use labels like "Independent Republican."[27]

Political Vigilance Is Still Required

But not all surrendered meekly to the period's state of relative tranquility, since there were those who hastened to remind their readers from time to time that vigilance was needed and that they were ready to return once again to the fight should one break out anew. Republican lawyer John Norvell, already mentioned, and printer Ignatius Cavins[28] were two such newspaper proprietors. In 1819, as they assumed the publication of one of the frontier's oldest newspapers, the Lexington *Kentucky Gazette*, they discussed the importance of remaining politically alert, especially during a period of seeming tranquility:

Even at the present day, though an organised and systematic opposition to the republican cause has ceased to exist, yet it may be probably still expected, that the introductory address of an editor should contain something on this subject. As far then as partyism may still prevail, on the old grounds of division, we pledge ourselves that the *Gazette* shall still be, as it ever has been, found on the republican side. . . . We shall occupy no half way ground; we recognise not the doctrine of 'amalgamation.' . . .The politician who would regard the present calm in party politics, as proceeding from an oblivion or abandonment of those principles, which produced our late inflammatory discord, would be entitled to very little respect for his wisdom and penetration. . . . The leaders of the opposition still retain their principles . . . [and in some places] we find them still pursuing their old practices.[29]

Another editor, William Alexander Rind, publisher of Georgetown's *Metropolitan*, likewise called for vigilance. His prospectus said: "The Editor . . . thinks that it would not only be politic, but absolutely necessary to add another watchman, if it be merely to rattle the windows and cry 'Awake, awake, all is not safe!'"[30]

JOURNALISTIC SHIFTS IN WORK PRACTICES AND CAREERS

A third body of research focused on whether journalists in this era altered their newspapers, trade practices, and careers in response to the period's calmer political environment. Such research revealed that not many newspaper conductors were forced out of the newspaper business as a result of the changes brought by this environment. Of the ninety-two newspaper proprietors whose careers were studied, sixty-nine remained in the newspaper publishing business throughout the period. The twenty-three who did leave did so for a variety of reasons, including the following: eight were deceased; two left in conjunction with the deaths of spouses or partners; seven left for new careers; and one of the group retired, probably due to old age. The remaining four left for other unknown reasons.

In addition to these findings, a review of the ninety-two careers showed that many appeared on the surface to be firmly established publishing and printing entrepreneurs with various degrees of flexibility and innovativeness. Most had been in the publishing business from an early age, having served long apprenticeships during their teens, and sixty of the ninety-two were involved in diverse printing and publishing enterprises, including the publication of books, magazines and pamphlets, and bookselling operations. It was common for these individuals to have been involved in multiple publishing business partnerships and other printing-related business ventures. Nine of the ninety-two simultaneously carried on other careers while publishing newspapers. Such careers included among other things university teaching, law, farming, and inventing.

The findings also suggest that changes in the political environment may have led some newspaper journalists to experiment with new types of newspapers. Of the ninety-two newspaper journalists studied, twenty-six started what for them were new types of newspaper periodicals. These included religious, literary, labor, women's, and farmers' newspapers, in addition to periodicals for juveniles.[31] New York state printer and newspaper publisher Frederick P. Allen, for example, who was involved in the issuance of at least six newspapers from 1811 to 1845, began publishing religious periodicals for the first time during the Era of Good Feelings. One of these ventures was a paper named the *Religious Reporter,* which he established along with copublisher Jared W. Copeland in April 1820. While the historical record does not reveal specifically why he chose to publish such newspapers, these enterprises might have come out of not just changes in the social and environment but out of changes in politics. [32]

In addition to starting new types of newspapers, some era editors adapted to the period's calmer political climate by changing their newspapers in other ways. James C. Dunn and William Alexander Rind, the proprietors of Georgetown's *National Messenger and Town and City Commercial Gazette,* were among this group. When faced in 1817 with the loss of their newspaper's primary political targets — Federalists — they altered the paper's size, appearance, and editorial character.[33] In their transformed paper's first issue, Dunn and Rind discussed how party conflict, which had "kept the Union for so many years in a state of perturbation," had abated and explained the impact of the comparative dearth of political material:

Universal tranquility deprives the journalist not only of the topics legitimate to the nature of his profession, but of that endless reciprocation of conflicting opinions which arise out of them. To attract public attention in stormy times, and to keep it from slumbering in the dead calm of universal and domestic tranquility, are efforts of very different natures. . . . The current politics of the day . . . will hardly saturate our columns or satisfy the curiosity of the public.[34]

As a result of such change, they said they were forced to include greater amounts than formerly of certain kinds of material in their newly designed newspapers, including the following:

It shall be our business therefore to provide articles of amusement and information in other departments of science for the perusal of our readers. In our columns will be found essays either original or selected, on moral, scientific and literary subjects; chosen pieces of poetry, occasional strictures on the drama, and notices of, and extracts from such new publications, as shall appear to us to be clearly deserving of that distinction; and in a word, all such selections of matter as newspapers generally communicate.[35]

Business mergers were also found to be a strategy of some newspaper journalists during the Era of Good Feelings. The merger of newspapers had been commonplace throughout the history of the business, but generally, such mergers did not occur between individuals from antagonistic parties. But with the disappearance of old political enemies came new business opportunities. In Alexandria, Virginia, late in the period, two previously antagonistic newspaper journalists, Samuel Snowden and William Fitzhugh Thornton teamed up to issue the *Alexandria Phenix* [sic] *Gazette*. [36] As their prospectus explained, where such a merger was impossible before, this new arrangement would help corroborate their claims that their paper would be more independent, just the kind they said their community needed. [37]

An example of a merger of another type occurred in Ohio, when John Bailhache and George Nashee, [38] merged Federalist and Republican newspapers. Publisher and editor Bailhache, dubbed "Mons. Belly-ache" by his fellow Ohioans, was a native of England where he served his apprenticeship. He arrived in the United States in 1810 and two years later launched his career in Cambridge, Ohio, where he would serve as a printer, newspaper publisher, businessman, judge, and public office holder. His first venture was to become part-owner of the *Fredonian*, a Republican paper published in Chillicothe, Ohio. The newspaper was financially successful throughout the War of 1812 because its readers were hungry for the reports of the military operations on the western frontier. But after the war, his readers lost interest in the newspaper and it began to fail. Finding himself deep in debt, he learned that the *Scioto Gazette*, another Republican paper and the oldest in the state, was for sale. He thought that if he purchased and merged it with the *Fredonian* he could garner enough readership from the two that he would make a go of it. So he bought it for $3,000 (half in cash; the rest a loan) and commenced publication of the consolidated newspaper under the name of the *Scioto Gazette and Fredonian Chronicle* in August 1815.

He was successful in this venture, but he made a bad financial decision when he invested in a local banking scheme. To recover from his reverses, he invested in a third newspaper, the *Supporter*, for sale in 1820. Although this paper was a Federal newspaper, considering the political times, he and its publisher, George Nashee, decided to consolidate their papers, titling the result *The Supporter and Scioto Gazette*. The plan was commenced in February 1821, with Nashee attending to the paper's financial department and Bailhache in charge of its editorial side. According to Bailhache:

As the line of demarkation [sic], which had previously divided the Republican and Federal parties, had then become nearly or quite obliterated, no difficulty was experienced in so conducting the new journal as to give general satisfaction to its readers; and our business flourished as well as could have been reasonably expected under the severe pecuniary embarrassments which then prevailed in Ohio. [39]

The research suggests that those who conducted newspapers during the Era of Good Feelings were on the whole an adaptable lot and were so firmly entrenched within the period's broader printing and publishing culture that few were forced to leave it when faced with the challenges that the altered political environment brought to their newspaper publishing ventures.

SUMMARY

This examination of newspaper histories, prospectuses, and the careers and trade practices of Era of Good Feelings newspaper journalists reveals how the period's shifting political climate confronted the members of this group with a considerable occupational challenge, one that resulted in some of the group member's reconstruction of journalistic occupational discourse, as well as adjustments in newspapers, careers, and trade practices. Some Federalist papers were closed during the period, serving as a symbol that reminded newspaper journalists that to survive, they must remain flexible enough to adjust to changing environmental conditions beyond their control. Others took steps to shift the political stances of their newspapers, alter their newspapers' formats to include different kinds of content, and experiment with what for them were new types of periodicals, such as religious, women's, labor, or other types of newspapers.

Certainly, these findings are not generalizable to every community across the nation, since the challenges brought by the Era of Good Feelings varied geographically. Certain regions of the country are well known as centers for an especially virulent brand of partisantism. For example, while New England is considered by historians as having been strongly Federalist, it also harbored pockets of intense Republicanism. Other communities, such as Cincinnati, were dominated almost entirely by one or the other party before the Federalist party collapsed. John Nerone,[40] who studied the early history of Cincinnati's publishing and printing industries, found it to be primarily Republican, at least until the middle of the 1820s. As a result, its newspapers were more community than politically focused. Such variations might help predict where the impact of the Era of Good Feelings might have been strongest.

But where its effects were felt most keenly, the Era of Good Feelings would indeed lead to significant alterations of discursive strategies, career directions, and trade practices, and these would have been totally abandoned when the nation returned to a two-party system. Just such a conclusion was reached by historian Stephen Botein, who explored a period of relative political calm and its impact on newspapers in England as part of his comparative study of the occupational ideologies of early English and American colonial presses.[41] Botein concluded that the British printing trade, having undergone a generation of bitter political disputes in the Walpole era, began to calm by the middle of the eighteenth century, and printers were forced to change their trade habits as a result. Experimentations with new types of publications, including nonpolitical essay journals, were among their new repertory of trade practices. The editor of one of these new periodicals, *The World*, said he would provide purely entertainment and spoke of a determination "not to meddle with religion or politics."[42] Botein concludes that these changes brought lasting effects. "Political peace did not endure into the 1760s, but by that time the character of many English journals would be fundamentally different," he wrote.[43]

The Era of Good Feelings may have contributed to a process already under-way in America publishing — the development of various new forms and styles of newspapers and other magazines. During the early decades of the century, religious, agrarian, and various other types of periodicals emerged for the first time. Historians have generally attributed their appearances to changes in the nation's social and cultural environments. But profound changes in the level of political conflict due to the collapse of the Federalist Party might also have en-couraged journalists to incorporate such innovations in their publishing enter-prises. As career-line analysis indicates, these ventures into new types of peri-odicals were often continued after the era's demise. Perhaps the effects of the collapse of the nation's multiparty system taught newspaper conductors a valu-able lesson. Recognizing that being so closely tied to political parties had left them in a vulnerable position when the party structure collapsed and a period of political conflict commenced, newspaper proprietors who published newspapers during the Era of Good Feelings learned that newspapers that offered exclu-sively political essays were especially vulnerable to changes in the political cli-mate.

These conclusions differ with those of many historians of the press who find that the newspaper industry and those involved in it were somewhat static dur-ing the early decades of the nineteenth century. In contrast to such characteri-zations of the press and its operators, this study shows that the emerging jour-nalistic group was a vital and responsive body. In addition, its findings suggest the possibility that changes in journalism traditionally thought of as not occur-ring until later may have emerged earlier in part as a result of political change associated with the Era of Good Feelings.[44]

Joseph T. Buckingham offers a final illustration. In his reminiscences on the histories of early American newspapers and their conductors, Buckingham pondered the seemingly early retirement of newspaper publisher Benjamin Rus-sell, in whose paper, the *Centinel*, as noted earlier, the term "Era of Good Feelings" first appeared. Buckingham interpreted Russell's 1828 retirement as perhaps coming out of a realization that newspapers had changed, whereas he had not:

The circulation of the *Centinel* had diminished, and other papers had sprung into exis-tence, and were gaining popularity with a younger generation. This might have operated unpleasantly on his feelings; and, probably, he foresaw that, without a change in his style of writing and general system of arranging his materials, in order to suit his paper to the taste of the "varying hour," its circulation would continue to diminish, until the establishment might be of little value; and that it would be better to sell it then, than to run the hazard of a poorer bargain when a sale would be unavoidable.[45]

Not all newspaper proprietors followed Russell's example and retired in the years following the Era of Good Feelings. In fact, having survived many of its challenges, some of them adopted different newspaper forms and ways of operating their businesses. It is difficult to believe that the innovations brought during the Era of Good Feelings would be totally reversed when the second party system and its accompanying partisanship sprang into existence in the middle of the 1820s. While many newspaper publishers certainly jumped right back into the political fray, future research might show that they also carried at least some of the innovations adopted in the period of political calm with them into the new era.[46]

NOTES

1. George Dangerfield, *The Era of Good Feelings* (New York: Harcourt, Brace and World, Inc., 1952), 98. According to historian Richard P. McCormick, when the national parties disintegrated, there was not much of a tendency toward the formation of state-oriented parties except in New York, Georgia, and Kentucky. See McCormick's essay "Political Development and the Second Party System," in *The American Party Systems*, Richard P. McCormick and William N. Chambers, eds. (New York: Oxford University Press, 1975); and Paul Goodman, "The First American Party System," in *The American Party Systems*, Richard P. McCormick and William N. Chambers, eds. (New York: Oxford University Press, 1975).

2. Dangerfield, *Era*, xiii.

3. W. David Sloan's *American Journalism History: An Annotated Bibliography* (Westport, CT: Greenwood Press, 1989) provides an annotated listing of the many books and articles that center on the party press in the first and second political party systems.

4. Historians, such as Culver H. Smith, *Press, Politics and Patronage* (Athens: University of Georgia Press, 1977); Donald H. Stewart, *The Opposition Press of the Federalist Period* (Albany: State University of New York Press, 1969); W. David Sloan, "The Early Party Press: The Newspaper Role in American Politics, 1788-1812," *Journalism History* 9 (Spring 1982): 18-24; Gerald J. Baldasty, "The Press and Politics in the Age of Jackson," *Journalism Monographs* 89 (August 1984); and Jerry W. Knudson, "Political Journalism in the Age of Jefferson," *Journalism History* 1 (Spring 1974): 20-23; and many others, have studied newspapers and their proprietors during the period labeled the party press era. Among their conclusions are the following: Newspapers from the 1780s until the middle of the nineteenth century were often filled with political materials, especially debates over politics; many of the period's newspapers were commonly imbued with party spirit and scurrility; newspaper proprietors were at times controlled through patronage systems by politicians, political parties and government officials; and the operators of the day's newspapers developed certain political communication journalistic innovation, such as the editorial, during the early nineteenth century.

Many historians have judged the party press harshly, such as Frank Luther Mott, who called the period of the party press an age of "Black Journalism" in *American Journal-*

ism 3d ed. (New York: Macmillan Co., 1962). More recently, W. David Sloan has argued that such depictions of the press are too harsh, since the scurrility inherent in press columns was natural for the times; see "Scurrility and the Party Press, 1789-1816," *American Journalism* 5 (1988): 98-112.

5. Information on the histories of Federalist newspapers was compiled from Edward C. Lathem, *Chronological Tables of American Newspapers, 1690-1820* (Barre, MA: American Antiquarian Society, 1972).

6. This group included newspapers publishers, conductors, and editors from each state of the nation, as well as from major population centers and small towns. In the selection of individuals for the study, an effort was made to be as representative as possible so as to learn about the "typical," rather than the "notable," newspaper conductor. A group of such journalists was selected from the index of newspaper conductors included in Clarence S. Brigham, *History and Bibliography of American Newspapers, 1690-1820* (Worcester, MA: American Antiquarian Society, 1947) and research was conducted at the American Antiquarian Society and other libraries and archives. Information was sought on these individuals' social and educational backgrounds; apprenticeships; printing and publishing business activities, including all the newspapers and other publishing enterprises they initiated or were otherwise involved in; and their political affiliations and possible office holding, among other things. Files were assembled on each, and brief biographical sketches were prepared.

7. Andrew Abbott, *The System of Professions: An Essay on the Division of Expert Labor* (Chicago: University of Chicago Press, 1988), 129.

8. Such prospectuses are part of a larger group of more than 200 such documents that the researcher has compiled and analyzed; these documents were issued from 1704 to the early twentieth century. The group is representative in that it includes examples of both daily and weekly newspapers, as well as examples from each state; towns and cities of all sizes; and newspapers of many different political positions and forms, including religious, labor, literary, and other categories of papers.

9. Dangerfield, *Era,* xiii. See also James A. Kehl, *Ill Feelings in the Era of Good Feelings* (Pittsburgh: University of Pittsburgh Press, 1956).

10. These papers were titled, more specifically, in West Chester, Pennsylvania, the *Chester and Delaware Federalist*, which issued its last number on December 31, 1817; in Greenfield, Massachusetts, the *Franklin Federalist*, also in 1817; in 1818, New Bern, North Carolina, the *Federal Republican* and St. Clairsville, Ohio's *Federalist;* in 1819, Fredericktown, Maryland's *Star of Federalism;* and in 1825, Baltimore's *Federal Gazette.*

11. For information on Abbey's life and career, see the American Antiquarian Society printer biography file, as well as sources such as Cleveland Abbe, *Abbe-Abbey Genealogy* (New Haven, CT: The Tuttle, Morehouse and Taylor Company, 1916), 189-90; John A. Haddock, *The Growth of a Century: A History of Jefferson County* (Philadelphia, PA: Sherman and Co., 1894), 302-03; Hamilton, *Country Printer.*

12. Haddock, *Growth,* 303.

13. Political scientists maintain that the nation has undergone five major shifts in the party system since the nation was formed, although some have discussed the possibility that we are currently in the midst of a sixth.

14. Joseph T. Buckingham, *Specimens of Newspaper Literature,* vol. 2 (Boston:

Charles C. Little and James Brown, 1850), 96-103.

15. More than 100 prospectuses issued from 1801 to 1830 has been reviewed, as well as others from earlier and later periods. A pervasive theme in such especially during the period of the party press was the pervasiveness and detrimental effects of party spirit and press scurrility.

16. For information on Norvell, see *National Cyclopedia of American Biography*, vol. 11 (Clifton, NJ: J. T. White, 1892), 500-501. Research was not conducted on Bache's career.

17. *Franklin Gazette,* 22 May 1819, 2.

18. Neither Green nor Bellamy were among the group of ninety-two journalists whose careers were compiled and studied in the research.

19. *Franklin Monitor,* 3 January 1819, 1.

20. A group of prospectuses issued in the fifteen years prior to the Era of Good Feelings shows such a tendency.

21. This is discussed in Brigham's *History and Bibliography* entries on the histories up to 1820 of the *Journal of the Times* and *Morning Chronicle.* Maund and Schaeffer employed well-known editor and poet Paul Allen as their paper's editor. Allen had previously edited the *Federal Republican and Baltimore Telegraph* but disagreed with his associates and left. There followed a period of poverty when he was imprisoned for a debt of thirty dollars. Schaeffer and Maund had earlier started the *Journal of the Times* to give him an editorial position, and the *Journal* was in 1819 turned into the *Morning Chronicle.* For more on Allen's literary career, including his involvement with newspapers, see the first volume of the *Dictionary of American Biography* (New York: C. Scribner's Sons, 1928-58), 202-03.

22. *Morning Chronicle and Baltimore Advertiser,* 8 April 1819.

23. Henry Swan Dana, *History of Woodstock, Vermont* (Boston; New York: Houghton Mifflin & Co., 1889), 249-51, 253, 269-71.

24. *American,* 7 February 1816, 1.

25. *Observer,* 11 January 1820, 1.

26. *York Recorder,* 17 February 1818, 2.

27. Haddock, *Growth.*

28. Cavins is a relatively obscure newspaper printer and publisher who lived and worked in Kentucky through much of the Era of Good Feelings. See *Kentucky State Historical Society Register* 33 (1935): 50.

29. *Kentucky Gazette,* 6 March 1819, 3.

30. *Metropolitan and Georgetown Commercial Advertiser*, 26 January 1820, 1.

31. Many of these types of newspapers and magazines originated in the early decades of the nineteenth century. The first religious periodical, for example, was started just several years before the Era of Good Feelings.

32. See its prospectus dated 8 April 1820, 1. Information about Allen's life and career is included in D. Hamilton Hurd's *History of Franklin County, New York* (Philadelphia, PA: J. W. Lewis & Co., 1880), 388-89; Frederick J. Seaver, *Historical Sketches of Franklin County and Its Towns* (Albany, NY: J. B. Lyon and Co., Printers, 1918), 715; an obituary, in the *Plattsburgh Republican,* 11 May 1878, 1.

33. *National Messenger and Town and City Commercial Gazette,* 27 October 1817, 2.

34. Ibid.

35. Ibid. Future research ought to probe how common this kind of editorial adjustment was during the Era of Good Feelings.

36. The careers of these two are discussed in Carroll H. Quenzel, *Samuel Snowden, a Founding Father of Printing in Alexandria* (Charlottesville, VA: Bibliographical Society of the University of Virginia, 1952); Snowden's career is discussed throughout, while see 20-23 for information on Thornton.

37. See prospectus issued in *Alexandria Phenix [sic] Gazette,* 1 January 1825, 2.

38. Bailhache's career is amply documented. Not only did he leave an unpublished autobiography, which is housed within the American Antiquarian Society's manuscript collection, but there are a number of biographical sketches on him, such as William L. Fisk, "John Bailhache: A British Editor in Early Ohio," *The Ohio Historical Quarterly* 67 (April 1958): 141-47.

For information on Nashee's career, see Alfred E. Lee, *History of City of Columbus, the Capital of Ohio,* vol. 1 (New York & Chicago, 1892), 423-24, 457-58, 470-71; Ruth Young White, ed., *We Too Built Columbus* (Columbus, OH: Stoneman Press, 1936), 82; obituary, *(Columbus) Ohio Monitor,* 19 May 1827.

39. Taken from a typed version of Bailhache's autobiography, American Antiquarian Society manuscript collection, 20.

40. John Nerone, *The Culture of the Press in the Early Republic: Cincinnati, 1793-1848* (New York; London; Garland Publishing, Inc., 1989).

41. Stephen Botein, "'Meer Mechanics' and an Open Press: The Business and Political Strategies of Colonial American Printers," *Perspectives in American History* 9 (1975): 127-225.

42. Ibid., 164.

43. Ibid.

44. Such is not universally accepted. John Nerone, in "The Mythology of the Penny Press," *Critical Studies in Mass Communication* 4 (1987): 376-404, discusses his view that many of our assumptions about the impact of the penny press are inaccurate.

45. Buckingham, *Specimens,* 102-03.

46. See Baldasty, "The Press and Politics in the Age of Jackson," and other sources on newspapers and journalists in the Jacksonian period annotated in Sloan, *American Journalism History.*

6

Conclusion and Implications of Historical Study of the Journalistic Occupational Group

In 1929, journalist E. W. Howe published an autobiography that described his life and career as a newspaper publisher and editor in Atchison, Kansas. Among his many stories was one about a relationship he had in the 1880s with a local politician nicknamed Old Spider. In a bid for elective office, Old Spider had tried, but failed, to buy Howe's support. When the editor refused to accept his $500 offer, the politician said, "They say I run Ed Howe. The facts are, he runs me."[1]

Old Spider's words portray not just the relationship of a particular politician to a journalist, but also exemplify the profound changes that journalism underwent during the eighteenth and nineteenth centuries. By the time Howe's autobiography was published in the 1920s, journalistic work was widely considered to be an important and powerful occupation, and some even considered it a profession. Valued especially for their contributions in the political realm, journalists, rather than politicians, would be entrusted by most Americans with the important task of providing the nation with political news and editorial opinion.

Even politicians, who a century before had not only frequently practiced journalism, but who often controlled newspapers, regarded political journalists as authoritative figures. As Old Spider had put it, editor Ed Howe ran him, rather than the other way around. Reflecting on this nearly fifty years later, Howe put a label on his refusal to accept Old Spider's financial offer. "I was always independent, sometimes too much so," he wrote.

Two centuries earlier, colonial Americans had few ideas about what constituted journalistic work, let alone concepts of journalism as an independent occupation. While printers and others performed journalistic work tasks early in the eighteenth century, these tasks did not yet have the cultural meaning and legitimacy they would later acquire. Occupational boundaries had not yet formed that would conceptually mark off areas of journalistic work. Those who performed journalistic tasks were more widely recognized as printers, postmasters, lawyers, political elites, and literary types than they were as journalists.

That journalists, rather than politicians, would become the nation's primary providers of political news and editorial opinion was not preordained, nor has the journalistic group ever been invulnerable from forces that from time to time have threatened their jurisdiction over such work. Indeed, as discussed in Chapter 1, some contemporary scholars are convinced that journalism is being fundamentally reshaped today in terms of its occupational roles and legitimacy. To understand contemporary and future journalistic work and occupational issues requires learning about how, and by whose agency, journalists became members of an occupation with particular roles and social position in the first place.

Americans' ideas about what it means to be a journalist began to assume occupational definition during the eighteenth and nineteenth centuries. A complex process involving those who performed journalistic tasks, the public, politicians and political authorities, and events and societal conditions, journalistic work came to be more clearly defined as an occupation in the colonial and post-Revolutionary War eras. The emergence of the newspaper, as well as clashes between newspaper printers and the authorities which culminated in the American Revolution, was an important part of this process. The occupation continued to be defined in the next century by developments such as the transformation of the newspaper industry into a commercially profitable and highly rationalized, organized, and mechanized enterprise.

But those who produced America's newspaper were also agents of occupational change, albeit unwitting ones, and it is this aspect of the occupational history of journalism that has been explored in this book. Discursive practices and routines of newspaper proprietors are part of the process whereby journalism assumed cultural and social meaning and organization. Pre-revolutionary newspaper journalists claimed in prospectuses that they would provide useful services, would not become embroiled in political matters, were authoritative and trustworthy, and held standards that would enable them to handle information in such a way that the public would not have reasons to complain. Although occasionally they would discuss their political roles, few newspaper proprietors did so until after the American Revolution. During and after the revolution, a discourse emerged that not only stressed the important political roles held by newspaper journalists, but the idea that journalists were independent operators, free from the control of politicians. The revolution's replacement of the colonial authoritarian political communication system with a more open and democratic one had made it possible for newspaper printers to operate more freely than they had been before the war.

While social and cultural boundaries had begun to coalesce around the concept of journalistic work during the eighteenth century, they were still only barely discernible by 1800. For journalists, rather than politicians, to be considered by most Americans as their prime providers of political news, the members of the emerging group needed to continue carving a niche for themselves in the broader political communication work system, and this process, while it began in the decades after the revolution, was an ongoing and important one throughout the nineteenth century.

To succeed in their newspaper enterprises, those who published and edited newspapers early in the nineteenth century were compelled to negotiate situations where they were often forced to both cater to, and at the same time, to resist the strong-willed politicians who they worked so closely with in their communities. Only too well did newspaper proprietors know that, although the public's appetite for political information in newspapers seemed to be growing, the citizenry had not yet developed an ethic of party politics that would lead them to tolerate even mild partisanism let alone the more heated political disputes that continually would break out in America. To become viable forces in their communities, those who practiced newspaper journalism were compelled to come to grips with questions that would go to the very heart of their group's occupational roles and societal duties in the political area: What political communication roles would be fulfilled by the producers of newspapers? Who should the public entrust with the responsibility to perform and control journalistic political communication tasks? What, if any, roles should politicians play in the production and dissemination of political communication in newspapers?

The answers to these questions are found in the occupational discourses newspaper publishers and editors constructed in printed and spoken forms of communication across the nineteenth century. Several of these forms of occupational communication — newspaper prospectuses and libel courtroom statements — have been studied here. Grounded in the social experiences of journalists who were ever cognizant of their positions relative to politics and politicians, several themes were pervasive within the journalistic occupational discourses these texts embodied: First, journalists are important, indeed, crucial, providers of certain categories of political communication; second, the public needs the political communication services of journalists, who will not only educate them politically, but will guard against politicians and government officials who might threaten democracy or act in their own interests instead of those of the public; third, while journalists are politically knowledgeable and have political principles, they are independent from the control of others and have standards for the handling of political information that they claim equip them to meet the public's political communication needs.

The nature of the relationship between journalists and politicians was almost always portrayed as being one of tension and conflict, and this was an important strategy in the process that led to elevation of the positions of journalists as providers of political journalism. Since journalists were often politicians themselves, and since politicians often funded or worked on newspapers, the members of the two groups were often close allies. But journalists' discursive portrayals of their relationships with politicians painted a different picture, one that glossed over these friendships in their emphasis on these disputes.

Considering the profound changes that America underwent during these two centuries, it is difficult to imagine that those who claimed independence in 1780 meant the same thing as those who claimed independence a century later. But regardless of when such statements were issued by America's journalists, or who specifically journalists claimed independence from, all essentially portrayed themselves as free and powerful societal entities. On a local community level, these discourses of independence would be useful to journalists as they sought patronage and readers in their communities.

Discursive appeals in prospectuses also equipped journalists with a weapon to use when they were forced to thwart the less routine and perhaps more serious challenges of politicians, such as the ones posed by those who sued them for libel. Courtroom libel testimony served the two groups occupationally, as well as legally. Examples of courtroom testimony revealed journalistic defenses against libel charges by politicians; arguments in those defenses said it was journalists' occupational duty, as well as their right, to conduct themselves as political communicators and commentators. In addition, libel courtroom statements of journalists and their legal counsel stressed the importance of journalistic political reporting, not just to those in local communities, but to the health of the nation. Politicians, on the other hand, disputed such contentions and argued their own rights to serve as arbiters of what was fair and legally permissible journalistic political communication.

Journalists' discursive positioning of themselves as independent entities also enabled them to negotiate major political systems changes, such as the collapse of the Federalist Party in the second decade of the nineteenth century. Data on the demise of newspapers and information gleaned from prospectuses and the biographies of newspaper journalists who worked during this period reveal that the political structural changes in the Era of Good Feelings likely affected the development of journalistic work. The collapse of the multi party system and the ensuing relative calm left journalists with a dearth of political controversy to report and comment on in their newspapers. The deaths of some of the period's Federalist newspapers served as a reminder of the commercial dangers of remaining too close to any particular political view. In addition, some of the period's journalists altered long-standing trade practices, started new types of newspapers, and changed their existing newspapers' editorial character and contents during the Era of Good Feelings. Although the calmness of the period was ultimately short lived, newspaper proprietors did not know how long it would last. Journalists were forced to seriously consider what alternative communication roles they might perform for the members of their communities.

Finally, journalists' construction of themselves as independent entities not only proved to be an effective strategy on the local level, but it constituted occupational meaning and boundaries in the broader social structure as well. Through the construction of a discourse that defined them occupationally, journalists ultimately carved out and maintained a niche for themselves in the broader political communication work domain over the nineteenth century, and this in turn, had ramifications for the position of journalists throughout society. Although changes have occurred since 1900, the structures of the contemporary journalistic occupation developed during the previous two hundred years.

QUESTIONS AND IMPLICATIONS

The research points up several implications, as well as raises important questions, that could be useful in future studies of the history of the journalistic occupational group and its work, and more generally of the press and its political role. The American Revolution profoundly affected the development of the journalistic occupational group. Not only did the work of journalists become a more crucial part of the nation's political communication, but the revolution placed those who accomplished such work in a more authoritative position. Political information, rather than another category of information, such as commercial news, would become the foundation on which journalists would seek to build their occupation's legitimacy.

This had a lasting impact on the group's history. For example, to acquire jurisdiction over political communication work, the members of the group had to convince the public that such work undertaken on its behalf was of supreme importance in the republic. But then later, when some journalists sought to change the functions and roles of newspapers (as in the 1820s and 1830s when some began publishing more types including ethnic and racial, labor, women's, religious, and other kinds of publications), they may have had to confront criticism by those journalists, who believed journalists' proper role to be largely political.

The research also suggests that scholars should look earlier than they have previously for the origins of the journalistic group's professional development. Professional work is defined as that which experts perform through manipulation of abstract knowledge to provide the public with services they cannot provide for themselves.[2] In addition, groups do not attain professional status unless they acquire clear authority over such abstract work tasks. In light of such a definition, it can be argued that a professional press model was developing as early as the late eighteenth century in conjunction with the events of the American Revolution, when through a highly abstract process, journalistic work became more closely linked to political communication.

At first blush, these findings appear to contradict portrayals of the press in previous work. For example, as was discussed in Chapter 1, scholars who discuss the origins of professional development generally do not detect traces much earlier than the late nineteenth century. In addition, historians have found the origins of the movement toward greater political independence in the period following the emergence of the penny press in the 1830s.

Of particular importance, the findings here suggest that while nineteenth-century newspaper journalists routinely communicated with their publics through political news and editorial materials, they were also simultaneously engaged in an ancillary communication process involving the issuance of messages that constructed definitions of journalistic work and jurisdictions of those conducting it.

It must be stressed here that any impact from this occupational communication process cannot be attributed to the simple conveyance of information. Instead, any impact of such rhetoric arose from the fact that the messages were embodied in occupational discourses that became almost ritualistic in nature. The cultural meaning of nineteenth-century journalistic political communication work, including diagnosis, inference, and treatment of the citizenry's information needs, was socially constructed through occupational practices of journalists.

It was not the purpose of the research to determine whether the members of a still young journalistic group in the early nineteenth century claimed to be building occupational boundaries of their group. Indeed, it seems safe to assume that some journalists wrote prospectuses only for themselves. Only later in the century, when many journalists became members of the nation's growing number of occupational associations would a clearer sense of group consciousness develop. Yet, taken as a whole, prospectuses and other practices that included messages identifiable as occupational in nature were part of a process that served to construct perceptions of the group's work, identity, and boundaries.

The model of press history articulated here provides a more complex prism through which to examine press-political relationships than that offered in many previous histories of journalism. Press historians generally have suggested that before the 1830s, the press was largely subservient to politicians; then, over the rest of the century, the journalists and politicians underwent an evolution in their power relationships, and the press was gradually transformed into a more independent institution.

Evidence found in the research presented here presents a different picture of the history of the press, which can be used to enhance previous conclusions of historians. To explain emergence of what has been viewed as a more independent press by the end of the nineteenth century, historians have studied the roles of certain forces, such as developing technologies, the Jacksonian democratic revolution, and the commercial advertising industry. All these developments affected the press and its relationships. But this study shows that events originating outside the work system, such as the American Revolution and changes in political structures exemplified by the Era of Good Feelings, along with other forces embodied in the work systems of journalists, also affected development of the journalistic work. In addition, looking at history through this theoretical framework helps reveal that the broad transformation of the press from a less to more independent entity was not a slow, steady progression toward more independence; rather, that transformation is better represented by a counterprogressive model; there were periods of advances in legitimacy that were later tempered because of events beyond the control of journalists, and there were periods of regressions of legitimacy.

Many historians have portrayed the watchdog journalist, sometimes known as the "fighting" journalist, as emerging in the late nineteenth century, contrasting that persona with the earlier more subservient type. This study indicates that the image of the "fighting" journalist emerged much earlier than historians have assumed. While early nineteenth-century journalists often were subservient to politicians because of dependence on their economic and social largesse, many of them at the same time engaged in a very public, rhetorical battle with politicians.

In fact, this adversarial relationship emerged even earlier in the eighteenth century in the disputes of printers and political and religious authorities over dissemination of newspapers and other printed materials that embodied controversial themes. The American Revolution brought journalists and politicians tightly together in the political communication work system, an occupational social structure that included work tasks and groups involved in the communication of political information. In addition to simply acquainting the public with the idea that printers, instead of political elites, were to be looked to as regular providers of political information in newspapers, journalists faced resistance in both friendly and opposing political camps.

But journalists also were forced to appease readers' distrust of politicians and discomfort with public displays of partisanship. That the founders of the new government established a system of political communication based on a set of more open, democratic principles did not change the fact that Americans needed a very long time to overcome their distaste, and even fears, that were inspired by rabid political partisanship. Journalists were involved in the dissemination of partisanship. Therefore, to establish themselves as political communicators, journalists as early as the American Revolution period claimed to be doing work that only independent journalists could do in such a way that it would meet the public's needs.

The rhetoric in this battle between journalists and politicians over which group should be looked to as the nation's primary issuers of political information in newspapers was fought in very simplistic terms. Prospectuses and libel courtroom statements published in public media glossed over important distinctions and hierarchies that existed within the actual workplaces in which journalists practiced their craft. The prospectuses examined were sometimes produced by newspaper publishers and sometimes by editors. But distinctions rarely appear in prospectuses; the authors write as if in one voice, for one group. Journalists are portrayed as representing all who practice journalism and all of society, even though this is a distortion. In addition, over the years subcategories of journalistic workers developed that had different amounts of power over their work. Reporters, for example, are generally not empowered with as much decision making as are editors. Women, African Americans, and others who involved themselves in journalistic work during the nineteenth century were also invisible in journalistic discourses that constructed journalism as occupation. This history of the discursive practices of mainstream newspaper journalists helps explain why until recently, the roles and contributions of women and others in journalism have been overlooked. Again, such distinctions as they existed or were developing did not appear in prospectuses or other occupational discourses of nineteenth-century mainstream journalists.

An important question coming out of this research is whether the origins of such problematic journalistic concepts like objectivity and news balance lie in the dynamics that precipitated occupational development. Schudson relates the origins of journalistic objectivity to the rise of an emphasis on science in the late nineteenth century, while Schiller puts them in the penny press era.[3] This research suggests that the idea that journalists are objective, that is, detached, and therefore better suited than others to be charged with the responsibility of present the public with views of the world may be linked to occupational development that began before the penny press era. Some journalists sought to convey the impression that they were independent from politicians as early as the American Revolution period, and such efforts continued through the nineteenth century. While some historians have already noted this, their analysis of the meaning of such independence is largely limited to politics. The argument here is that one can also view independence as a stance that one would want to take if one were seeking to distinguish oneself occupationally as well. If one accepts the premise that objectivity may have been a hybrid standard that grew out of claims of journalistic independence, the evidence collected in this research points to the possibility that notions that later were labeled as objectivity may have been born earlier than previously thought.

The model presented in Chapter 1, a broad one that addresses many aspects of journalism's occupational and professional development, offers much promise for future studies of journalists and their work. In its examination of two historical periods — the American Revolution and Era of Good Feelings — and two categories of communication — prospectuses and libel courtroom testimony — the findings presented here indicate a beginning.

A crucial aspect of the social construction of work jurisdictions, for example, were journalists' sensitivities to the public's concern about the scurrility and partiality of political rhetoric. Such sensitivity, along with other forces journalists had to contend with, played roles in shaping journalistic work. Population changes in nineteenth-century America undoubtedly played a role, including the movement of people west and south and the growth of urban centers. These and other developments merit study, as well as other rhetorical forms and strategies that journalists likely developed to meet their occupational goals.

This study raises important questions about the role of changes in the political system and the transformation of the political culture in the development of journalistic work. Although the effects of the American Revolution and Era of Good Feelings have revealed much about how developments in politics affect occupations like journalism, future scholarship could explore other similar areas, such the public perception of politics and dissemination of political communication. Early in the nineteenth century, politics was largely informal, more akin to family social structures than the more impersonal societal structures. Not well thought of, political office was not sought after. But by the end of the century, politics and politicians had become more popular than they had ever been in America. No longer disdained, as they had been earlier in the century, politicians nevertheless were still often ruthlessly criticized. And popular politics was considered the lifeblood of America; more citizens voted in late nineteenth-century elections than during any other period in American history.[4] The impact of this on the public's perception of journalists, and ultimately the development of journalistic work, merits study.

Questions also arise here about the meaning of independence in journalistic statements in late eighteenth-, and early nineteenth-century prospectuses. Such ideas proliferated in early America, since journalists claimed independence from politicians not only in newspaper prospectuses and libel courtroom statements, but also in other published forms of communication. Masthead slogans, for example, sometimes carried this idea. The *Antioch (Illinois) News*, on 19 January 1893, carried the slogan: "Independence in all things, neutral in nothing, and for the right as we understand the right to be." Newspaper titles also featured the word "independent." Examples from across the two centuries include: *The Independent Whig*, in Philadelphia, in 1724; *The Independent Reflector*, in New York, in 1753; the *Independent Ledger, and the American Advertiser*, in Boston, in 1778; the *Independent Press and Freedom's Advocate*, in Cincinnati, Ohio, in 1822; the *Independent Inquirer*, in Brattleboro, Vermont, in 1834; *The Independent-Leader*, in Bridgeport, Connecticut, 1890; and *The Independent Voter*, in Toledo, Ohio, in 1905.

An examination of the statements in prospectuses reveals an important similarity among most, whether issued in 1775, 1800, or 1900. It is clear that most journalists were concerned chiefly with their independence from some political entity.[5] There were, however, subtle differences. The nature and locus of the political entity journalists claimed independence from changed. During periods of extreme crisis, such as the American Revolution, the authors of journalistic statements on political independence said they would work to be free from the control of tyrants, but the nature of such tyranny differed depending on whether one was a Patriot or a Tory. Later, during the crises that culminated in the 1798 Alien and Sedition Acts and the War of 1812, the locus of the tyrants depended on whether the author was a Republican or Federalist.[6] As the nation's multiparty system developed and Americans gradually overcame fears about being invaded by tyrants from across the seas, the authors claimed they were independent from politicians, whatever the party, in their communities.

Despite these differences, journalists' statements nevertheless were similar in that authors meant to differentiate themselves from politicians, political parties, and/or factions. Irrespective of the nature of the political entities journalists pitted themselves against, from before the American Revolution, they were involved in differentiating themselves from one type or another of politicians and/or political systems. All of the statements, despite subtle differences, can be construed as part of a process that led to the construction of a model of a politically independent press.

Finally, questions naturally arise about the duration of the struggles between journalists and politicians and whether journalists achieved full jurisdiction over their political communication work. The struggles between the two groups continue; neither journalists nor politicians have acquired full jurisdiction over the dissemination of political information since the American Revolution created a communication system meant to involve both the citizens and their representatives.

But while the competitive struggle has never ended, its intensity has varied depending on events and circumstances in the more general political and social environment. This research looked at the impact of only the American Revolution and the political changes of the Era of Good Feelings, but other events affected the relationship of journalists and politicians. Only when one or the other group achieves full jurisdiction or becomes disinterested in the control and manipulation of the political information that enters the public arena might jurisdictional struggles between them cease — and then perhaps only briefly.

The nature of the jurisdictional settlement between journalists and politicians is more difficult to address. Certainly, journalists sought full jurisdiction over political communication work, since every occupational group aims for complete, legally established control over its work. But more likely, journalists, who have never wrested complete control of the issuance of political information from politicians, because they have never been able to break all their dependencies on them, have had to settle for a less powerful form of jurisdiction.

While newspaper journalists were able to break away from dependence on politicians for financial support because they increasingly developed other support and became more socially legitimate, they could never fully stop depending on politicians for political knowledge. Full jurisdiction of journalists over political communication work has never been possible for various reasons, chief among them the fact that the knowledge system on which their work depends — knowledge of politics — is to some extent in the hands of politicians and government officials. Because journalism is based on gathering and publishing facts, journalists must acquire political knowledge, either through direct observation or from others within the political system. While journalists can acquire some political knowledge through direct observation, they are unable to acquire all such knowledge that way. Thus, politicians have a tool they can use to deprive journalists of political knowledge, and this makes full jurisdiction impossible for journalists.

Perhaps an even more crucial reason why journalists have never gained full jurisdiction over political communication work is that politicians, not journalists, are structurally closer to the reigns of power in government. All too often, especially during political crises, journalists have been painfully reminded that they serve the public at the pleasure of the state. Libel law, emergency war powers acts, and other legal and constitutional impediments have made it impossible for journalists to fully control their work.[7] Hence, while journalists, like all aspiring professionals, desire full jurisdiction over political communication in newspapers and other media, they cannot achieve it completely because of these important links to the politicians and the historical realities of the American democratic and legal systems.

But neither are journalists fully subordinated to politicians. Formal and informal mechanisms have developed as journalists have sought to control their work. Examples of informal supports include the accumulation of public acceptance and the diverse political communication forms that provide some flexibility in dependence on political sources. In editorial writing, journalists can afford to be less dependent on political sources than they can in political news, where the attribution standards today require that journalists depend heavily on political sources. Examples of more formal structural mechanisms are the constitutional protections afforded by the First Amendment to the United States Constitution and favorable court decisions, such as *New York Times vs. Sullivan*.[8]

A number of different forms of jurisdictional settlements are possible: full jurisdiction; complete subordination of one group under the other; divisions of labor that splits jurisdiction into interdependent parts; the sharing of jurisdictions, wherein interdependent groups share an area without division of labor; advisory settlements, where one group is allowed advisory control over certain aspects of the work; and divisions of jurisdiction based on the nature of clients.[9] Among these, since neither full jurisdiction nor total subordination seem appropriate, the settlement that appears most to fit journalists and politicians is the sharing of a jurisdiction, wherein interdependent groups share an area without a formal division of labor.

But regardless of whether journalists have been granted full jurisdiction over their work, the power of the occupational discourses they constructed encouraged most Americans to accept their basic tenets by 1900. The strength of the ideas embodied within journalistic occupational discourse may explain why reporters, despite their low pay and difficult working conditions, often did not greet the idea of banding together in trade unions with much enthusiasm. As journalists, a group with an aura that smacked of lofty purposes, intellectualism, and power, why would they want to associate with trade unionists? In addition, the power of the discourse might also help explain why mass communication scholars and teachers of journalism have so stubbornly adhered to its liberal progressive vision of journalism and journalists in their histories of journalism and journalism textbooks.[10]

Because of the legal and constitutional protections in various twentieth-century U. S. Supreme Court decisions, contemporary journalists likely have more jurisdiction over their political communication work than their nineteenth-century predecessors had. Despite this, any power journalists may have amassed over their work is always subject to erosion because of shifts within the environment and campaigns launched by politicians who seek to curtail journalistic authority. The Washington political press corps today complains because members of the Clinton administration and other politicians and government officials, aided by 1990s technology, have been able to by-pass journalists seeking to serve the public through traditional journalistic forms. Politicians and executive and governmental power structures have used television and radio talk shows to get to the people with their messages. Such a strategy precipitated by changes in technology has touched off a jurisdictional struggle between journalists and politicians, which will be played out in the years to come.[11] The ability of future journalists to maintain authority over their political communication roles will largely depend on their willingness to confront those in the political communication community who invade their work turf and on their constant reassessment and reconstruction of their discursive strategies.

NOTES

1. E. W. Howe, *Plain People* (New York: Dodd, Mead and Co., 1929), 141.

2. Andrew Abbott, *System of Professions: An Essay in the Division of Labor* (Chicago: University of Chicago, 1988), 8.

3. Dan Schiller, *Objectivity and the News: The Public and the Rise of Commercial Journalism* (Philadelphia: University of Pennsylvania Press, 1981); Michael Schudson, *Discovering the News: A Social History of American Newspapers* (New York: Basic Books, 1978).

4. Thomas T. Mackie, *The International Almanac of Electoral History* (New York: Free Press, 1974).

5. In addition, in the later decades studied, there were a few who broadened their definition of journalistic independence to include independence from business interests, such as one journalistic author who claimed that he was not controlled by the railroad interests who wielded much power within his broader community. Another journalistic author, setting up a newspaper in Mandan, North Dakota, said that, while cattle was king, he would not be controlled by cattle interests and their concerns alone. See the prospectus of the *Bad Lands Cow Boy* (Medora, ND, 1884).

6. See, for example, the following prospectuses, which discuss the War of 1812: *Albany (New York) Argus* (1812); *Rhode-Island American* (Providence, 1813); *Rhode-Island American* (Providence, 1814).

7. See, for example, the following: Randall P. Bezanson, Gilbert Cranberg, and John Soloski, *Libel Law and the Press* (New York: Free Press, 1987); H. C. Peterson and Gilbert Fite, *Opponents of War, 1917-1918* (Seattle, WA: University of Washington Press, 1957); Paul L. Murphy, *The Meaning of Freedom of Speech: First Amendment Freedoms from Wilson to FDR,* Contributions in American History Series (Westport, CT: Greenwood Press, 1972).

8. *New York Times vs. Sullivan,* 376 U.S. 254 (1964). See also Jeremy Cohen, *Congress Shall Make No Law* (Ames, IA: Iowa State Univesity Press, 1989); J. Edward Gerald, *The Press and the Constitution* (Minneapolis, MN: University of Minnesota Press, 1948); Rodney Smolla, *Suing the Press* (New York: Oxford University Press,

1986).

9. Abbott, *System of Professions*, 8-9.

10. See Chapter 1 of Hanno Hardt and Bonnie Brennen, eds., *Newsworkers: A History of the Rank and File* (Minneapolis, MN: University of Minnesota Press, 1995), for a critique of journalism history in terms of its blindness to the histories of the rank and file.

11. Michael Schudson, "The Limits of Teledemocracy," *American Prospect* 11 (Fall 1992): 41-45; Patricia L. Dooley and Paul G. Grosswiler, "'Turf Wars': The New Media and the Struggle for Control of Political News," *The Harvard International Journal of Press/Politics* 2 (Summer 1997): 31-51; speech of David Broder, presented at the annual conference of the Silha Center at the University of Minnesota, April, 1996; speech of David Lamb, presented at the annual conference of the Maine Association of Journalists, 25 April 1993.

Appendix: Newspaper Prospectuses

EIGHTEENTH CENTURY

Boston News-Letter (17 April 1704)
Boston Gazette (21 December 1719)
American Weekly Mercury (Philadelphia; 22 December 1719)
New England Courant (Boston; 7 August 1721)
New England Weekly Journal (Boston; 20 March 1727)
Pennsylvania Gazette, or the Universal Instructor (Philadelphia; 1 October 1728)
Weekly Advertiser/Pennsylvania Journal (Philadelphia; 2 December 1742)
Occasional Reverberator (New York; 7 September 1753)
New Hampshire Gazette (Portsmouth; 7 October 1756)
Weyman's New York Gazette (16 February 1759)
Providence (Rhode Island) Gazette and Country Journal (20 October 1762)
Georgia Gazette (Savannah; 7 April 1763)
Connecticut Courant (Hartford; 29 October 1764)
Pennsylvania Chronicle (26 January 1767)
Boston Chronicle (21 December 1767)
Connecticut Journal and New Haven Post Boy (23 October 1767)
Essex Gazette (Salem, Massachusetts; 2 August 1768)
New York Chronicle (8 May 1769)
Pennsylvania Packet (Philadelphia; 28 October 1771)
Censor (Boston; 30 November 1771)
Continental Journal and Weekly Advertiser (Boston; 30 May 1776)
Independent Ledger and American Advertiser (15 June 1778)
New-York Gazetteer (4 August 1783)
Vermont Journal (Windsor; 7 August 1783)
Independent Journal (New York; 17 November 1783)
Massachusetts Centinel and Republican Journal (Boston; 1 March 1784)
New-Haven (Connecticut) Gazette (6 May 1784)
Carlisle (Pennsylvania) Gazette & Western Repository of Knowledge (17 August 1785)
Middlesex Gazette (Middletown, Connecticut; 8 November 1785)
New-Haven Gazette and the Connecticut Magazine (15 February 1786)

Newport (Rhode Island) Gazette (1 March 1787)
Albany (New York) Journal (2 February 1788)
Federal Gazette & Philadelphia Evening (16 October 1788)
General Advertiser (Philadelphia; 4 October 1790)
Massachusetts Mercury (Boston; 1 January 1793)
Baltimore Daily Intelligencer (28 October 1793)
Centinel of the North-Western Territory (Cincinnati; 9 November 1793)
Hartford (Connecticut) Gazette (13 January 1794)
Columbia (South Carolina) Gazette (14 January 1794)
Massachusetts Mercury (Boston; 8 April 1794)
Federal Orrery (Boston; 20 October 1794)
Eagle; or, Dartmouth Centinel (Hanover, New Hampshire; 6 April 1795)
Courier (Boston; 1 July 1795)
Oriental Trumpet (Portland, Maine; 22 August 1796)
Centinel of Freedom (Newark, New Jersey; 5 October 1796)
Polar Star; Boston Daily Advertiser (6 October 1796)
The Bee (New London, Connecticut; 14 June 1797)
Commercial Advertiser (New York City; 2 October 1797)
Journal of the Times (Stonington, Connecticut; 10 October 1790)
Western Spy (Cincinnati; 28 May 1799)
Constitutional Telegraph (Boston; 2 October 1799)

NINETEENTH CENTURY: 1800-1830

National Intelligencer (Washington, D.C.; 3 November 1800)
True American (Trenton, New Jersey; 10 March 1801)
Newburyport (Massachusetts) Herald (4 August 1801)
New York Evening Journal (16 November 1801)
Litchfield (Connecticut) Gazette (16 March 1802)
Kentucky Gazette (Lexington; 2 April 1802)
Greenfield (Massachusetts) Gazette (7 June 1802)
Weekly Visitor or Ladies' Miscellaney (New York City; 9 October 1802)
Farmers' Cabinet (Amherst, New Hampshire; 11 November 1802)
Charleston (South Carolina) Courier (10 January 1803)
Democrat (Boston; 4 January 1804)
Suffolk Gazette (Sag Harbor, New York; 20 February 1804)
Saratoga Advertiser (Ballston Spa, New York; 12 November 1804)
Lancaster (Pennsylvania) True American (12 June 1805)
Boston Courier (13 June 1805)
The Witness (Litchfield, Connecticut; 14 August 1805)
Genesee Messenger (Canandaigua, New York; 25 November 1806)
True Republican (New London, Connecticut; 1 July 1807)
Western Star (Lebanon, Ohio; 13 February 1807)
American Patriot (Concord, New Hampshire; 18 October 1808)
Carthage (Tennessee) Gazette (13 August 1808)
Clarion (Nashville, Tennessee; 26 January 1808)
Portland (Maine) Gazette (12 September 1808)
Supporter (Chillicothe, Ohio; 6 October 1808)

American Advocate (Hallowell, Maine; 18 October 1809)
The Balance (Albany, New York; 4 January 1809)
Boston Daily Advertiser (5 June 1809)
Boston Patriot & American Republican (3 March 1809)
Columbian (New York City; 14 October 1809)
Connecticut Mirror (Hartford; 10 July 1809)
Green-Mountain Farmer (Bennington, Vermont; 17 April 1809)
Independent American & Columbian Advertiser (Washington, D.C.; 11 July 1809)
American Advocate (Hallowell, Maine; 23 January 1810)
Orange County Patriot (Goshen, New York; 9 March 1809)
Fredonian (Boston; 20 February 1810)
Republican Farmer (Bridgeport, Connecticut; 25 April 1810)
Pennsylvania Republican (Harrisburg; 3 December 1811)
Weekly Messenger (Boston; 25 October 1811)
Western Intelligencer (Worthington, Ohio; 17 July 1811)
Courier (Georgetown, Washington, D.C.; 20 May 1812)
The Pilot (Boston; 25 September 1812)
The Yankee (Boston; 3 January 1812)
Troy (New York) Post (2 September 1812)
Albany (New York) Argus (26 January 1813)
Carthage (Tennessee) Gazette (12 February 1813)
Washington (Tennessee) Republican (13 April 1813)
Rhode Island American (Providence; 8 October 1813)
Rhode-Island American (Providence; 15 April 1814)
Weekly Recorder (Chillicothe, Ohio; 5 July 1814)
Petersburg (Virginia) Daily Courier (21 September 1814)
Spirit of Pennsylvania (Easton; 16 June 1815)
Niagara Journal (Buffalo, New York; 4 July 1815)
Saratoga Courier (Ballston Spa, New York; 6 December 1815)
Liberty Hall and Cincinnati Gazette (11 December 1815)
City and Carolina Gazettes (Charleston, South Carolina; 6 January 1816)
The American (Hanover, New Hampshire; 7 February 1816)
Middlesex Gazette (Concord, Massachusetts; 20 April 1816)
Vermont Gazette (Bennington; 18 June 1816)
The Times (Hartford, Connecticut; 1 January 1817)
National Messenger (Washington, D.C.; 27 October 1817)
Weekly Visitor and Ladies' Museum (New York City; 1 November 1817)
York (Pennsylvania) Recorder (17 February 1818)
Paris (Kentucky) Instructor (2 May 1818)
American Advocate (Hallowell, Maine; 25 July 1818)
Cleaveland [sic] (Ohio) Gazette & Commercial Register (31 July 1818)
Blakeley Sun & Alabama Advertiser (15 December 1818)
Franklin Monitor (Charlestown, Massachusetts; 3 January 1819)
Kentucky Gazette (Lexington; 6 March 1819)
Alabama Courier (Clairborne; 19 March 1819)
Morning Chronicle & Baltimore (Maryland) Advertiser (8 April 1819)
Middlesex Gazette (Concord, Massachusetts; 7 May 1819)
Southern Evangelical Intelligencer (Charleston, South Carolina; 27 March 1819)

Franklin Gazette (Philadelphia; 22 May 1819)

Edwardsville Spectator (Illinois; May 1819)

Hamilton (New York) Recorder (11 June 1819)

(Jackson) Missouri Herald (25 June 1819)

Town Gazette & Farmer's Register (Clarksville, Tennessee; 5 July 1819)

Rhode Island American & General Advertiser (Providence; 6 July 1819)

St. Louis (Missouri) Enquirer (13 August 1819)

York (Pennsylvania) Recorder (28 September 1819)

Arkansas Gazette (Arkansas Post, Arkansas Territory; 20 November 1819)

Florence (Arkansas) Gazette (Prospectus published in the 27 November 1819 issue of
    the *Clarksville Gazette*)

*Manufacturers' & Farmers' Journal, Providence (Rhode Island) & Pawtucket Adver-
    tiser* (3 January 1820)

Lexington (Kentucky) Public Advertiser (5 January 1820)

Columbian Advocate and Franklin Chronicle (Worthington, Ohio; 7 January 1820)

The Mountaineer (Easton, Pennsylvania; 7 January 1820)

Woodstock (Vermont) Observer (11 January 1820)

Clarksville (Tennessee) Gazette (20 January 1820)

The Metropolitan & Georgetown Commercial Advertiser (Washington, D.C.; 26 January
    1820)

Orange Farmer (Goshen, New York; 12 February 1820)

National Gazette & Literary Review (Philadelphia; 5 April 1820)

Western Spy and Literary Cadet (Cincinnati; 29 April 1820)

New York Statesman (Albany; 16 May 1820)

Illinois Gazette (Shawneetown; 27 May 1820)

Western Carolinian (Salisbury, North Carolina; 13 June 1820)

Village Register & Norfolk County Advertiser (Dedham, Massachusetts; 16 June 1820)

Missourian (St. Charles; 24 June 1820)

Patron of Industry (New York City; 28 June 1820)

Hancock Gazette (Belfast, Maine; 6 July 1820)

American Farmer (Baltimore; 25 August 1820)

Montgomery (Alabama) Republican (25 August 1820)

Clarion (Nashville, Tennessee; 5 September 1820)

Republican Chronicle (Ithaca, New York; 6 September 1820)

Maine Intelligencer (Brunswick; 23 September 1820)

(Harrisburg) Pennsylvania Intelligencer (Prospectus published in the 1 December 1820
    issue of the *Mountaineer*)

(Bath) Maine Gazette (8 December 1820)

American Statesman (Boston; 6 February 1821)

Charleston (South Carolina) Mercury (1 January 1822)

Northern Intelligencer (Plattsburgh, New York; 7 May 1822)

National Republican and Ohio Political Register (Cincinnati; 1 January 1823)

Alexandria (Virginia) Phenix [sic] Gazette (1 January 1825)

Patriot (Greensboro, North Carolina; 24 April 1826)

Plattsburgh (New York) Times (12 February 1827)

Waldo Democrat (Belfast, Maine; c. 1827)

Ladies' Port Folio (Boston; 1 January 1828)

Missouri Republican (St. Louis; 25 March 1828)

The Atlas (New York City; 20 September 1828)
Greensborough (North Carolina) Patriot (23 May 1829)
Evening Transcript (Boston; 24 July 1830)

NINETEENTH CENTURY: 1870-1900

The New Era (Washington, D.C.; 13 January 1870)
Boston Daily Globe (4 March 1872)
The Daily Graphic (New York City; 4 March 1873)
Mankato (Minnesota) Free Press (16 April 1873)
Bismarck (North Dakota) Tribune (11 July 1873)
The Anti-Monopolist (Bloomington, Illinois; 14 August 1873)
Whitehall Sentinel (Published in an unidentified New England state; 23 September
     1875)
Ashland (Wisconsin) Weekly Eagle (2 March 1876)
The People's Rights (Nashua, Iowa; 4 July 1878)
Schoolcraft County Pioneer (Manisque, Michigan; 29 April 1880)
The Exodus (Washington, D.C.; 1 May 1880)
Rural Citizen (Jacksboro, Texas; 4 June 1880)
Topeka (Kansas) Tribune (24 June 1880)
Los Angeles Daily Times (4 December 1881)
District Post (Postville, Iowa; 10 August 1882)
Saturday Evening Post (Burlington, Iowa; 19 August 1882)
The Mortar (New Harmony, Indiana; 12 May 1883)
Cleveland (Ohio) Gazette (25 August 1883)
The Times (Salt Lake City; 1 October 1883)
The Grit (Washington, D.C.; 21 December 1883)
Bad Lands Cow Boy (Medora, North Dakota; 7 February 1884)
Elsie (Michigan) Leader (16 August 1884)
Rockbridge County News (Lexington, Virginia.; 7 November 1884)
Elsie (Michigan) Sun (9 January 1885)
Menominee (Michigan) Democrat (7 November 1885)
The Alaskan (Territory of Alaska; 7 November 1885)
The Advocate (Los Angeles; 17 April 1886)
The News (Newberry, Michigan; 10 June 1886)
Osceola County Democrat (Reed City, Michigan; 28 July 1886)
Weekly Pelican (New Orleans, Louisiana; 4 December 1886)
Admire City (Kansas) Free Press (7 January 1887)
Evening Statesman (Marshall, Michigan; 15 January 1887)
Admire City (Kansas) Free Press (27 May 1887)
Tahlequah (Indian Territory) Telephone (10 June 1887)
Ashland (Wisconsin) Sunday News (25 September 1887)
American Citizen (Topeka, Kansas; 23 February 1888)
Advocate (Leavenworth, Kansas; 25 August 1888)
Imlay City (Michigan) Times (30 November 1888)
Pacific Union (San Francisco and San Jose; 5 January 1889)
Guthrie (Oklahoma) Getup (29 April 1889)
The Amery (Wisconsin) Echo (14 June 1889)

Weekly Sentinel (Dothan, Alabama; 4 June 1890)
Amherst (Wisconsin) Advertiser (16 September 1890)
Sunday Morning Star (Marquette, Michigan; 12 October 1890)
Weekly News (New Harmony, Indiana; 20 November 1890)
Alger County Democrat (Munising, Michigan; 4 April 1891)
Hanover (Michigan) Local (13 June 1891)
Times-Observer (Topeka, Kansas; 4 September 1891)
Wason (Colorado) Miner (12 December 1891)
Southern California Guide (16 January 1892)
Amherst (Wisconsin) Advocate (22 February 1893)
Hawaiian Star (Honolulu; 28 March 1893)
Advance (Admire, Kansas; 8 April 1893)
Agra (Kansas) News (22 July 1893)
Menominee (Michigan) Journal (26 August 1893)
Agra (Kansas) News (21 October 1893)
The Morning Sun (Tahlequah, Indian Territory; 6 November 1893)
East Dubuque (Iowa) Register (2 February 1894)
Newberry (Michigan) Enterprise (8 February 1894)
Lodi (Wisconsin) Enterprise (16 February 1894)
Leavenworth (Kansas) Herald (17 February 1894)
Agra (Kansas) News (27 October 1894)
Agra (Kansas) News (1 March 1895)
Broad Ax (Salt Lake City; 31 August 1895)
Southern Democrat (Blountsville, Alabama; 18 October 1895)
Admire (Kansas) Journal (1 November 1895)
National Reflector (Wichita, Kansas; 8 December 1895)
Independent News (Girard, Kansas; 18 May 1896)
Algoma (Wisconsin) Press (6 October 1897)
Kansas Razoo (Agra, Kansas; 4 December 1896)
Adair County News (Columbia, Kentucky; 3 November 1897)
Marshall (Michigan) News (11 March 1898)
The Pioneer (Muscogee, Indian Territory; 24 June 1898)
Antigo (Wisconsin) Journal (17 September 1898)
(Agra) Kansas Breeze (22 September 1898)
Toledo (Ohio) Saturday Night (22 April 1899)
Cripple Creek (Colorado) Daily Press (17 June 1899)
Apple River (Wisconsin) Advance (27 September 1899)
Gold Digger (Nome, Alaska; 25 October 1899)
Daily News (Marshall, Michigan; 30 October 1899)
The Herald (Menominee, Michigan; 1899)
Woodsville (New Hampshire) News (5 January 1900)
Searchlight (Wichita, Kansas; 2 June 1900)
Adirondack News (Utica & Old Forge, New York; 4 July 1900)
Los Angeles Democrat (20 September 1900)
Huntsville (Alabama) Star (1900)

Bibliography

BOOKS

Abbe, Cleveland. *Abbe-Abbey Genealogy*. New Haven, CT: The Tuttle, Morehouse and Taylor Company, 1916.

Abbott, Andrew. *The System of Professions: An Essay on the Division of Labor*. Chicago: University of Chicago Press, 1988.

Abbott, Philip. *In States of Perfect Freedom: Autobiography and American Political Thought*. Amherst, MA: University of Massachusetts Press, 1987.

Abrams, Philip. *Historical Sociology*. Ithaca, NY: Cornell University Press, 1982.

Altschull, J. Herbert. *Agents of Power: The News Media in Human Affairs*. New York: Longman, 1984.

Ames, William H. *A History of the "National Intelligencer."* Chapel Hill, NC: University of North Carolina Press, 1972.

Anderson, Elliott, and Mary Kinzie, eds. *The Little Magazine in America: A Modern Documentary History*. Yonkers, NY: Pushcart, 1978.

Bailyn, Bernard. *The Ideological Origins of the American Revolution*. Cambridge, MA: Harvard University Press, 1967.

Bailyn, Bernard, and John B. Hench, eds. *The Press and the American Revolution*. Worcester, MA: American Antiquarian Society, 1980.

Baldasty, Gerald J. *The Commercialization of the News in the Nineteenth Century*. Madison, WI: University of Wisconsin Press, 1992.

Balk, Alfred. *A Free and Responsive Press*. New York: Twentieth Century Fund, 1973.

Beaumont, W. Newhall. *The History of Photography from 1839 to Present*. New York: Museum of Modern Art, 1982.

Bennett, W. Lance. *News: The Politics of Illusion*. White Plains, NY: Longman, 1988.

Berelson, Bernard, Paul F. Lazarsfeld, and William McPhee. *Voting: A Study of Opinion Formation in a Presidential Campaign*. Chicago: University of Chicago Press, 1954.

Berger, P. L., and T. Luckmann. *The Social Construction of Reality*. London: Allen Lane, 1966.

Beringer, Richard R. *Historical Analysis: Contemporary Approaches to Clio's Craft*. New York: Wiley, 1978.

Bezanson, Randall P., Gilbert Cranberg, and John Soloski. *Libel Law and the Press.* New York: Free Press, 1987.

Binkley, Wilfred E. *American Political Parties: Their Natural History.* New York: Knopf, 1963.

Blanchard, Margaret A. "Filling the Void: Speech and Press in State Courts Prior to *Gitlow*." In *The First Amendment Reconsidered.* Ed. Bill F. Chamberlin and Charlene J. Brown. New York: Longman, 1982.

Bledstein, Burton. *The Culture of Professionalism.* New York: Norton, 1976.

Bleyer, William G. *Main Currents in the History of American Journalism.* Boston: Houghton Mifflin, 1927.

Bloch, Maurice. *Political Language and Oratory in Traditional Society.* London; New York: Academic Press, 1975.

Boardman, Samuel L. *Peter Edes, Pioneer Printer in Maine.* Bangor, ME: Printed for the DeBurians, 1901.

Bonadio, Felice A., ed. *Political Parties in American History.* Vol. 2, *1828-1890.* New York: G. P. Putnam's Sons, 1974.

Bond, Donovan H., and W. Reynolds McLeod, eds. *Newsletters to Newspapers: Eighteenth-Century Journalism.* Morgantown, WV: West Virginia University, 1977.

Borden, Morton. *Parties and Politics in the Early Republic: 1789-1815.* New York: Crowell, 1967.

Botein, Stephen. "Printers and the American Revolution." In *The Press and the American Revolution.* Ed. Bernard Bailyn and John B. Hench. Worcester, MA: American Antiquarian Society, 1980.

Boyce, George, James Curran, and Pauline Wingate, eds. *Newspaper History: From the Seventeenth Century to the Present Day.* Beverly Hills, CA: Sage, 1978.

Bradley, Joseph F. *The Role of Trade Associations and Professional Business Societies in America.* University Park, PA: Pennsylvania State University Press, 1965.

Bridenbaugh, Carl. *Cities in the Wilderness: The First Century of Urban Life in America, 1625-1742.* New York: Knopf, 1955.

Brigham, Clarence S. *History and Bibliography of American Newspapers, 1690-1820.* Worcester, MA: American Antiquarian Society, 1947.

Brown, Richard D. *Knowledge Is Power: The Diffusion of Information in Early America, 1700-1865.* New York; Oxford: Oxford University Press, 1989.

————. *Modernization: The Transformation of American Life, 1600-1865.* New York: Hill & Wang, 1976.

Brown, Robert E. *Middle-Class Democracy and the Revolution in Massachusetts, 1691-1780.* Ithaca, NY: Cornell University Press, 1955.

Buckingham, Joseph Tinker. *Specimens of Newspaper Literature.* 2 vols. Boston: Charles C. Little and James Brown, 1850.

Bunnell, A. O., comp. *New York Press Association, Authorized History for Fifty Years, 1853-1903.* Dansville, NY: F. A. Owen Publishing Co., 1903.

Buranelli, Vincent, ed. *The Trial of Peter Zenger.* New York: New York University Press, 1957.

Burke, Peter. *Sociology and History.* London: George Allen and Unwin, 1980.

Burrage, Michael, and Rolf Torstendahl, eds. *Professions in Theory and History.* London: Sage, 1990.

Campbell, Karlyn Kohrs. *The Rhetorical Act.* Belmont, CA: Wadsworth, 1982.

Caplow, Theodore. *The Sociology of Work*. Minneapolis, MN: University of Minnesota Press, 1953.

Carey, James. *Communication as Culture: Essays on Media and Society*. Boston: Unwin Hyman, 1989.

Carr-Saunders, A. M., and P. A. Wilson. *The Professions*. Oxford: Clarendon Press, 1933.

Chaffee, Steven H., ed. *Political Communication: Issues and Strategies for Research*. Beverly Hills, CA: Sage, 1975.

Chambers, William H., and Philip C. Davis. "Party Competition and Mass Participation: The Case of the Democratizing Party System, 1824-1852." In *The History of American Electoral Behavior*. Ed. Joel H. Silbey, Allan G. Bogne, and William H. Flanigan. Princeton, NJ: Princeton University Press, 1978.

Chambers, William H., and Walter Burnham, eds. *The American Party Systems: Stages of Political Development*. New York: Oxford University Press, 1967.

Chartier, Roger. "Texts, Printing, Readings." In *The New Cultural History*. Ed. Lynn Hunt. Berkeley, CA: University of California Press, 1989.

Chartier, Roger, ed. *The Culture of Print: Power and the Use of Print in Early Modern Europe*. Trans. Lydia G. Cochrane. Princeton, NJ: Princeton University Press, 1989.

Chase, James. *Emergence of the Presidential Nominating Convention, 1789-1832*. Urbana, IL: University of Illinois Press, 1973.

Chess, Wayne A., and Julia M. Norlin. *Human Behavior and the Social Environment: A Social Systems Model*. Needham Heights, MA: Allyn and Bacon, 1988.

Chomsky, Noam. *Deterring Democracy*. London: Verso, 1991.

Clark, Charles E. *The Public Prints: The Newspaper in Anglo-American Culture, 1665-1740*. New York: Oxford University Press, 1994.

Coggeshall, W. T. *The Newspaper Record, Containing a Complete List of Newspapers and Periodicals in the United States, Canadas and Great Britain*. Philadelphia, PA: Lay and Brother, 1856.

Cohen, Jeremy. *Congress Shall Make No Law*. Ames, IA: Iowa State University Press, 1989.

Cohen, Jeremy, and Timothy Gleason. *Social Research in Communication and Law*. Sage CommText Series. Newbury, CA.: Sage, 1990.

Collingwood, R. G. *The Idea of History*. New York: Oxford University Press, 1956.

Condit, Lester. *A Pamphlet about Pamphlets*. Chicago: University of Chicago Press, 1939.

Cook, Elizabeth C. *Literary Influences in Colonial Newspapers, 1704-1750*. New York: Columbia University Press, 1912.

Cortner, Richard C. *The Supreme Court and the Second Bill of Rights*. Madison, WI: University of Wisconsin Press, 1981.

Cranfield, G. A. *The Press and Society: From Caxton to Northcliffe*. London: Longman, 1978.

Cullen, John B. *The Structure of Professionalism*. New York; Princeton, NJ: Petrocelli Books, 1978.

Curti, Merle. *The Growth of American Thought*. New York: Harper & Row, 1964.

Dana, Henry Swan. *History of Woodstock, Vermont*. Boston; New York: Houghton Mifflin, 1889.

Dangerfield, George. *The Era of Good Feelings*. New York: Harcourt, Brace and World, 1952.

Davidson, Philip. *Propaganda and the American Revolution*. Chapel Hill, NC: University of North Carolina Press, 1941.

Dennis, Jack, ed. *Socialization to Politics: A Reader*. New York: Wiley, 1973.

Denzin, Norman K. *Interpretive Biography*. Sage University Paper Series on Qualitative Research Methods. Beverly Hills, CA: Sage, 1989.

Deutsch, Karl. *The Nerves of Government*. New York: Free Press, 1963.

Dexter, Franklin B. *Biographical Sketches of the Graduates of Yale College with Annals of the College History*. 6 vols. New York: H. Holt and Company, 1885-1912.

Dicken-Garcia, Hazel. *Journalistic Standards in Nineteenth-Century America*. Madison, WI: University of Wisconsin Press, 1989.

Dijk, T. A. van. *Text and Context: Explorations in the Semantics and Pragmatics of Discourse*. London: Longman, 1977.

Dill, William Adelbert. *Growth of Newspapers in the United States*. Lawrence, KS: University of Kansas, 1928.

Dillon, Merton L. *The Abolitionists: The Growth of a Dissenting Minority*. DeKalb, IL: Northern Illinois University Press, 1974.

Dingwall, Robert, and Philip Lewis, eds. *The Sociology of the Professions: Lawyers, Doctors and Others*. London: Macmillan Press, 1983.

Donohue, George A., Phillip J. Tichenor, and Clarice N. Olien. *Community Conflict and the Press*. Beverly Hills, CA: Sage, 1980.

Drechsel, Robert E. *News Making in the Trial Courts*. New York: Longman, 1983.

Duniway, Clyde A. *The Development of Freedom of the Press in Massachusetts*. New York: Longmans, Green & Company, 1906.

Duranti, Alessandro. "Oratory." In *International Encyclopedia of Communications*. 1992 ed., s.v. "Oratory."

Durkheim, Emile. *The Division of Labour in Society*. New York: Macmillan, 1933.

————. *Professional Ethics and Civic Morals*. London: Routledge, 1957.

Eisenstein, Elizabeth. *The Printing Revolution in Early Modern Europe*. 2 vols. Cambridge; New York: Cambridge University Press, 1983.

Elliott, Philip. "Media Organizations and Occupations: An Overview." In *Mass Communication and Society*. Ed. James Curran, Michael Gurevitch, and Janet Woollacott. Beverly Hills, CA: Sage, 1979.

Ely, John Hart. *Democracy and Distrust: A Theory of Judicial Review*. Cambridge: Harvard University Press, 1980.

Emery, Edwin. *History of the American Newspaper Publishers Association*. Minneapolis, MN: University of Minnesota, 1949.

Emery, Edwin, and Michael Emery. *The Press in America*. 7th ed. Englewood Cliffs, NJ: Prentice Hall, 1992.

Flower, Milton E. *John Dickinson, Conservative Revolutionary*. Charlottesville, VA: University Press of Virginia, 1983.

Form, William H. "Occupations and Careers." In *International Encyclopedia of The Social Sciences*. 1968 ed., s.v. "Occupations and Careers."

Formisano, Ronald P. *The Birth of Mass Political Parties: Michigan, 1827-1861*. Princeton, NJ: Princeton University Press, 1971.

Frank, Joseph. *The Beginnings of the English Newspaper*. Cambridge: Harvard University Press, 1961.

Franklin, Benjamin. *The Autobiography of Benjamin Franklin, The Unmutilated and Correct Version, Compiled and Edited with Notes by John Bigelow*. New York; London: G. P. Putnam's Sons, Knickerbocker Press, 1927.

Franklin, Benjamin. *Boston Printers, Publishers and Booksellers: 1640-1800*. Boston: G. K. Hall & Co., 1980.

Freidson, Eliot. *Profession of Medicine: A Study of the Sociology of Applied Knowledge*. New York: Dodd, Mead, 1970.

Genovese, Eugene. *The World the Slaveholders Made*. New York: Pantheon Books, 1969.

Gerald, J. Edward. *The Press and the Constitution*. Minneapolis, MN: University of Minnesota Press, 1948.

Gilmore, William J. *Reading Becomes a Necessity of Life*. Knoxville, TN: University of Tennessee Press, 1989.

Gleason, Timothy. *The Watchdog Concept: The Press and the Courts in Nineteenth-Century America*. Ames, IA: Iowa State University Press, 1990.

Golding, Peter. "Media Professionalism in the Third World: The Transfer of an Ideology." In *Mass Communication and Society*. Ed. James Curran, Michael Gurevitch, and Janet Woollcott. London: Edward Arnold Press, 1977.

Goodman, Paul. "The First American Party System." In *The American Party Systems*. Ed. Richard P. McCormick and William N. Chambers. New York: Oxford University Press, 1975.

Griffin, Joseph. *History of the Press of Maine*. Brunswick, ME: The Press, 1872.

Haddock, John A. *The Growth of a Century: A History of Jefferson County*. Philadelphia, PA: Sherman and Co., 1894.

Hage, George. *Newspapers on the Minnesota Frontier, 1849-1860*. St. Paul, MN: Minnesota Historical Society, 1967.

Hall, David D. "The World of Print and Collective Mentality in Seventeenth-Century New England." In *New Directions in American Intellectual History*. Ed. John Higham and Paul K. Conkin. Baltimore, MD: Johns Hopkins University Press, 1979.

Hall, David D., and John B. Hench, eds. *Needs and Opportunities in the History of the Book: America, 1639-1876*. Worcester, MA: American Antiquarian Society, 1987.

Hall, Stuart, D. Hobson, and P. Willis, eds. *Culture, Media, Language*. London: Hutchinson, 1980.

Hamilton, Milton W. *The Country Printer: New York State, 1785-1830*. New York: Columbia University Press, 1936.

Hardt, Hanno, and Bonnie Brennen, eds. *Newsworkers: Toward a History of the Rank and File*. Minneapolis, MN: University of Minnesota, 1995.

Harris, Michael, and Allen Lee, eds. *London Newspapers in the Age of Walpole*. Rutherford, NJ: Fairleigh Dickison University Press, 1987.

———. *The Press in English Society from the Seventeenth to the Nineteenth Centuries*. Rutherford, NJ: Farleigh Dickinson University Press, 1968.

Heap, Nick, Ray Thomas, Geogg Einan, Robin Masson, and Hughie MacKay. *Information, Technology and Society*. Thousand Oaks, CA: Sage, 1995.

Heide, Walther. *Die alteste gedruckte Zeitung.* Mainz: Verlag der Gutenberg-Gesellschaft, 1931.

History of Ross and Highland Counties. Evansville, IN: Williams Brothers, 1880.

Hoe, Robert. *Short History of the Printing Press.* New York: R. Hoe and Company, 1902.

Hoerder, Dirk. *Crowd Action in Revolutionary Massachusetts, 1765-1780.* New York: Academic Press, 1977.

Howe, E. W. *Plain People.* New York: Dodd, Mead and Co., 1929.

Hudson, Frederick. *Journalism in the United States from 1690 to 1872.* New York: Harper and Brothers, 1873.

Hughes, Everett C. *Men and Their Work.* Glencoe, IL: Free Press, 1958.

———. *The Sociological Eye: Selected Papers.* Chicago; New York: Aldine-Atherton, 1971.

———. "The Professions." In *The Professions in America.* Ed. Kenneth S. Lynn. *Daedalus* Library Series. Boston: Houghton-Mifflin Co., 1965.

Humphrey, Carol Sue. *This Popular Engine: New England Newspapers During the American Revolution: 1775-1789.* Newark, DE: University of Delaware Press, 1992.

Hurd, D. Hamilton. *History of Franklin County, New York.* Philadelphia: J. W. Lewis & Co., 1880.

Jacobs, Wilbur R. *Dispossessing the American Indian.* Norman, OK: University of Oklahoma Press, 1972.

Jamieson, Kathleen Hall, and Karyl Kohrs Campbell. *The Interplay of Influence: News, Advertising, Politics, and the Mass Media.* Belmont, CA: Wadsworth Publishing, 1997.

Jebb, Richard Claverhouse. "Ancient Organs of Public Opinion." In *Essays and Addresses.* Cambridge: University Press, 1907.

Jensen, Klaus Bruhn, and Nicholas W. Jankowski, eds. *A Handbook of Qualitative Methodologies for Mass Communication Research.* London; New York: Routledge, 1991.

Jensen, Merrill. *The New Nation: A History of the United States During the Confederation, 1781-1789.* New York: Knopf, 1950.

Johnson, Malcolm. "Professional Careers and Biographies." In *The Sociology of the Professions: Lawyers, Doctors and Others.* Ed. Robert Dingwall and Philip Lewis. London: The Macmillan Press, 1983.

Johnson, Terence J. *Professions and Power.* London: Macmillan (British Sociological Association), 1972.

Johnston, Elma Lawson. *Trenton's Newspapers, 1778-1932.* Trenton, NJ: Trenton Times Newspapers, 1932.

Jordan, Winthrop D. *White over Black: American Attitudes Toward the Negro, 1550-1812.* Chapel Hill, NC: University of North Carolina Press, 1968.

Joyce, William L., David D. Hall, Richard D. Brown, and John B. Hench, eds. *Printing and Society in Early America.* Worcester, MA: American Antiquarian Society, 1983.

Kairys, David. "Freedom of Speech." In *The Politics of Law: A Progressive Critique.* Ed. David Kairys. Rev. ed. New York: Pantheon Books, 1990.

Kammen, Michael. *People of Paradox: An Inquiry Concerning the Origins of American Civilization.* New York: Oxford University Press, 1972.

Kaplan, Louis, James T. Cook, Clinton L. Colby, Jr., and Daniel C. Haskell. *A Bibliography of American Autobiographies*. Madison, WI: State Historical Society of Wisconsin, 1962.

Kehl, James A. *Ill Feelings in the Era of Good Feelings*. Pittsburgh: University of Pittsburgh Press, 1956.

Kessler, Lauren. *The Dissident Press: Alternative Journalism in American History*. Sage Commtext Series. Beverly Hills, CA: Sage, 1984.

Kielbowicz, Richard. *News in the Mail: The Press, Post Office and Public Information*. Westport, CT: Greenwood Press, 1989.

Kimball, Penn. "Journalism: Art, Craft or Profession?" In *The Professions in America*. Ed. Kenneth S. Lynn. *Daedalus* Library Series. Boston: Houghton-Mifflin, 1965.

Kraus, Sidney, and Dennis Davis. *The Effects of Mass Communication on Political Behavior*. University Park, PA: Pennsylvania State University Press, 1976.

Larson, Magali Sarfatti. *The Rise of Professionalism*. Berkeley, CA: University of California Press, 1977.

———. "Profession." In *International Encyclopedia of Communication*. 1989 ed. s.v. "Profession."

Latham, Edward C. *Chronological Tables of American Newspapers, 1690-1820*. Barre, MA: American Antiquarian Society, 1972.

Leab, Daniel J. *A Union of Individuals: The Formation of the American Newspaper Guild, 1933-1936*. New York: Columbia University Press, 1970.

Lee, Alfred E. *History of City of Columbus, the Capital of Ohio*. Vol. 1. New York; Chicago: Munsell & Co., 1892.

Lee, Alfred McClung. *The Daily Newspaper in America: The Evolution of a Social Instrument*. New York: Macmillan, 1937.

Lee, James Melvin. *Instruction in Journalism in Institutions of Higher Education*. Bulletin No. 21. Washington, D.C.: U.S. Department of the Interior, Bureau of Education, 1918.

Leith, James A. *Media and Revolution: Moulding a New Citizenry in France During the Revolution*. Toronto: Canadian Broadcasting Corporation, 1968.

Lemon, James T. *The Best Poor Man's Country*. Baltimore, MD: Johns Hopkins University Press, 1972.

Leonard, Thomas C. *Power of the Press: The Birth of American Political Reporting*. New York: Oxford University Press, 1986.

Levy, H. Phillip. *The Press Council: History, Procedures and Cases*. New York: St. Martin's Press, 1967.

Levy, Leonard W., ed. *Emergence of a Free Press*. New York: Oxford University Press, 1985.

———. *Freedom of the Press from Zenger to Jefferson*. Indianapolis, IN: Bobbs-Merrill, 1966.

Lindemann, M. *Deutsche Presse bis 1815*. Berlin: Colloquium Verlag, 1969.

Lipset, Seymour Martin. "History and Sociology: Some Methodological Considerations." In *Sociology and History: Methods*. Ed. Seymour Martin Lipset and Richard Hofstadter. New York: Basic Books, 1968.

Lord, Myra B. *History of the New England Woman's Press Association*. Newton, MA: Graphic Press, 1932.

Luckmann, T. and P. L. Berger. *The Social Construction of Reality.* London: Allen Lane, 1966.

Lynn, Kenneth S., ed. *The Professions in America. Daedalus* Library Series. Boston: Houghton-Mifflin Co., 1965.

Lynch, James A. *Epochal History of the International Typographical Union.* Indianapolis, IN: International Typographical Union, 1925.

Mackie, Thomas T. *The International Almanac of Electoral History.* New York: Free Press, 1974.

Maier, Pauline. *From Resistance to Revolution: Colonial Radicals and the Development of American Opposition to Britain, 1765-1776.* New York: Knopf, 1972.

Marx, Karl, and F. Engels. *The German Ideology.* London: Lawrence & Wishart, 1965.

McCombs, Maxwell E., and Donald L. Shaw. *The Emergence of American Political Issues: The Agenda-Setting Function of the Press.* St. Paul, MN: West Publishing, 1977.

McCormick, Richard P. "Political Development and the Second Party System." In *The American Party Systems.* Ed. Richard P. McCormick and William N. Chambers. New York: Oxford University Press, 1975.

———. *The Second American Party System: Party Formation in the Jacksonian Era.* Chapel Hill, NC: University of North Carolina Press, 1966.

McCormick, Richard P., and William N. Chambers, eds. *The American Party Systems.* New York: Oxford University Press, 1975.

McFarland, Gerald W. *Mugwumps, Morals and Politics, 1884-1920.* Amherst, MA: University of Massachusetts Press, 1975.

McKerns, Joseph P., ed. *Biographical Dictionary of American Journalism.* Westport, CT: Greenwood Press, 1989.

Miller, John C. *Crisis in Freedom: The Alien and Sedition Acts.* Boston: Little, Brown, 1951.

———. *The Federalist Era, 1789-1801.* New York: Harper, 1960.

———. *Origins of the American Revolution.* Boston: Little, Brown, 1943.

Miller, Perry. *The New England Mind: From Colony to Province.* Cambridge: Harvard University Press, 1953.

———. *The New England Mind: The Seventeenth Century.* Boston: Beacon Press, 1961.

Morgan, Edmund S. *The Birth of the Republic, 1763-1789.* 3d ed. Chicago: University of Chicago Press, 1959.

———. *Political Parties Before the Constitution.* Chapel Hill, NC: University of North Carolina Press, 1972.

———. *The Puritan Dilemma: The Story of John Winthrop.* Boston: Little, Brown, 1958.

———. *The Stamp Act Crisis.* Chapel Hill, NC: University of North Carolina Press, 1953.

Morris, Richard B. *Government and Labor in Early America.* New York: Columbia University Press, 1946.

Mott, Frank Luther. *American Journalism.* 3d ed. New York: Macmillan, 1962.

———. *A History of American Magazines.* 5 vols. Cambridge: Harvard University Press, 1938-1968.

Murphy, Paul L., ed. *The Meaning of Freedom of Speech: First Amendment Freedoms from Wilson to FDR.* Contributions in American History Series. Westport, CT: Greenwood Press, 1972.

———. *Political Parties in American History.* Vol. 3, 1890-Present. New York: Putnam, 1974.

Nash, Gary. *The Urban Crucible: Social Change, Political Consciousness, and the Origins of the American Revolution.* Cambridge: Harvard University Press, 1979.

Nerone, John. *The Culture of the Press in the Early Republic: Cincinnati, 1793-1848.* New York; London: Garland Publishing, 1989.

Nevins, Allan. *American Press Opinion, Washington to Coolidge.* Boston: Heath, 1928.

———. "Journalism." In *Encyclopaedia of Social Sciences.* 1933-1935 ed., s.v. "Journalism."

———. *Ordeal of the Union.* 4 vols. New York: Scribner, 1947-1971.

Nichols, Roy F. *The Invention of the American Political Parties.* New York: Macmillan, 1967.

Nye, Russell B. *Fettered Freedom: Civil Liberties and the Slavery Controversy, 1830-1860.* East Lansing, MI: Michigan State College Press, 1963.

O'Dell, Forest. *The History of Journalism Education in the United States.* New York: Columbia University Teachers College, 1935.

Olney, James. *Studies in Autobiography.* New York; Oxford: Oxford University Press, 1988.

———, ed. *Autobiography: Essays, Theoretical and Critical.* Princeton, NJ: Princeton University Press, 1980.

Ong, Walter J. *Orality and Literacy: The Technologizing of the World.* London; New York: Methuen, 1982.

Orwell, George, and Reginald Reynolds, eds. *British Pamphleteers.* 2 vols. London: A. Wingate, 1948-1951.

Oswald, John Clyde. *A History of Printing: Its Development Through Five Hundred Years.* New York: Appleton and Company, 1928.

Paine, Robert, ed. *Politically Speaking: Cross-Cultural Studies of Rhetoric.* Philadelphia: Institute for the Study of Human Issues, 1981.

Parenti, Michael. *Inventing Reality.* New York: St. Martin's Press, 1993.

Parrington, Vernon L. *Main Currents in American Thought.* Vol. 1. New York: Harcourt Brace Jovanovich, 1927.

Parsons,Talcott. "Professions." In *Encyclopedia of the Social Sciences,* 1968 ed., s.v., "Professions."

———. "Professions and Social Structure." In *Essays in Sociological Theory.* Rev. ed. Glencoe, IL: Free Press, 1954.

———. *The Social System.* New York: Free Press, 1964.

Patterson, Thomas E. *The Mass Media Election: How Americans Choose Their President.* New York: Praeger, 1980.

Pavlik, John P., and Everett E. Dennis. *Demystifying Media Technology.* Mountain View, CA: Mayfield, 1993.

Peterson, H. C., and Gilbert Fite. *Opponents of War, 1917-1918.* Seattle, WA: University of Washington Press, 1957.

Polanyi, Karl. *The Great Transformation.* Boston: Beacon, 1957.

Pollard, James E. *The Presidents and the Press.* New York: Macmillan, 1947.

Pratte, Alf. *A Critical History of the American Society of Newspaper Editors 1922-1990.* Washington, D.C.: American Association of Newspaper Editors, 1992.

Pray, Isaac C. *Memoirs of James Gordon Bennett*. New York: Stringer and Townsend, 1866; rpt. New York: Arno Press and the New York Times Company, 1970.

Price, Warren C. *The Literature of Journalism, An Annotated Bibliography*. Minneapolis, MN: University of Minnesota Press, 1959.

Quenzel, Carroll H. *Samuel Snowden, A Founding Father of Printing in Alexandria*. Charlottesville, VA: Bibliographical Society of the University of Virginia, 1952.

Raum, John O. *History of the City of Trenton, New Jersey*. Trenton, NJ: W. T. Nicholson and Co., Printers, 1871.

Ritzer, George. *Man and His Work: Conflict and Change*. New York: Appleton-Century-Crofts, 1972.

Rivers, William, et al. *Backtalk: Press Councils in America*. San Francisco: Canfield Press, 1972.

Roos, Patricia A. "Professions." In *Encyclopedia of Sociology*. 1992 ed., s.v., "Professions."

Rosenberg, Norman L. *Protecting the Best Men: An Interpretive History of the Law of Libel*. Chapel Hill, NC: University of North Carolina Press, 1986.

Rosewater, Victor. *History of Cooperative News-Gathering in the United States*. New York: Appleton-Century-Crofts, 1930.

Rude, George F. E. *Ideology and Popular Protest*. New York: Pantheon Books, 1980.

Ryan, Mary. "The American Parade: Representations of the Nineteenth-Century Social Order." In *The New Cultural History*. Ed. Lynn Hunt. Berkeley, CA: University of California Press, 1989.

Salz, Arthur. "Occupation." In *Encyclopaedia of the Social Sciences* 1933-1935 ed., s.v. "Occupation."

Schellenger, Harold K. *An Era of Newspaper Organization: Development of the Buckeye Press Association, 1895-1908*. Columbus, OH: Ohio Historical Society, 1939.

Schiller, Dan. *Objectivity and the News: The Public and the Rise of Commercial Journalism*. Philadelphia, PA: University of Pennsylvania Press, 1981.

Schlesinger, Arthur M. *The Colonial Merchants and the American Revolution, 1763-1776*. New York: Columbia University Press, 1917.

———. *Prelude to Independence: The Newspaper War on Britain, 1764-1776*. New York: Alfred A. Knopf, 1958.

Schudson, Michael. *Discovering the News: A Social History of American Newspapers*. New York: Basic Books, 1978.

———. "Political Communication." In *International Encyclopedia of Communications*. 1992 ed., s.v. "Political Communication."

———. "The Profession of Journalism in the United States." In *The Professions in American History*. Ed. Nathan O. Hatch. Notre Dame, IN: University of Notre Dame, 1988.

Scott, Donald M. "The Profession that Vanished: Public Lecturing in Mid-Nineteenth-Century America." In *Professions and Professional Ideologies in America*. Ed. Gerald L. Geison. Chapel Hill, NC: University of North Carolina Press, 1983.

Scott, Joan Wallach. *Gender and the Politics of History*. New York: Columbia University Press, 1988.

Seaver, Frederick J. *Historical Sketches of Franklin County and Its Towns*. Albany, NY: J. B. Lyon and Co., Printers, 1918.

Seitz, Don C. *The James Gordon Bennetts: Father and Son, Proprietors of the "New York Herald."* Indianapolis, IN: Bobbs-Merrill, 1928.

Shaaber, Matthias A. *Some Forerunners of the Newspaper in England, 1476-1776*. Philadelphia, PA: University of Pennsylvania Press, 1929.

Siebert, Fredrick. *Four Theories of the Press*. Urbana, IL: University of Illinois Press, 1956.

———. *Freedom of the Press in England, 1476-1622*. Urbana, IL: University of Illinois Press, 1952.

Skocpol, Theda, ed. *Vision and Method in Historical Sociology*. New York: Cambridge University Press, 1984.

Smith, Anthony. *The Newspaper: An International History*. London: Thames and Hudson, 1979.

Smith, Culver H. *The Press, Politics and Patronage*. Athens: University of Georgia Press, 1977.

Smith, James M. *Freedom's Fetters: The Alien and Sedition Laws and American Civil Liberties*. Ithaca, NY: Cornell University Press, 1956.

Smith, Jeffery A. *Printers and Press Freedom: The Ideology of Early American Journalism*. New York: Oxford University Press, 1988.

Smolla, Rodney. *Suing the Press*. New York: Oxford University Press, 1986.

Spengemann, William C. *The Forms of Autobiography*. New Haven; London: Yale University Press, 1980.

Steele, Ian K. *The English Atlantic, 1675-1740: An Exploration of Communication and Community*. New York: Oxford University Press, 1986.

Steirer, William F. "Riding 'Everyman's Hobby Horse': Journalists in Philadelphia, 1764-1794." In *Newsletters to Newspapers: Eighteenth-Century Journalism*. Ed. Donovan H. Bond and W. Reynolds McLeods. Morgantown, WV: West Virginia University, 1977.

Stephens, Mitchell. *A History of News*. New York: Penguin Books, 1988.

Stevens, John D., and Hazel Dicken-Garcia. *Communication History*. Sage CommText Series. Beverly Hills, CA: Sage, 1980.

Stewart, Donald H. *The Opposition Press of the Federalist Period*. Albany, NY: State University of New York Press, 1969.

Sutton, Albert A. *Education for Journalism in the United States From Its Beginning to 1940*. Evanston, IL: Northwestern University, 1945.

Tebbel, John W. *A History of Book Publishing in the United States*. Vol. 1. New York: Bowker, 1972.

Thomas, Isaiah. *The History of Printing in America, with a Biography of Printers*. 2d ed. rprt. New York: B. Franklin, 1967.

Tilly, Charles. *As Sociology Meets History*. New York: Academic Press, 1981.

———. *Big Structures, Large Processes, Huge Comparisons*. New York: Russell Sage Foundation, 1984.

———. "Collective Action in England and America, 1765-1775." In *Tradition, Conflict, and Modernization: Perspectives on the American Revolution*. Ed. Richard Maxwell Brown and Don E. Fehrenbacher. New York: Academic Press, 1977.

Ver Steeg, Clarence L. *The Formative Years, 1607-1763*. New York: Hill and Wang, 1964.

Vollmer, Howard M., and Donald L. Mills. *Professionalism*. Englewood Cliffs, NJ: PrenticeHall, 1966.

Von Klarwill, Victor, ed. *The Fugger News Letters*. 2 vols. New York: G. P. Putnam's & Sons, 1924-1926.

Warner, Michael. *The Letters of the Republic: Publication and the Public Sphere in Eighteenth-Century America*. Cambridge; London: Harvard University Press, 1990.

Weber, Max. *Economy and Society*. Ed. G. Roth and C. Wittich. New York: Bedminster Press, 1968.

Weed, Thurlow. *Autobiography of Thurlow Weed*. Ed. Harriet A. Weed, Rprt. ed. New York: DaCapo Press, 1970.

White, Ruth Young, ed. *We Too Built Columbus*. Columbus, OH: Stoneman Press, 1936.

Williams, Raymond. *Communications*. Harmondsworth: Penguin, 1962.

———. *The Long Revolution*. New York: Columbia University Press, 1975.

———. "The Press and Popular Culture: An Historical Perspective." In *Newspaper History from the Seventeenth Century to the Present Day*. Ed. George Boyce, James Curran, and Pauline Wingate. Beverly Hills, CA: Sage, 1978.

Williams, William Appleman. *The Contours of American History*. Cleveland, OH: World Publishing, 1961.

Wood, Gordon S. *The Creation of the American Republic, 1776-1787*. Chapel Hill, NC: University of North Carolina Press, 1969.

Wroth, Lawrence C. *The Colonial Printer*. Portland, ME: Southworth-Anthoensen Press, 1938.

Zinn, Howard. *Declarations of Independence: Cross-Examining American Ideology*. New York: HarperCollins, 1990.

ARTICLES AND MONOGRAPHS

A Faithful Report of the Trial of the Cause of Philip R. Arcularius. New York: Kirk for Dornin, 1807.

Allison, Marianne. "A Literature Review of Approaches to the Professionalism of Journalists." *Journal of Mass Media Ethics* 1 (Spring/Summer 1986): 5-19.

Baldasty, Gerald J. "The Press and Politics in the Age of Jackson." *Journalism Monographs* 89 (August 1984).

Baldasty, Gerald J., and Jeffrey B. Rutenbeck. "Money, Politics and Newspapers: The Business Environment of Press Partisanship in the Late 19th Century." *Journalism History* 15 (Summer/Autumn 1989): 60-69.

Beam, Randall. "Journalism Professionalism as an Organizational-Level Concept." *Journalism Monographs* 90 (1990): 1-43.

Ben-David, Joseph. "Professions in the Class System of Present Day Societies." *Current Sociology* 12 (1963): 247- 98.

Blum, Terry C., Paul M. Roman, and Deborah M. Tootle. "The Emergence of an Occupation." *Work and Occupation* 15 (February 1988): 96-114.

Botein, Stephen. "'Meer Mechanics' and an Open Press: The Business and Political Strategies of Colonial American Printers." *Perspectives in American History* 9 (1975): 127-225.

Breed, Warren. "Social Control in the Newsroom: A Functional Analysis." *Social Forces* 33 (1955): 326-35.

Clark, Charles E. "Boston and the Nurturing of Newspapers: Dimensions of the Cradle." *New England Quarterly* 64 (1991): 243-71.

———. "'Metropolis' and 'Province' in Eighteenth-Century Press Relations: The Case of Boston." *Journal of Newspaper and Periodical History* 5 (Autumn 1989): 2-16.

———. "The Newspapers of Provincial America." *Proceedings of the American Antiquarian Society* 100 (1990): 367-89.

Clark, Charles E., and Charles Wetherell. "The Measure of Maturity: The Pennsylvania Gazette, 1728-1765." *William and Mary Quarterly* 3d series, 61 (1989): 279-303.

Coldwell, Thomas. "Professionalization and Performance Among Newspaper Photographers." *Gazette* 20 (1974): 71-81.

Dooley, Patricia L. "Minnesota Publishers and Editors as Elected Officials, 1923-1938: A Comparison of Journalistic Rhetoric and Conduct." *Journalism Quarterly* 71 (Spring 1994): 64-75.

Dooley, Patricia L., and Paul G. Grosswiler. "'Turf Wars': The New Media and the Struggle for Control of Political News." *The Harvard International Journal of Press/Politics* 2 (Summer 1997): 31-51.

Erickson, John E. "One Approach to the Cultural History of Reporting." *Journalism History* 2 (Summer 1975): 40-42.

Fisk, William L. "John Bailhache: A British Editor in Early Ohio." *The Ohio Historical Quarterly* 67 (April 1958): 141-47.

Gieryn, Thomas F., George M. Bevins, and Stephen C. Zehr. "Professionalization of American Scientists: Public Science in the Creation/Evolution Trials." *American Sociological Review* 50 (June 1985): 392-409.

Gifford, C. A. "Ancient Rome's Daily Gazette." *Journalism History* 2 (Winter 1975-1976): 106-9.

Gillis, D. Hugh. "Broadcasting as Profession: A Socio-Economic Approach." *Journal of Broadcasting* 11 (1966-1967): 73-82.

The Great Libel Case. Geo. Opdyke agt. Thurlow Weed. A Full Report of the Speeches of Counsel, Testimony, Etc., Etc. New York: The American News Company, 1865.

The Great Libel Case. Report of the Criminal Prosecution of the News and Courier for Libelling Sheriff and Ex-Congressman C. C. Bowen. Charleston, SC: *News and Courier*, 1875.

The Great Libel Suit; David S. Bennett v. James N. Matthews and James D. Warren Buffalo, NY: Matthews and Warren, 1870.

Greenwood, Ernest. "Attributes of a Profession." *Social Work* 2 (July 1957): 44-55.

"The Growing Independence of American Journalism." *Century Magazine* (March 1888): 801.

Gutman, Herbert G. "Work, Culture, and Society in Industrializing America." *American Historical Review* 73 (June 1973): 531-87.

Hodges, Louis W. "The Journalist and Professionalism." *Journal of Mass Media Ethics* 1 (Spring/Summer 1986): 32-36.

Janowitz, Morris. "Professional Models in Journalism: The Gatekeeper and Advocate." *Journalism Quarterly* 52 (1975): 618-26.

Kaul, Arthur J. "The Proletarian Journalist: A Critique of Professionalism." *Journal of Mass Media Ethics* 1 (Spring/Summer 1986): 47-55.

Kentucky State Historical Society Register 33 (1935): 50.

Kielbowicz, Richard. "Newsgathering by Printers' Exchanges Before the Telegraph." *Journalism History* 9 (Summer 1982): 42-48.

Kim, Chong Lim, and Jun Hwanh Oh. "Perceptions of Professional Efficacy Among Journalists in a Developing Country." *Journalism Quarterly* 51 (1974): 73-78.

Klegon, Douglas. "The Sociology of Professions: An Emerging Perspective." *Sociology of Work and Occupations* 3 (August 1978): 259-83.

Knudson, Jerry W. "Political Journalism in the Age of Jefferson." *Journalism History* 1 (Spring 1974): 20-23.

Kronus, Carol L. "The Evolution of Occupational Power: An Historical Study of Task Boundaries Between Physicians and Pharmacists." *Sociology of Work and Occupations* 1 (February 1976): 3-37.

Krause, Elliott A. "Book Review." *Sociology of Work and Occupations* 6 (May 1979): 251-53.

McCombs, Maxwell E., and Donald L. Shaw. "The Agenda-Setting Function of Mass Media." *Public Opinion Quarterly* 36 (1973): 176-87.

McLeod, Jack and Searle E. Hawley. "Professionalization Among Newsmen." *Journalism Quarterly* 41 (1964): 583-90.

———. "Professionalization of Latin American and U.S. Journalists." Parts 1 and 2. *Journalism Quarterly* 46 (1969): 583-90, 784-89.

Menanteau-Horta, Dario. "Professionalism of Journalists in Santiago de Chile." *Journalism Quarterly* 44 (1967): 715-24.

Miller, Linda Patterson. "Poe on the Beat: 'Doings of Gotham' as Urban, Penny Press Journalism." *Journal of the Early Republic* 7 (Summer 1987): 164.

Millerson, Geoffrey. "Dilemmas of Professionalism." *New Society* 4 (June 1964): 5.

Nayman, Oguz. "Professional Orientations of Journalists: An Introduction to Communicator Analysis Studies." *Gazette* 19 (1973): 195-202.

Nayman, Oguz, Blaine K. McKee, and Dan L. Lattimore. "PR Personnel and Print Journalists: A Comparison of Professionalism." *Journalism Quarterly* 54 (1977): 492-97.

Nerone, John. "The Mythology of the Penny Press." *Critical Studies in Mass Communication* 4 (1987): 376-404.

Nevins, Allan. "Journalism." *Encyclopaedia of Social Sciences* 1933-1935 edition, s.v. "Journalism."

Nord, David Paul. "Intellectual History, Social History, Cultural History." *Journalism History* 67 (Winter 1990): 645-58.

———. "Teleology and News: The Religious Roots of American Journalism, 1630-1730." *Journal of American History* 77 (1990): 9-38.

Park, Robert E. "The Natural History of the Newspaper." *American Journal of Sociology* 29 (November 1923): 273-89.

Parker, Peter. "The Philadelphia Printer: A Study of an Eighteenth-Century Businessman." *Business History Review* 40 (Spring 1966): 24-26.

Pickett, Calder M. "Technology and the New York Press in the Nineteenth Century." *Journalism Quarterly* 35 (Summer 1960): 398.

Prince, Carl E. "The Federalist Party and Creation of a Court Press, 1789-1801." *Journalism Quarterly* 53 (1976): 238.

Report of the Case of Joshua Stow vs. Sherman Converse, for a Libel. New Haven: S. Converse, 1822.

Report of the Case of Timothy Upham Against Hill and Barton. Dover, DE: George. W. Ela, 1830.

Report of the Trial of Charles N. Baldwin for a Libel. New York: C. N. Baldwin, 1818.

Review of the Report of the Case of the Commonwealth versus David Lee Child, for Publishing in the Massachusetts Journal a Libel on the Honorable John Keyes. Boston: J. H. Eastburn, Printer, 1829.

Ritter, John A., and Matthew Leibowitz. "Press Councils: An Answer to Our First Amendment Dilemma." *Duke Law Journal* 24 (December 1974): 845-70.

Roth, Julius. "Professionalism: The Sociologist's Decoy." *Sociology of Work and Occupations* 1 (February 1974): 6-23.

Runcie, John F. "Occupational Communication as Boundary Mechanism." *Sociology of Work and Occupations* 1 (November 1974): 419-44.

Schudson, Michael. "The Limits of Teledemocracy." *American Prospect* 11 (Fall 1992): 41-45.

Schuneman, R. Smith. "The Photograph in Print: An Examination of New York Daily Newspapers." *Journalism Quarterly* 42 (Winter 1965): 43.

Schwartz, Mildred A. "Historical Sociology in the History of American Sociology." *Social Science History* 11 (1987): 1-16.

Schwarzlose, Richard A. "Harbor News Association: Formal Origin of the AP." *Journalism Quarterly* 45 (Summer 1968): 253-60.

Shaw, Donald. "At the Crossroads: Change and Continuity in American Press News 1820-1860." *Journalism History* 8 (Summer 1981): 38-50.

―――. "News Bias and the Telegraph: A Study of Historical Change." *Journalism Quarterly* 44 (Spring 1967): 3-12.

Skocpol, Theda. "Social History and Historical Sociology: Contrasts and Complementarities." *Social Science History* 11 (1987): 17-30.

Sloan, W. David. "The Early Party Press: The Newspaper Role in National Politics, 1788-1812." *Journalism History* 9 (Spring 1982): 18-24.

―――. "Scurrility and the Party Press, 1789-1816." *American Journalism* 5 (1988): 98-112.

Smythe, Ted Curtis. "The Reporter, 1880-1900: Working Conditions and Their Influence on the News." *Journalism History* 7 (Spring 1980): 1-10.

Stephens, Mitchell. "Sensationalism and Moralizing in 16th- and 17th-Century Newsbooks and News Ballads." *Journalism History* 12 (Autumn/Winter 1985): 92-95.

Stevens, John D. "Sensationalism in Perspective." *Journalism History* 12 (Autumn/Winter 1985): 78-79.

The Strong-Bennett Libel Suit. Brooklyn, New York, 1866.

Sydnor, Charles S. "The Beginning of Printing in Mississippi." *Journal of Southern History* 1 (February 1935): 49-55.

Sztompka, Piotr. "The Renaissance of Historical Orientation in Sociology." *International Sociology* 1 (March 1986): 321-37.

Taeuber, Irene Barnes. "Changes in the Content and Presentation of Reading Material in Minnesota Weekly Newspapers 1860-1929." *Journalism Quarterly* 9 (September 1932): 280-89.

To the Press of the United States, and Especially To the Press of State of New York. Hoboken, NJ: George Wilkes, 1851.

Trial of the Hon. Maturin Livingston Against James Cheetham for a Libel. New York: S. Gould, 1807.

Trial of William J. Snelling. Boston: Printed for the Reporter, 1834.

Tuchman, Gaye. "Making News by Doing Work: Routinizing the Unexpected." *American Journal of Sociology* 79 (July 1973): 110-30.

———. "Professionalism as an Agent of Legitimation." *Journal of Communication* 28 (Winter 1978): 106-13.

Wallace, Michael. "Changing Concepts of Party in the United States: New York, 1815-1828." *American Historical Review* 74 (1968): 453-91.

Weinthal, Donald S., and Garrett J. O'Keefe. "Professionalization Among Broadcast Newsmen in an Urban Area." *Journal of Broadcasting* 18 (1974): 193-209.

Wilensky, Harold. "The Professionalization of Everyone?" *American Journal of Sociology* 70 (September 1964): 137-58.

Wilson, B. R. "Sociological Methods in the Study of History." *Transactions of the Royal Historical Society* 21 (1972): 101-18.

Yodelis, Mary Ann. "The Press in Wartime: Portable and Penurious." *Journalism History* 3 (Spring 1976): 2-6.

———. "Who Paid the Piper? Publishing Economics in Boston, 1763-1775." *Journalism Monographs* 38 (February 1975).

Yodelis, Mary Ann, and Gerald J. Baldasty. "Criticism of Public Officials and Government in the New Nation." *Journal of Communication Inquiry* 4 (Winter 1979): 53-74.

DISSERTATIONS, THESES, UNPUBLISHED PAPERS AND SPEECHES

Baldasty, Gerald J. "The Political Press in the Second American Party System: The 1832 Election." Ph.D. diss, University of Washington, 1978.

Bradley, Patricia. "No 'Meer Mechanic': William Bradford and the Search for Legitimacy." Paper presented at the annual meeting of the American Journalism Historians Association, Philadelphia, Pennsylvania, 1991.

Brennen, Bonnie. "Newsworkers During the Interwar Era: A Critique of Traditional Media History." Paper presented at Qualitative Studies Division, Annual Convention Association for Education in Journalism and Mass Communication, Kansas City, Missouri, 1993.

Broder, David. Speech presented at a conference sponsored by the Silha Center for the Study of Media Ethics and Law, School of Journalism and Mass Communication, University of Minnesota, April, 1996.

Connery, Thomas B. "Fusing Fictional Technique and Journalistic Fact: Literary Journalism in the 1890s," Ph.D. diss., Brown University, 1984.

Dooley, Patricia L. "Minnesota Journalists as Elected Officials, 1923-1938: An Historical Study of an Ethical/Conflict of Interest Question." Master's thesis, University of Minnesota, 1985.

Finnegan, John Robert, Jr. "Defamation, Politics, and the Social Process of Law in New York State, 1776-1860." Ph.D. diss., University of Minnesota, 1985.

Groth, Lynne Marie. "The Journalistic Standard of Attribution: An Historical Study of the Change in Attribution Practices by Journalists Between 1890-1924." Master's thesis, University of Minnesota, 1989.

Jennings, Kenneth Q. "Political and Social Force of the New Jersey Press Association, 1857-1939." Master's thesis, Columbia University, 1940.

Lamb, David. Speech presented at the annual conference of the Maine Association of Journalists, University of Maine, Orono, 25 April 1993.

Mirando, Joe. "Journalism's First Textbook: Creating a News Reporting Body of Knowledge." Paper presented at a meeting of the Association for Education in Journalism and Mass Communication, Kansas City, Missouri, 1993.

Mueller, Milton. "The Currency of the Word: War, Revolution and the Temporal Coordination of Literate Media in England, 1608-1655." Ph.D. diss., University of Pennsylvania, 1986.

Rutenbeck. Jeffrey B. "The Rise of Independent Newspapers in the 1870s: A Transformation in American Journalism." Ph.D. diss., University of Washington, 1990.

Ward, Henry H. "Ninety Years of the National Newspaper Association." Ph.D. diss., University of Minnesota, 1977.

Index

Abbey, Dorephus, 111
Abbey, Seth Alden, 111, 115
Abbott, Andrew, 6-8, 32-33 n.6, 38 n.65, 42 n.113, 43 n.120
Abolitionist movement, 23
Accuracy, journalistic, 54
Advertising, 26-27, 73-74, 139
Advocacy journalism, 23
African-American newspapers, 79
Agency of journalists, 21, 45
Alexandria Phenix [sic] Gazette, 118
Alien and Sedition Acts, 57, 63, 133
Alleghany Federalist, 111
Allen, Frederick P., 117
Allen, Paul, 123 n.21
American, 114-15
American Advocate, 111
American Citizen, 93
American Patriot, 80
American Revolution: Boston printers during, 46-47; effects on newspapers, 12, 16, 73; effects on political communication systems, 63-64, 71, 109-10, 127, 131; role in journalistic occupational development, 20, 30-31, 45, 59-64, 71, 126-27, 129-30
American Watchman, 100
American Weekly Mercury, 68 n.54
Antioch (Illinois) News, 133

Arcularius, Philip R., 95-96
Associated Press, 15
Associations, occupational, 5, 7, 16-17, 21, 26, 75, 130
Attribution, journalistic, 36 n.47, 135
Autobiography, 27, 39 n.75

Bache, Richard, 113-14
Bailhache, John, 118, 124 n.38
Balance, news, 132
Baldasty, Gerald J., 108 n.37
Baldwin, Charles N., 96
Barton, Cyrus, 98-99
Belfast (Maine) Gazette, 71
Bellamy, Elisha, 114
Bennett, George C., 102
Bennett, James Gordon, 41 n.100
Bennett vs. Matthews, 104
Bertrand, Peter, 83
Biography, 27, 29, 31
Blakeley (Alabama) Sun, 28
Boston Courier, 78-79
Boston Gazette, 46-47, 51
Boston News-Letter, 46-47
Boston printers, 46-47
Botein, Stephen, 48-49, 119-20
Bowen, Christopher Columbus, 98
Bradford, Andrew, 68 n.54
Bradford, William, 53

Brooker, William, 46-47, 51
Brown, Andrew, 61
Buckingham, Joseph T., 39 n.75, 113, 120-21
Buffalo Elevator Association, 103
Burr, Aaron, 100, 107 n.24

Camera, 21, 23
Campbell, John, 46-47, 49, 50-53
Careers, journalistic, 31, 116-20
Carthage (Tennessee) Gazette, 89 n.36
Cavins, Ignatius, 116, 123 n.28
Charleston (South Carolina) Courier, 81
Charlestown (South Carolina) Mercury, 81
Checkley, John, 67 n.45
Cheetham, James, 93, 99-100
Chester and Delaware Federalist, 122 n.10
Child, David Lee, 104-5
Childs, George W., 27
Civil War, 16, 30, 74-75
Clarksville (Tennesee) Gazette, 27
Clinton administration, 136
Codes of ethics, 4, 8, 16
Coleman, William, 95-97
Columbian, 76, 80
Columbian Advocate and Franklin Chronicle, 89 n.36
Columbian Centinel, 109-10, 113, 120-21
Columns, journalistic, 27-28
Commercial Advertiser, 102, 104
Commonwealth of Boston vs. Snelling, 100-1
Connecticut Journal, 96
Converse, Sherman, 96-98
Cooperative news gathering, 73, 87-88 n.11
Copeland, Jared W., 117
Crowell, Timothy B., 80
Cullen, John B., 7
Cushing, Joseph, 86

Daily Advertiser, 105
Daily and Weekly Federal Republican, 111

Daily Times, 102
Dawson, Captain F. W., 98
Day, Matthias, 74, 83, 85
Derrida, Jacques, 32 n.6
Dicken-Garcia, Hazel, 108 n.37
Dickinson, John, 19
Douglass,William, 67 n.45
Duane, William, 93, 106 n.1
Dunn, James C., 117
Dwight, Theodore, 90 n.40

East Dubuque (Illinois) Register, 27
Edes, Peter, 61
Editorials: as journalistic products and tasks, 13, 15-16, 18-19, 24-25; during eighteenth century, 58, 64; during Era of Good Feelings, 113; during nineteenth century, 72, 75, 77-78; journalistic providers of, 4, 9, 125-26, 129, 135; on journalistic libel plaintiffs, 104-5
Edwardsville (Illinois) Spectator, 89 n.36
Era of Good Feelings: as a shift in political system, 30-31; deaths of political newspapers during, 112; defined, 111; journalists and their trade practices during, 116-19; naming of, 110, 113; role in journalistic occupational development, 109, 128, 130, 132, 134. *See also* Prospectuses; Republican party
Essays: as a journalistic treatment, 27-29; in American Revolution, 16; in early journalism, 15; in Era of Good Feelings, 112, 114, 119-20; in nineteenth century, 72-73, 77-78, 81, 83, 85; nonjournalistic contributors of, 19
Essex Gazette, 62
Etheridge, Samuel, 62
Evening Journal, 99
Evening Post, 95
Evening Transcript, 90 n.37, 91 n.62

Farmer's Cabinet, The, 86, 91 n.62
Federal Gazette (Baltimore), 122 n.10
Federal Gazette (Philadelphia), 61

Federal Republican, 122 n.10

Federalism, 111

Federalist, 122 n.10

Federalist party: disintegration of during Era of Good Feelings, 30, 109-11; reaction of Federalist editors to newspaper coverage of President Monroe's Boston visit, 113; reaction of Federalist editors to party's disintegration, 115, 117-20, 128; regional variations in strength of, 119

Fellowes, Ephraim, 71, 80

First Amendment, 17, 63, 94, 135

Fitzgerald, John, 27

Florence Gazette, 83

Foucault, Michel, 32 n.6

Fowle, Daniel, 52, 54

Franklin, Benjamin, 27, 39 n.75, 41-42 n.101, 47, 64 n.1, 66 n.14

Franklin, James, 46, 50, 52-54, 59, 67 n.45

Franklin Federalist, 122 n.10

Franklin Gazette, 113-14

Franklin Monitor, 114, 91 n.62

Fredonian (Boston), 80

Fredonian (Chillicothe, Ohio), 118

Freidson, Eliot, 8

Gazette, 85-86

Gazette and Western Repository of Knowledge, 60

Genessee Messenger, 76

Goddard, William, 68 n.54, 68 n.56

Great Transformation, The, 20, 39 n.77, 39 n.78

Green, Bartholomew, 46

Green, Thomas, 62, 114

Greensborough (North Carolina) Patriot, 91 n.62

Griffin, Joseph, 12-13

Grit, The, 89 n.36

Gutenberg, Johann, 20

Hall, David, 47

Hall, Samuel, 62, 70 n.91

Hancock (Maine) Gazette, 80

Hardt, Peter, 115

Harris, Benjamin, 67 n.48

Hartford Courant, 73

Hearst, William Randolph, 75

Henderson (Minnesota) Independent, 26

Heroes, journalistic, 27

Hill, Horatio, 98-99

History of Ross and Highland Counties, Ohio, 28

Holt, Charles, 80

Holt, William, 80

Hosmer, Charles, 90 n.40

Howe, Edward W., 125

Hughes, Everett C., 4-5

Impartiality, journalistic, 54, 84-86

Independence, journalistic. 25, 61, 82-84, 128-33, 136 n.5

Independent Inquirer, 133

Independent-Leader, The, 133

Independent Ledger and the American Advocate, 133

Independent Press and Freedom's Advocate, 133

Independent Reflector, The, 133

Independent Voter, The, 133

Independent Whig, The, 133

Information work system, 22

Inverted pyramid news form, 16

Jefferson, Thomas, 74

Johnson, Terence J., 6

Jordan, Ambrose L., 105

Journal, The, 84

Journalistic jurisdiction: contests over, 21-22, 126; defined, 11, 16; future of, 2, 136; importance of in histories of occupations and professions, 21; in nineteenth century, 24; role of occupational communication in establishment of, 22; vulnerability of, 22, 126. *See also* Journalistic occupation

Journalistic knowledge, 12, 14-15, 19, 36 n.47

Journalistic legitimacy: 1-4, 6-9, 11, 13, 17, 21-22, 24-25, 28, 50, 53, 63-64, 125-26, 129-31. *See also* Journalistic jurisdiction

Journalistic occupation: as represented in journalistic occupational communication, 28-29, 126-27, 130, 133-34; defined, 3, 11; explanatory model used in this book, 9-29, 126, 130; historical and cultural evolution of, 11, 125-29; impact of broader environments on, 20, 126, 132-33; journalistic occupational communication, role of and examples, 24-29, 126; mass communication and journalism scholars on, 8-9, 137 n.10; political roles of, 1-2. *See also* Journalistic occupational communication; Journalistic occupational development

Journalistic occupational communication: defined, 3, 24-25; impact on public, 26; in eighteenth century, 3, 45, 49, 63, 126, 129; in jurisdictional disputes, 24-25; in legal sphere, 3, 22, 24, 26, 93-106; in nineteenth century, 3, 71-87, 126-29; in public sphere, 3, 22, 25-26; in workplace, 3, 22, 26, 104-5; printed and oral forms, 25-28; role in journalistic occupational development, 3-4, 24-26, 29, 126-28, 130, 133-35. *See also* Era of Good Feelings; Libel trials; Prospectuses

Journalistic occupational development: boundary emergence and maintenance, 3, 5-7, 9, 11; during eighteenth and nineteenth centuries, 125-27; during Era of Good Feelings, 110, 119-21; in eighteenth century, 45-46, 48, 63; in libel trials, 93-95, 105-6; in nineteenth century, 74, 86-87. *See also* Occupational development; Professionalization

Journalistic work: as fulfillment of human need, 11-12; cultural stages of, 11-16; debates on its occupational or professional status, 4, 11; defined, 3; diagnosis stage, 14-16; inference stage, 15-16; social structural aspects of, 16-19; treatment stage, 16

Journalistic work specialties, 17, 19, 23, 28, 39 n.75

Journalistic work tasks: abstract and technical dimensions of, 12-15, 18, 22; acquisition of cultural meaning and legitimacy, 125-26; distribution and dissemination, 18, 39 n.75; division of printing and editing, 13, 36 n.45; editing, 19; emergence from journalistic work's cultural stages, 17; observation and information gathering, 18, 36 n.47; political tasks in libel trials, 95-98; political tasks in prospectuses, 50-51; printing, 12-13, 18; publishing, 18; reporting, 15, 18; writing, 19

Journalists: as members of an emerging occupation, 3; as orators, 28; as political communicators, 1, 76-87, 126; as political educators, 78, 80-81; as the nation's political protectors, 78-80; defined, 2, 11; dependence on nonjournalists for information, 15, 134; evolution of passive to proactive, 15; importance of in America, 98-101; in early-America, 15; involvement in politics, 72, 106 n.2; pre-American work products of, 17, 20; relationships to business leaders, 104, 108 n.37; relationships to politics and politicians, 1-2, 61, 82-84, 102-4; 130, 134; social responsibilities of, 81; standards of, 84-86; status vis-à-vis politics, 73; support for peers, 104-5

Journal of the Times, 114

Keimer, Samuel, 50-51, 53-54
Kentucky Gazette, 116
Keyes, John, 104-5
Kimball, Penn, 8
Kline, George, 60
Kneeland, Samuel, 51-53

Lancaster (Pennsylvania) True American, 89 n.36
Larson, Margali Sarfatti, 7-8, 34 n.24, 39 n.77

Law: defined, 93-94; role of in journalistic occupational development, 7, 21, 134-35

Legal sphere, 3, 8, 22, 24, 26, 93-106

Legitimacy, and authority, of journalists. *See* Journalistic jurisdiction

Lewis, John E., 77

Libel law, 101, 106 n.5, 134-35

Libel trials: as sites of jurisdictional contests, 26; 93, 95, 105; journalistic occupational communication within, 3, 26, 29-31, 94-101, 105, 127-28, 131-33; newspaper coverage of, 104-5, 127-28; political relationships of opponents in, 102-5; prevalence of in nineteenth century, 93-94; transcripts of, 107 n.10

Licentiousness, journalistic, 84

Livingston, Maturin, 99-100

Looker, James H., 79, 81

Los Angeles Daily Times, 79

Mann, Jacob, 74, 83, 85

Marschalk, Andrew, 83-84, 90 n.5

Massachusetts Centinel and Republican Journal, 60, 62

Massachusetts Mercury, 62

Masthead slogans, 27

Matthews, James W., 102-4

Maund, Thomas Martin, 114, 123 n.21

Meigs, Josiah, 62

Melsheimer, Charles T., 115

Metropolitan and Georgetown Commercial Advertiser, 116, 91 n.62

Middlesex (Connecticut) Gazette, 62

Miller, Samuel, 59

Miller, W. N., 77

Millerson, Geoffrey, 6

Missouri Herald, 89 n.36

Mob violence, 69 n.72

Monroe, James, 109, 111, 113

Morford, Edmund, 81

Morning Chronicle and Baltimore Advertiser, 114

Muckracking, 75

Mueller, Milton, 48

Nashee, George, 119

National Intelligencer, 72, 89 n.37, 90-91 n.62

National Messenger and Town and City Commercial Gazette, 117

National Reflector, The, 79

National Republican and Ohio Political Register, 79

Nerone, John, 119

New England Courant, 46, 50, 67 n.45

New England Galaxy, 101

New-England Weekly Journal, 51, 53

New-Hampshire Gazette, 52, 54

New Hampshire Patriot and Star Gazette, 98-99

New Journalism, 75

Newport (Rhode Island) Gazette, 61

News: broadcast, 9; councils, 17; defined, 11, 35 n.38; early forms of, 16-17, 38 n.63, 63; gathering, 17-18; local, 16, 37 n.56; models, 35-36 n.41; political, 1-2, 4, 9, 24, 28-29, 46, 58, 64; providers of, 12, 46, 51, 53-54, 64; public need for, 12, 15-16. *See also* Journalistic work tasks

News, The (Newberry, Michigan), 89 n.36

Newspaper industry: in professional work systems, 13; in the eighteenth century, 47, 63, 65 n.10, 71; in the nineteenth century, 15, 19, 44, 72-73, 75, 119-20, 126

Newspapers: as precipitators of journalistic occupational development, 46-49, 126; commercialization, 73-75, 108 n.37; contents, 24, 48, 75; coverage of libel trials, 104-5; deaths of during collapse of Federalist party, 111; early examples of, 20; economic supports, 1, 24, 53, 73-74, 87 n.7; effects of American Revolution on, 12, 59-60; effects of Era of Good Feelings on, 117, 119-21; English origins, 49; histories, 28; in nineteenth century, 72-75, 88-89 n.24, 123 n.31; mergers, 118-19; periodicity, 48; political roles, 1-2, 12, 24, 71-72; power and utility, 61-62; prospectuses, 26; shift away

from sensationalism, 75; short-lived
nature of, 112. *See also* Journalistic
occupational communication; Pro-
spectuses
News story, 12-16, 104-5
New-York Columbian, The, 76
New York Evening Journal, 89 n.36,
89 n.37
New York Times, 75
New York Times News Service, 15
New York Times vs. Sullivan, 135
Northern Intelligencer, 91 n.62
Norvell, John, 113-14, 116

Obituaries, 27
Objectivity, 132
Occasional Reverberator, The, 54
Occupation: defined, 3, 38 n.64
Occupational boundaries: defined, 7, 9;
emergence and maintenance, 1-3, 5-
7, 9, 11; importance of in group
emergence and legitimization, 7-8,
29; role of occupational communication in development of, 2-3, 89.
See also Journalistic occupational
boundaries
Occupational communication: defined,
3. *See also* Era of Good Feelings;
Journalistic occupational communication; Libel trials; Prospectuses
Occupational competition, 3, 9, 21-23.
See also Journalistic jurisdiction;
Journalistic occupational communication
Occupational development, 3, 9. *See
also* Journalistic occupational development; Professionalization
Occupational group: agency of group
members, 3, 5; as a culturally-
contingent concept, 3; competition
between, 3, 9, 21-24; development,
1, 3, 9-11, 29; emergence, 3, 29;
legitimacy, 6, 8. *See also* Journalistic occupation; Professionals
Occupational knowledge, or meaning,
3
Occupational sociology, 33 n.7
Ochs, Adolph, 75

Opdyke, George, 99
Orange County Patriot, 80, 90 n.37
Oratory, public, 28, 57

Paine, Thomas, 58, 100, 107 n.24
Pamphlets, 58
Parker, James, 54
Parsons, Talcott, 33 n.7
Partisanism, 84-85, 110
Party press era, 90 n.61, 121-22 n.4
Pennsylvania Gazette, 47, 51, 54
*Pennsylvania Gazette, or the Universal
Instructor*, 50
Pennsylvania Journal, 53
Penny press, 23, 124 n.44, 129, 132
Photojournalism, 9, 19, 23
Poems, 27
Political communication: defined, 22,
56, 69 n.65; government and politi-
cal news, 54; in colonial New Eng-
land, 53-54; participatory forms, 57;
prescriptive and nonprescriptive
forms, 56; printed forms, 57-58;
work tasks, 56
Political communication systems, 55-
57
Political communication work system:
competition within, 22-24; defined,
22, 56; settlements, 22, 24, 134-35;
task divisions within, 24; vacancies
within, 23. *See also* American
Revolution; Era of Good Feelings;
Journalistic jurisdiction
Political systems: party development,
121 n.1; shifts in, 122 n.13. *See also*
American Revolution; Era of Good
Feelings; Federalist party; Republican party
Politicians: as early journalistic correspondents, 15; as part of political
communication work system, 22;
defined, 2; in jurisdictional compe-
titions with journalists, 24; relationship to journalists, 1; use of newspaper as vehicle of political communication, 1. *See also* Era of Good
Feelings; Libel trials; Prospectuses

Press freedom: clashes over as precipitators of journalistic development, 45, 58-59

Press models: business, 73-75, 108 n.37; political, 72-73; social institutional, 72

Printer-journalist in eighteenth century, 47-48, 52-54, 62

Printers' guilds, 16-17, 37 n.60

Printing: as precipitator of journalistic occupational development, 46-49; effects of, 20, 23; in early America, 20

Professional development, 4-8, 22

Professionalization: Abbott on, 7-8; historical analysis of, 5; in journalism and mass communication scholarship, 8-9; power (monopolist) model, 6-8; role of agency in, 5; role of boundary emergence and maintenance in, 7; trait theory, 4-6, 33 n.8

Professionalization of science, 34 n.26

Professionals: as defined by Abbott, 6, 12; as defined by power theorists, 5-8; as defined by trait theorists, 4; compared to occupations, 12

Professional work systems, 21-24

Prospectuses: defined, 26; described as an occupational routine, 26, 49, 71, 75, 87 n.2, 88 n.17; in eighteenth century, 49-55, 60-62; in Era of Good Feelings, 112-117, 119-21; in nineteenth-century, 76-86; role of in occupational and professional development, 22, 26, 49-50; 66-67 n.27, 74-75, 126-27; samples used in this book explained, 29. *See also* American Revolution; Era of Good Feelings; Journalistic occupational communication

Providence Gazette & Country Journal, 68 n.54, 68 n.56

Public: acceptance of journalists, 29, 63-64, 73; criticism of journalists, 1-2, 126; effects on editors, 73; mistrust of politicians, 61; need for journalistic work products, 63-64, 68 n.49; relationship to journalism,

27; sensitivity to displays of partisanism, 2, 73, 110

Public Occurrences, 67 n.48

Public relations experts, 15, 22-23

Pulitzer, Joseph, 75

Religious Reporter, 117

Remuneration of journalists, 16, 18-19, 47, 53

Republican Chronicle, 96

Republican party, 74, 109, 111, 113-14, 118-19, 133

Retrospect of the Eighteenth Century, 59

Reynolds, George, 60

Rind, William Alexander, 116-18

Rockbridge County News, 89 n.36

Rosenberg, Norman, 94

Roth, Julius A., 5-6

Russell, Benjamin, 60, 62, 113, 120-21

Saratoga Advertiser, 89 n.36, 89-90 n.37

Saturday Evening Post, 84, 89 n.36

Schaeffer, Frederick G., 114, 123 n.21

Schiller, Dan, 132

Schoolcraft County Pioneer, 89 n.36

Schudson, Michael, 132

Scioto Gazette, 28, 118

Scioto Gazette and Fredonian Chronicle, 118

Scott, Joan Wallach, 32 n.6

Searchlight, The, 77

Simpson, William R., 80

Snelling, William J., 100-1

Snowden, Samuel, 118

Social class, 46, 48

Specimens of Newspaper Literature, 113

Spooner, Alden, 60, 76, 80

Spooner, Judah, 76

Spooner's Vermont Journal, 76

Stamp Act, 57, 59, 60-61

Star of Federalism, 122 n.10

State and Local Histories, 28

State vs. Bowen, 104

Stevens, John A., 76

Stow, Joshua, 96

Strong, Demas, 102
Supporter, 118
Supporter and Scioto Gazette, 118

Talk shows, 136
Technology: and work task subjectiv-
ity, 14; as a precipitator of work
system disturbances, 23; journalists'
access to, 21; role in occupational
development, 20, 23, 136
Television news work, 39 n.75
Thornton, William Fitzhugh, 118
Topeka (Kansas) Tribune, 89 n.36
Trade practices, journalistic. *See* Era of
Good Feelings
Training (apprenticeships) of journal-
ists, 8, 16-17, 28, 46-48, 63, 66 n.14
Treaty of Paris, 70 n.83
True, Benjamin, 78-79, 90 n.38
True American (New London, Con-
necticut), 76, 80
True American (Trenton, New Jersey),
74, 83, 85

Upham, Timothy, 98-99
U. S. Supreme Court, 17, 135

Values: expressions of in journalistic
occupational communication, 27-28;
journalistic, 11, 17; normative, 7; of
professional groups, 13
Vermont Gazette, 76
Vermont Journal, 60, 76
Virginia Gazette, 47
Voting, in colonial America, 55, 57

Waldo (Maine) Gazette, 71
Walpole era, 119
Warden, William, 60, 62
War of 1812, 133
Warren, James D., 102-4
Washington (Mississippi) Republican,
83-84
Washington press corps, 136
Watson, David, 114-15
Weed, Thurlow, 18, 99
Weyman, William, 53
Whitman, Benjamin, 100-1

Wilkes, George, 105
Wilson, James Jefferson, 83, 85
Woodstock (Vermont) Observer, 115
Woodward, Moses H., 62
World, The, 120

York (Pennsylvania) Recorder, 115
Young, Alexander, 62

Zenger, John Peter, 27, 54, 59

About the Author

PATRICIA L. DOOLEY is Assistant Professor at the Elliott School of Communication at Wichita State University, Wichita, Kansas.

ISBN 0-313-30062-3

90000>

EAN

9 780313 300622

HARDCOVER BAR CODE